SPOTTING
THE TREND

An Entrepreneur's Success Story

JENNY CHANG

ISBN: 978-1-4834-3279-3 (sc)
ISBN: 978-1-4834-3281-6 (hc)
ISBN: 978-1-4834-3280-9 (e)

Library of Congress Control Number: 2015910056

Because of the dynamic nature of the Internet, any web addresses or links contained in this book may have changed since publication and may no longer be valid. The views expressed in this work are solely those of the author and do not necessarily reflect the views of the publisher, and the publisher hereby disclaims any responsibility for them.

Any people depicted in stock imagery provided by Thinkstock are models, and such images are being used for illustrative purposes only. Certain stock imagery © Thinkstock.

Lulu Publishing Services rev. date: 09/14/2015

CONTENTS

Section Four: Culture in Practice
Business Clad in Cultural Armor

Weathering Change, Piloting Transformation

Steve Chang
Founder and Chairman, Trend Micro Incorporated

One question people have invariably asked me since Trend Micro was started is whether this "husband-wife" business of ours was hurting our marriage. I think this book is just about the best response that Jenny could have possibly given to this question.

Our roles as cofounders never threatened to turn Trend Micro into a myopic family endeavor. In the pages that follow, Jenny gives many examples of how we have valued corporate culture from the very beginning and how we worked to build a corporate culture capable of nourishing and sustaining Trend Micro's foundational values, corporate communication style, and innovative dynamism through the changes in management and internationalization that were sure to come. The eventual change in leadership was part of the initial equation, and we held dear to the principle that no one at any level of the company should ever be irreplaceable. This naturally obviated the issues and problems that often confront the "family business." While we *are* husband and wife, our respective professional roles were clearly defined and designed to foster positive synergy. After taking our start-up public, we waited a full seven years to ensure that Trend Micro was grounded firmly in its own set of positive core values and communication style before finally taking the carefully considered decision to step back and let others assume leadership.

In 2005, after relinquishing my CEO position and all executive responsibilities at Trend Micro, I launched a new venture in the social-enterprise sector. Little did I realize that a brief four months later, Trend Micro would be embroiled in the "594 Incident"—a disaster that almost drove it out of business. However, even at the height of the crisis, I stayed my hand and resisted the instinctive urge to again take charge of the situation. Eva Chen was the new CEO, and I reiterated to her my position that she alone held full authority and responsibility. I knew that if I'd pushed myself back onto center stage, it would have mortally savaged Jenny and my long-cherished ideal of true succession.

Transformation is part and parcel of the Trend Micro business model and a tangible fact of life for Jenny, Eva, and me. For me, the transformative process conjures up an image of Tarzan swinging from vine to vine beneath the forest canopy. To move forward, he releases his hold on one vine to clasp onto the next, and during each transition, the jungle king is necessarily empty-handed. It is a moment of pronounced uncertainty fringed with a certain measure of fear. But, continuing to cling to the safety of the first vine would leave him spinning in circles and make forward momentum impossible. Thoughts like this helped me to stay supportively behind the scenes during the 594 Incident, even while the value of Trend Micro stock collapsed, key customers threatened to desert, and media coverage turned bitingly critical. The Trend Micro vine was now in Eva Chen's firm grasp, and at the same time she was learning how to move it forward, Jenny and I were learning to manage the anxiety-riddled gap between letting go and catching our next vine.

While this was a time filled with doubt and uncertainty, I also recognized it as the necessary "moment of truth" faced by all entrepreneurs. If I hadn't stepped back and had rather stepped up to help resolve the crisis and other future company problems, I would have deprived my successor of critical learning opportunities and most likely ended up with what we all feared the most: a "coddled" company afraid and ultimately unable to grow and expand on its own.

It pleases me greatly that Jenny has chosen to share in such a detailed and honest fashion Trend Micro's quarter century of development.

Effectively managing "internationalization" and transforming business models to meet new knowledge-economy challenges and opportunities are regular agenda topics in many corporate boardrooms today. Trend Micro has dealt with these issues from the very start, and Jenny gives readers the real story, inside and out. We willingly share here Trend Micro's secrets of success—our "family jewels," if you will, in hopes that those concerned about or responsible for steering companies forward will come to appreciate the formative influence of culture on business management. The value of the individual permeates Trend Micro's global operations. It has helped see us through countless challenges and across many bumpy roads. Looking back on our experience affirms our convictions and our perseverance.

Although this book may not be a standard MBA curriculum material, it does give an honest, concise look into Trend Micro's experiences throughout the past twenty-five years. I truly hope it will become a valued reference on how to manage and overcome crises, on why corporate competitive strategies are almost never fully implemented, and, when the time comes, on how to help an incoming president or CEO catch the next vine forward.

However, in my humble opinion, while this work stands on its own as a business-management book, it also distinguishes itself as a well-crafted work of literature.

Jenny holds an undergraduate degree in Chinese, and one of her youthful ambitions was to be a professional writer and author. The demands of entrepreneurship saw this dream shelved for more than two decades. Jenny's long-hidden talents burst forth in this book, her maiden effort. As both business entrepreneur and author, Jenny deftly works between both roles to give readers a clear picture of events, an insightful and emotive understanding of Eva Chen, a remarkably clear and accurate analysis of her husband, and an honest reflection on her own thoughts, experiences, and growth. Furthermore, Jenny's personal involvement in so many of Trend Micro's key policy decisions gives this work added value as a candid, behind-the-scenes look at corporate operations.

Today, neither Jenny nor I deal with the day-to-day operations of Trend Micro. For me, this book reads like the memoirs of one who has seen and experienced much and is now eager to share with younger generations. For many years, I've seen the world of business as a training ground for personal and spiritual growth. For Jenny, her writing is her spiritual training ground. The pages that follow may be seen as Jenny's personal transformation and an honest record of how we managed Trend Micro's succession and our hopes for its future. Now, she is free to escape the cares of commerce and explore her literary and cultural passions. This book tells the story of my transformation as well, and I, too, am now free to depart the field of high-tech battle and invest time and passion in my next cause: social enterprise.

At this point, all that remains is to voice my great respect to Eva Chen, who remains in fine fighting form on the business battlefield, and my heartfelt wishes to my wife and former colleague Jenny Chang for success and fulfillment in all her current and future literary endeavors. As for me, I look with excitement on a future surely filled with new and meaningful endeavors that will certainly be accomplished with others who share similar ideals and passions. Might this be you? Look me up! Good works and much fun await!

A Debt of Gratitude to the Universe, My Family, My Mentors, and All Who Have Made This Day Possible!

Giving a task your undivided, devoted attention puts one in a state of mind that I can only characterize as contented tranquility. It is a state that runs parallel with, yet separately from the ordinary "me"—almost as if my mind was beyond my control and tracking a preset course into a yet unknown future.

The giddy, elated mood I've been in for the past three months has put me squarely into just such a state. Although I've been in meetings, given interviews, taught courses, and done studio work during this period, my mind has been elsewhere ... pleasantly distracted. This book has consumed the entirety of my attention.

This is my third book on the subject of Trend Micro. Despite my own nagging doubts about the need and value of yet another book in the virtual "sea" of books out there, about whether anybody would really be interested in a book on my entrepreneurial and business experience, and about today's publishing market, I gave in wholly and unapologetically to my desire to once again dive into writing. I thus wrote the one hundred thousand-plus words that follow not for my readers, for the publisher, or for Trend Micro, but rather solely for selfishly personal reasons.

This is the story of how my husband Steve and I built a business from the ground up and how we later handed this successful "baby" over to others in order to launch new chapters in our respective lives. This path of ours, intentionally or otherwise, created, nourished, and promoted an incomparable corporate culture. This ingrained cultural framework gave our business the tenacious flexibility that saw the entire Trend Micro team through its darkest hours. Experience shows the power of culture to be palpable and business culture to be so much more than just a means to an end or an emotive cry to battle. Core values embedded within a company's culture can and deserve to be the "North Star" that keeps business on a steady course forward.

ACKNOWLEDGEMENTS

While this book is solely my own work, it would have been much poorer without the support and involvement of so many to whom I owe a great debt of gratitude.

First and foremost, I wish to thank not a person, but the universal powers that have blessed me with my physical and spiritual capacities, guided my every step forward, and given me incredible friendships and contacts along the way.

Next, I want to thank my "king"—my loving husband. Thank you for temporarily suspending your urges to engage me in conversation or take me traveling and for allowing me the quietude necessary to explore my inner self and experiences. Thank you for your gentle and deft ducking of my occasional writer's-block-inspired outbursts and hot-headedness. You eagerly awaited each of my drafts and carefully developed and shared with me your insightful comments. Your loving participation both touched me deeply and helped me turn thoughts and words into literature. We are partners on life's road, and this book is ours together.

After my husband, I wish to thank my parents. I thank my dearly departed father for his understanding and loving support. His serene acceptance of death was instrumental in firing my love and passion for life. I credit my father as well for my inherent optimism, which recognizes and obeys the rules of nature's way. I thank you, too, my dear mother. You have been my role model from the very beginning and a great supporter of my ambitions to write. I know that you will read this and take pride in your daughter's latest literary effort. I have always striven to attain the fulfillment you longed for but were prevented from achieving due to the tenor of the conservative times in which you grew up. I have striven to live the expansive, self-made life you have always wished for me.

Of course, I also wish to thank my brothers. You are my greatest supporters, unfailingly "have my back," and make each return home a warm and loving experience. I thank my sister for sharing our entrepreneurial path with us and for so courageously taking the helm when we stepped down. While you may be known around the world as one of the most decisive women in business today, you remain for me as always my adoring, warmhearted sister.

I reserve special thanks for my two wonderful sons. You knew I was negligent in many of my motherly responsibilities, and you never complained. You grew up and learned to come confidently into your own. As emerging entrepreneurs, you are now trying out your new wings, and I must resist my natural motherly urges to get involved and be protective. My sons, you are also the reason for which I've written this book, and I hope you glean useful insights and inspiration from the words within.

I want next to thank all of my many teachers. It has been my great fortune to benefit from the guidance and advice of so many leading lights! First and foremost, I wish to thank Kenneth Pai. It was his writings that solidified my own literary interests and ambitions in youth. During the most conflicted time of my life, his reinterpretation of the Ming classic *Peony Pavilion* drew me into its beautiful world and helped me better understand myself. You have been a teacher and longtime friend. Your pithy comment, "Vividly written," after reading my first work *@Trend Micro* from cover to cover was the greatest affirmation of my writing I could ever hope for.

Great respect and appreciation also deservedly goes to my dear Chun-ming Huang. You gave me the strongest encouragement and guidance throughout my literary journey. Your tart remark, "Jenny … *what are you waiting for?*" helped me realize it was only my lack of confidence that was holding me back. I would never again give up so easily. You've taught me with great patience how to develop my characters and use dialogue to develop their personalities. While I listened attentively, my own limitations necessarily make my writing fall short of its potential. For this, I ask your forgiveness and understanding. I have also not forgotten your exhortation, "You write and I write. I write and you write. We write together!" Chun-ming, I await your next novel, *Three-Legged Piggy*, with well-deserved anticipation.

For my dear mentor Hsun Chiang, thank you for your companionship and for working with me these recent years. You taught me to unwind and appreciate the omnipresent beauty in nature. Your inexhaustible reserve of stories has taught me the richness of literature and life. Your friendship along life's path has been a true blessing, and I thank you for your abiding, heartfelt encouragement.

To I-yun Hsin, I am indebted and grateful to you for teaching us to weave Buddhist, Taoist, and Confucian wisdom into our lives, for helping us appreciate the wisdom of "nothing done, nothing left undone," and for helping us sprout wings and learn to fly. It is my deepest wish to be as you are: unfettered and free!

I also cannot end without expressing my deep appreciation for Carl Gustav Jung. While we have never met, it was you who introduced me to my inner being and to the "collective unconscious" of humanity. Your pioneering writings on synchronicity awakened me to the influence of providence. You helped me plumb the depths of my private dreamland.

Finally, I want to thank my many friends!

Thank you to all of my friends at Trend Micro, both past and present, in Taiwan, China, Japan, the United States, Germany, and the Philippines who agreed to be interviewed for this book. Your vibrant descriptions were critical to developing the narrative that follows. You were magnanimously generous in sharing your experiences, warts and all, and you helped me achieve the necessary critical detachment from my subject matter. The story within is the life story of Trend Micro. Thus, as peerless colleagues and valued comrades, it is *your* story as much as it is ours. It has been my honor to share this road with each one of you, and the memories shall remain with me always.

I've saved my final acknowledgments for those friends who have contributed most to making this book possible. Thank you to Trend Education Foundation Executive Director Sheng-tsung Chang for his deft blend of encouragement, provocation, and admonition. You never once gave up on me and were always there to give support, lend a sympathetic ear, and handle my myriad burdens so that I could continue writing. Your unblinking faith gave me the courage and strength to continue. For this, I remain grateful beyond words.

Thank you to Sophia Tseng, my radiantly charming chief editor. You and I had the pleasure of working together before as coeditors of Kenneth Pai's *Peony Trilogy*. My faith in you to handle my own book has not been misplaced. You were the steady helmsman of this project, reading each new draft and giving me your honest critique. While it was often infuriating at the time, I now look back on our creative process and all its innumerable revisions with an appropriate sense of respectful awe and deep gratitude. Thank you, Sophia, for your inimitable editorial skills and for bringing together such an editorial "dream team" for this project. Thank you also for letting Hsiang-lin and Tuo-cheng stay on with the project after finishing the first manuscript draft.

Thank you Jeff Miller for the wonderful English translation work in this book. Jeff Miller has been a full-time translator, editor and writer since 2007. He currently divides his time between Keelung and Taitung, both along Taiwan's beautiful East Coast. Jeff's diverse career includes previous positions with the American Institute in Taiwan (AIT), Accenture Consulting, and Unisys, among others. He loves the freedoms of freelancing as well as the opportunity and the honor to work with people throughout Taiwan. Outside of work, Jeff's passions include cycling, photography, homesteading, and his talented & awesomely cool daughter, Tara.

Thank you also to Jung-wen Wang and Yuan-Liou Publishing. In spite of the inclement conditions in today's publishing market, I greatly appreciate your decision to go ahead and publish this rather idiosyncratic work.

Finally, having thanked all those who helped make me who I am and make this book possible, it is only natural to thank you, the reader. Thank you for selecting this book out of the many you might otherwise have chosen. Although I don't pretend to know what inspired you, I sincerely hope the words within provide the foundations for a lasting and positive relationship.

Jenny Chang
October 7, 2013

The Beginning

In the beginning, he was a wild, free spirit that enjoyed spending hours at a time losing himself in seemingly aimless walks across Fu Jen University's campus grounds. Then one day, on a visit with his parents to see family friends in the Central Taiwan town of Jiji, he met their eldest granddaughter, who had cut class and arrived home early. They quickly escaped the dull conversations of their elders, and he burst forth with spellbinding stories about a recent camping trip to Europe. Tickled by his animated presentation, she eventually put a firm grip on his shoulders, pulled a seat over, sat down in front of him, and said, "Okay, now. Take your time. I'm listening!" It seemed to do the trick. He had found his moorings, and they settled into wonderful reminiscing.

In the beginning, she lived the sheltered life of a "good" girl. Being raised in a bustling, multigenerational home under her grandparent's protective, strict rules gave her values steeped in traditional mores and decorum. In hindsight, it should have come as no surprise that he would turn her world topsy-turvy. Instinctively aware of her helplessness in the face of temptation, he made his first move. "I've got books by Lu Xun and Lao She," he said. "Want to read them?"

Banned books! she thought. *Who would say no to them?* In reading and returning those books one after another, she stepped ever further into his world—his excitingly stimulating world. His life was a place far removed from and so much bigger than her familiar, rules-bound existence, but it was somewhere she had longed to go for as long as she could remember. It seemed only natural, then, for her to answer with a speechless nod when he eventually popped the question and said, "Marry me! Let's see the four corners of the world together!"

His impulsive inability to slow down, to shift even temporarily into a lower gear, took her by surprise. He was driven to compete—to invest his very last ounce of talent in proving his worth to himself and to others. He invariably chose the risky road and wasn't put off in the least at the prospect of getting lost along the way. "Safe and easy" held no allure. He was the master of his own destiny, and he marched confidently forward toward the goal of starting up his own company.

For his part, he didn't realize how cloistered and innocent of the world his new wife was. She was a devoted adherent of love's all-conquering power. While terrified of risk and of getting lost, she took blind comfort in his confidence and followed him into the unknown. His delectable dreams sustained her. She followed the lilting melodies of his magic flute and optimistically saw only exciting potential in every new risk and dangerous turn along the way. She set aside her own literary ambitions to invest herself fully in his entrepreneurial dream, both to see the dream to fruition and to fulfill the vows of innocent love.

She was very different from her younger sister because, while she resembled her mother in looks, she had her father's incurable optimism. Her sister was the opposite, looking more like Dad while inheriting Mom's tenacious fortitude. They were always close and got along well together. A favorite prank was to call up friends and pretend to be each other. The younger sister loved joining the couple on their adventures, and, like her older sister, admired the *je ne sais quoi* quality that made her brother-in-law special. For his part, he sensed the younger sister's talents but did not yet know how to help those talents shine. As he saw beneath her calm façade the deep-seated yearnings to give wings to her creativity, he invited her to join them on their entrepreneurial journey. No one would have guessed that this graduate in philosophy from Cheng Chi University was destined for great things in the field of software development or that she would appear on a shortlist of the most influential names in global information security.

Just like that, a boy from rural Pingtung County and two wide-eyed sisters from Taichung formed an entrepreneurial pact. They would go on to form an antivirus-software empire valued at some US$5 billion. A multiyear recipient of Taiwan's most valuable international brand award, the company has achieved more than anyone expected. In recent years, Harvard Business School (HBS) has used their entrepreneurial story as a case study in transnational businesses.

"Against all the odds, they've somehow succeeded!" an eminent professor at National Taiwan University's School of Business once remarked with surprise. "Considering current business theories, who would have seen the potential in this entrepreneurial startup? They had someone with a master's in IT in charge of sales, a Chinese BA responsible for global marketing, and a philosophy BA responsible for product R & D. But they made it work and in the process, they created a new model of international corporate management. I have my doubts whether someone with an advanced degree in business management could have pulled off what they did!"

At each stage along the way, there were always venture capitalists with major companies and private funds looking to invest in, or to buy out, their growing venture. But temptation never led them astray from the inceptive commitment to self-management. Only ten years after it was founded, the company became one of the top three leaders in Internet security in the world. It went public on the Tokyo Stock Exchange and was soon added to the Nikkei Index. The value created by these three has long since exceeded the wildest expectations of its initial shareholders.

Capitalist principles place the interests of the shareholder above all else and mandate that firms pursue the highest return on all investments. The three thus worked tirelessly within the rules of the market to earn and keep the trust of their many investors, small shareholders and global fund managers alike.

The demands of success unavoidably brought the three to revisit their innermost motives and hopes for the company. Return on investment had never really been a consideration on the difficult road to entrepreneurial success. For them, the hoped-for "returns" had always been more personal in nature. He wanted to be the captain of his own destiny, she wanted to explore life's potential, and her younger sister wanted a place in which to invest her creative energies. Thus, in the realm of management, their thoughts and discussions seemed invariably to get tangled up in human-centered ideals and issues of self-fulfillment. Some of the perennial questions asked were: *How can we make our employees and ourselves happier in order to make the most of our collective potential? Can we foster scenarios that are truly win/win, where my success is inclusive and where your successes can take flight within my business? Can we operate in a way that allows all in the company to balance the needs of work and family? Is there a way to let all employees express their natural talents and be their natural, relaxed selves at work? And is it possible to get them all to set down their personal motives and make the success of the team their top priority?*

However, while they explored the process of building an ideal company, their products still had to help clients resolve problems, their revenues still had to grow, their profit margins still had to remain steady, and hopefully, the value of their stock would steam ever higher. These were the rules of competition in the business "jungle" and were fundamental to continued survival.

Positive appraisals of management performance are essential for any firm wanting to successfully compete and grow into the future. Cooperative marketing agreements and competition for award recognition are part and parcel of strategies looking to build brand image and strengthen global brand value. Thus, over time, their company earned popular titles such as the "star of Asia" and "coolest company," and their executives were honored by titles such as "most influential female executive." Despite the newness of the company, the founders' unique contributions as business professionals earned them lifetime achievement awards. Such accolades were par for the course as the business tested new, unprecedented heights.

However, with neither fame nor fortune woven into the corporate DNA and none of the three well trained in corporate management, the company needed something else to distinguish itself in the marketplace. Fortunately, he had the vision to accurately assess future market trends and the canny ability to convince others, while she possessed worldly wisdom and empathy and knew how to lead teams to get things done, and her younger sister possessed extraordinary creative and planning abilities. They furthermore shared as a team unmatched passion and singularity of purpose. They were highly practical and fully committed, yet not overly concerned about losses and gains. Finally, they had an infectious enthusiasm that naturally brought others into their orbit and created powerfully cohesive team dynamics.

It was in this amalgam of distinct yet complementary leadership styles that a new corporate culture gradually emerged.

He was the anxious one who always got things done. "Change" defined him, and nothing ever kept him in one place for long.

Tact and persistence featured prominently in her arsenal. She willingly took the indirect approach and discussed issues *ad infinitum* to build relationships and understanding.

The younger sister's fresh style let her see patterns and potentials that she could use to create new things and ideas from "nothing." She shunned well-trodden paths in favor of creating new directions.

The company's "3C" culture of Change, Communication, and Creativity reflected the characters of its founders. Despite the fact that such culture was deep-rooted and acted as a defining part in this growing venture, no one had considered that it would play such a vital role in the company's very existence, influence key decisions, or make the organization ultimately more cohesive than it had ever been before.

After all, isn't corporate culture something announced by management—something posted on the notice boards and tirelessly flogged at staff meetings? It sets expectations that are rarely achieved in practice and may, in fact, never accurately define the company's core values anyway. Is it possible for this to be a practical tool for creating value?

It is natural to take established business-management theory with a grain of salt and want to make revisions in practice. However, these three founders never strayed from their original ideal of keeping people at the heart of the organization. Thus, however big it got and however great the challenges, the company remained a cohesive confederation of like-minded individuals investing their learning and skills to overcome each problem in their path. Thus, management is the art of managing people, with systems and regulations in place only as supporting roles.

Across the years, the three have never strayed from their foundational ideals and have given their company an Asian philosophical core clad in practical Western scientific fundamentals. A corporate culture steeped in Chinese tolerance has accommodated the disparate influences of Japanese persistence, Latin American optimism, American adventurousness, and European rationalism. They take pride in their company's supranational character and work to maintain their distinctive culture. For the past twenty-five years, this core set of values has helped the company not just to survive but also to grow and expand in today's fast-paced, fast-changing Internet age.

The company founded by these three individuals is the now globe-girding Trend Micro Inc.

His name is Steve Chang, Trend Micro Chairman and a tireless promoter of social enterprises.

"She" is me, Jenny Chang, Trend Micro Chief Cultural Officer (COO). My work focuses on the blending of technology and culture with a passion for advancing education in the realms of culture and art.

The younger sister, my sister, is Eva Chen, Trend Micro CEO and a perennially creative trailblazer on the international stage.

Note: A September 22, 2003, article in *Businessweek* entitled "Borders are So 20th Century" adopted University of Michigan Professor CK Prahalad's four-stage model of corporate internationalization. In stage one, a firm operates in one country and exports its products. In stage two, a firm sets up branch operations outside of the home country in order to address local business needs. In stage three, a firm relocates a part or parts of its core operations to other countries. Finally, in stage four (the supranational stage), the executive functions of the firm are conducted virtually, with senior executive officers located in countries offering the strongest competitive advantage in terms of human resources, funding, costs, distance to key customers, and so on. Trend Micro Inc. is the focus of this article. Although the process of transforming a multinational enterprise into a transnational enterprise represents a difficult management challenge, transnational corporations are the wave of the future.

ENTREPRENEURING & MANAGING TRANSNATIONAL BUSINESS

CHAPTER 1

Three in One

We registered Trend Micro in California in 1988 with a combined out-of-pocket investment of $5,000. Eva then set up Trend Micro Inc. in Taiwan the following year. On our own initiative, the three of us put together a company that grew quickly into a global provider of the world's most advanced antivirus software solutions.

Maybe it will be best to begin at the beginning, with my marriage to Steve.

The year was 1979, and Allentown, Pennsylvania, provided the backdrop for this memorable event.

Having already announced our engagement to friends and relatives in Taiwan, we made the impulsive decision to seal the deal soon after we returned to school in the United States. I wore the azure-blue *cheongsam* (a close-fitting, traditional Chinese dress) that my mother insisted I bring with me, and Steve wore his brother-in-law's charcoal-black suit. Accompanied by Steve's sister and a close friend, we arrived at the home of the local justice of the peace at the appointed time to swear our oaths of marriage. The judge donned his black robe of office and, with Bible in hand, commenced the ceremony.

Not long into the formalities, the judge stopped abruptly in midsentence, turned to us, and asked, "You both understand English?" in a low voice that I half imagined might have been meant to keep God from listening in. We quickly nodded as we worked to quiet our own nagging angst that Buddha may not, after all, look so kindly on a wedding ceremony held in the absence of family and friends and beyond the formalities of Chinese tradition.

It was the year I graduated from university in Taiwan, and I had arrived in the United States to study information technology. Steve was already a year into his studies for a doctorate in information sciences at Lehigh University in Pennsylvania. His talents let him graduate easily with a bachelor's in applied mathematics from Fu Jen Catholic University, where his grades had secured him a full scholarship and a job as a teaching assistant. My undergraduate degree was in Chinese literature. A lifelong aversion to math and science made my upcoming graduate studies all the more challenging. I knew I would have a tough slog ahead to make a success of my new academic venture.

Our engagement in Taiwan was sealed by the agreement of my easygoing fiancé, Steve, to a steadily increasing list of demands from my grandmother. Just as tensions were ready to boil over on both sides of the aisle, we whisked ourselves away for graduate studies in the United States.

Seeking to avoid the fiasco almost certain to come from a big family wedding, we kept it simple and got married by ourselves. After reading a few Bible verses, asking us, "Do you …" in turn, and signing the certificate on the dotted line, the judge concluded the ceremony as quickly as it had begun. We went to the license bureau to register our marriage and left with a bag filled with newlywed gifts. The generosity caught me off guard. We were newbie residents and not yet even taxpayers! We opened the bag to find a smorgasbord of commercial samples that included laundry detergent, household cleaner, wiping cloths—everything a startup family needed. The most valuable and thoughtful gift was a jumbo-sized bottle of aspirin. Perhaps the giver knew of the barrage of headaches that awaited me not far down the road!

My biggest immediate headache was Steve's bullheaded insistence on blazing his own trail. His biggest headache was my inveterately romantic take on life and stubborn innocence of life's hard realities.

"You've got no clue," and "You grew up too sheltered" were two insights he seemed very happy to share with me on an all-too-regular basis. My frequent retorts mocked his inexplicable attraction to hardship: "You'd rather surrender at the gates of hell than walk heaven's highway."

2

It was fortunate for both of us, then, that we had Eva, my more levelheaded, smarter younger sister. After earning her bachelor's in philosophy from National Chengchi University, graduating with a dual master's in international management and information management from the University of Texas at Dallas, and working for a stint as a product manager at Acer, Eva made the gutsy decision to jump ship and join us in setting up a new business. She took responsibility for our all-important Taiwan operations, helped balance our shortcomings, and, in the end, certainly saved this husband-wife team from a lot of unnecessary grief.

Unique Name, Unique Brand

I was the second child in my family, with an older brother, a sister three years my junior, and a baby brother eight years younger. Eva's original name in Chinese, Yi-fen, was our grandmother's choice. It was a clever play on words that basically meant, "Two daughters in a row are enough already! Give us a boy now." Apparently, it worked. Mom later gave birth to a strapping baby boy. Eva, the bearer of this plea for another male heir, suffered from frequent dizzy spells as a youth, and after our grandmother passed away, she officially changed her Chinese name from Yi-fen to Yi-hua, turning her name from a call for separation into a proclamation of brilliance. Her health actually did change for the better around this time. Today, however, Eva insists there was a more straightforward reason for her name change: "Yi-hua just sounded closer to my English name, Eva." Eva was the name we had chosen together when she was at university. She always loved its powerful simplicity. It also perfectly complemented her burgeoning entrepreneurial spirit.

As I was the eldest granddaughter in my family, my grandfather had asked a fortune-teller to choose a propitious name for me. I was never overly fond of my name as a child. Even my Chinese teachers at school often misread the "chin" in my name "Yi-chin," and my classmates regularly miscopied my "Yi" as another Chinese character "qia." Even my last name, Chen, seemed tiresomely common. I regularly asked Mom why I couldn't just adopt her stylishly simple last name of Ting. While my carefully chosen name had the perfect number of brush strokes and connoted "hidden fortune," it left me cold.

My then-boyfriend Steve chose "Jenny" as my English name for me before I went abroad to study. Although simple and nondescript, it had the advantages of being both easy to remember and to use in conversation.

Conversely, our company and the various products I named, such as *Global Views Monthly* magazine, Trend Micro, and PC-cillin did all manage to achieve impressive success.

As the first grandson in his family, Steve also had his Chinese name chosen by his grandfather. It was a simple and straightforward reference to a tablet above the gate of one of the many palaces in the Forbidden City, which read: "Decency, Honesty, and Magnanimity." It aptly describes Steve's approach to all of his responsibilities. His father's family had lived for generations in the Changhua area before moving to Pingtung in the southernmost part of Taiwan. His father ran a struggling construction business until "at someone's suggestion," he switched careers and opened Pingtung City's first bowling alley, which gave the family the comforts of a middle-class lifestyle. Steve helped pick up stray bowling pins at the bowling alley from a young age and began a lifelong relationship with entrepreneurialism that has continued ever since.

An American priest working at Fu Jen University gave Steve his English name, which means "smart and quick-witted." It was by coincidence that many of the superstars of the emerging IT industry, led by Apple Inc.'s Steve Jobs (who was just one year younger than my Steve), were also named Steve. There was something in Steve's blood that made him averse to settling into anything resembling a routine. He went into computers because they were then at the cutting edge of science and technology. He took his first job with an entrepreneurial startup in New York as a database software engineer in order to learn how to do computer-based market analysis. Soon after, he abandoned his plans for a PhD and returned to Taiwan to work for Hewlett-Packard as a sales engineer—a position that gave him client experience and insights into Taiwan's tremendous IT growth prospects.

Before founding Trend Micro, Steve had been president of the Taiwan distributor of a US-based mini-PC company and an investor in a money-losing nightclub. He had also sold another of his startups, Vassar Tech, a manufacturer of UPS systems, to Hitachi. The first real jackpot in his career came in 1987 with the sale of T-Lock, a software lock system designed to prevent software theft, to the California-based information-security firm Rainbow Technologies. While the sale provided a tidy sum, it was a modest amount, not quite enough to buy a house.

Going Viral

"We're going to be seeing a lot more of these viruses," I remember Steve announcing to me one day. We were in California and had just begun getting some much-needed market traction for T-Lock. We were living in a creaky old house that Steve's mother would soon tear down and rebuild. His comment came while I was in the midst of vacuuming the carpet, trying to keep the pervasive dust away from our two baby boys. Detached from the commotion that surrounded him, he remained glued to his computer screen, reading article after article for hours, lifting his head only occasionally to share some tidbit of new information he found interesting. I responded to his pronouncement with acrid disinterest.

"Viruses?" I said. "Computers get viruses? You'd better stay clear of that computer, then."

"Microsoft's OS is an open platform. Anyone who knows programming can develop software to run on it. This includes *virus* software." Over the din of my continued vacuuming, he continued his commentary. "See! There are already five or six known viruses. Each causes its own set of problems. One causes your computer to shut down; another makes characters on the screen disappear. They go from computer to computer on floppy disks, so they can spread fast."

I decided to stop vacuuming and vent my growing frustration. "It's nothing to do with you. We're starting to get good sales for T-Lock, and Eva's helping you get things moving in Asia. Don't you dare start focusing on other things now." I regretted my words almost immediately after they had left my mouth. I should have learned by then to never, *ever* say no to Steve. His offbeat logic invariably interprets denial as a challenge to be met rather than a line not to be crossed.

Just like that, Steve put me in charge of T-Lock affairs while he organized a team of like-minded, entrepreneurial software engineers, including Charles Lee and Li-fu Liang, to work with Eva in Taiwan on his new dream of creating an antivirus software business.

We paid our $5,000 to register Trend Micro in California in 1988. Eva registered the business in Taiwan the following year. The world's newest and most advanced antivirus firm had at the time just one major competitor, McAfee, a company that has since changed hands several times, involved its founder John McAfee in multiple lawsuits, and is now a wholly owned subsidiary of Intel. We were in Southern California, and McAfee was in Northern California. We often exchanged data on virus detections and helped each other improve operations. It was a competitive but comfortable relationship. Computer virus protection was, after all, an entirely new industry. Fortunes were difficult to predict, and the atmosphere was ripe with buoyant camaraderie.

The two companies approached the problem of virus protection from two distinct technological angles. McAfee focused primarily on identifying new viruses, extracting the malicious code, and securing naming rights. They would then hype the dangers of each new virus outbreak to stoke anxiety among computer users. For our part, after studying its basic functions, Trend Micro focused on beating each newly identified virus at its own game. We built intelligent "virus traps" and analyzed common behaviors within virus groups in order to create effective preventive measures. Further, we focused on making our software interface more intuitive and easier to manipulate and use. We generally kept a low profile, worked quickly to release free virus-removal tools, and tried not to hype issues in order to avoid being perceived as taking advantage of others' problems.

This low-key attitude was one of the very first bricks in the foundation of a new breed of corporate culture.

Intel Royalty Fees

Few expected this game of digital cat and mouse to grow so big so fast. It wasn't long before new competitors such as Symantec and Norton joined the fray. At its peak, market competition glowed white-hot, with more than five hundred companies vying for their slice of the antivirus pie.

Trend Micro has remained firmly grounded in its technical strengths and has been the "tip of the spear" in antivirus software, providing innovative, effective antivirus solutions for the historical gamut of operating systems including stand-alone DOS, Apple, Windows, Novell NetWare, networking platforms, Internet-based applications, and today's various smartphone OS platforms. Many top media outlets counted Trend Micro among the world's leading "technology vision" companies, going so far as to say we were the "best-kept secret" in virus protection. We did maintain a low-key approach to sales and restricted our strategic alliance partners to the biggest names in IT, including Intel Corporation.

(Table 2: Threat Landscape and Innovation)

Intel, together with Microsoft, has dominated the global IT industry for more than three decades. When servers were first launched, Intel created a network applications department that, while ostensibly working on networking software, was actually dedicated to pushing growth in demand for server hardware as a way to sell more of its IC chips. They truly operated at a higher frequency than most businesses. Intel's senior executive at the time, a solidly credentialed entrepreneur, insightfully recognized the growth potential in Trend Micro's unique antivirus solution for servers. He signed a five-year reciprocal contract with our company that made Intel the exclusive distributor of Trend Micro's server antivirus software outside of Asia.

The distributorship agreement gave Trend Micro a 17 percent royalty on all of its products sold by Intel, making us perhaps the very first company in Asia to actually *collect* money from Intel! This important and substantial new revenue stream gave us the funds needed to expand globally, and it raised Trend Micro's profile within the industry.

But our hopes and goals went beyond money and reputation.

"Stay determined. We're building success," was something Steve often said to encourage our engineers stationed in Provo, Utah. "We know innovation. We have the best technologies. But *they* have the comprehensive software development SOP that captures the whole process—from idea generation to module development, testing and user interface design, all the way to marketing and sales. Each step is an essential part of the whole. You're here at the source. Please don't come back empty-handed. Persevere for a while longer and really master the skills available here!" He had to give constant encouragement and pep talks to our engineers, who had been so long away from home. I truly empathized with their sacrifices and hardship.

Intel's corporate culture differed diametrically from Trend Micro's foundational emphasis on caring and compromise. Theirs reflected the "typically American" focuses on confrontation, discipline, and competition, embodied in the image of a gladiator locked in a life-and-death struggle against competitors both within and without, facing challenges with only two possible outcomes: victory or defeat.

Their internal meetings often featured hotheaded arguments. Our engineers often got caught in the crossfire and, not infrequently, were fingered as scapegoats. Situations like these simply made their assignment all the more onerous.

By the close of our five-year strategic agreement, we had not only mastered each step of the software development and marketing process; we had also had a strong taste of US "big corporate" culture. Both the good and the bad provided valuable lessons for Trend Micro's growing international business.

Trend Micro had spread its wings and was ready to fly. As the largest antivirus solutions provider in Asia, we made preparations to list Trend Micro on the Tokyo Stock Exchange.

Our InterScan Internet antivirus software would never again share a bed with Intel. Whatever the difficulties ahead, this time we were flying solo! Eva's successful development of Trend Micro's proprietary On-the-Fly technology (1) sealed the decision not to renew the strategic alliance with Intel. Eva then moved her family to Northern California and jumped headfirst into the deep end of Silicon Valley's cutthroat competition to hone her innovative skills. For our part, Steve and I moved to Japan to create Trend Micro's new international organization and to further deepen our penetration in the Asian market. As Trend Micro's business took flight, the lost royalty payments from Intel seemed increasingly insignificant. It was not long before they received little more than a passing thought.

In the run-up to our Tokyo listing in 1998, Intel requested at the end of our alliance contract that we share our latest version of InterScan. We responded with an agreement to continue providing the previous version for another two years to ensure continued support for InterScan users in Europe and the Americas. Intel did not respond kindly to this apparent rebuff and began covert contacts with our competitors. We had regained full control over our technology and the freedom to market beyond Asia—especially in key European and American markets. Free of Intel's shadow, we could finally take to the skies and fly as fast and as far as our wings would take us.

By the close of the twentieth century, frenetic competition among the more than five hundred companies in the antivirus solutions segment had whittled the field down to just three truly international competitors. These included merger-and-acquisition fueled Symantec, McAfee's successor Network Associates, and innovation-driven Trend Micro Inc.

The Japan "Snowball Effect"

When Trend Micro and Intel signed their strategic alliance in 1991, Japan was Asia's largest market, with the region's most advanced IT environment and a healthy emphasis on security. The Intel agreement spurred our decision to move the family to Japan in order to concentrate on developing Trend Micro's Asia-market sales. Our kids attended an international school, and I worked on learning Japanese. I diligently memorized new vocabulary three mornings every week, blended them with my limited grammatical skills, and used as much as I could in the office during the afternoon. I also organized and taught an English conversation class for our Japanese colleagues.

Having grown up in the United States, our two boys were used to their freedoms and had little patience for the polite niceties that defined so much of Japanese culture. Each day, I accompanied them to school by bicycle. Sometimes I had to sit patiently as their teachers lectured me on proper discipline. I enjoyed helping out on the occasional school trip. I have loved the outdoors since childhood but never learned a good sense of direction. When I was just three years old, I managed to wander away and get lost in Jiji for a whole day. How I was finally found and delivered safely home in tears by the police has been a story told and retold by family and friends ever since. In the unfamiliar landscape around my new home in Japan, although I could ask directions, I almost never understood the reply. I regularly lost my way in the seemingly endless warren of streets and alleys and lost my carefully maintained composure on more than a few occasions.

Steve, on the other hand, slipped into our new situation like a chameleon, successfully using an improvised amalgam of English, Chinese, his few Japanese phrases, and a liberal dose of hand movements to get his messages across. He bought out Trend Micro's local distributor and charged full steam into the Japanese market in true *henna gaijin* (crazy foreigner) fashion.

"Trend Micro will be Japan's largest software company!" Steve once announced to the whole office, standing atop a chair. At the time, the "whole office" comprised all eight employees from Trend Micro's newly acquired distributor. Only one could speak English, and the accountant was the only one with a university degree. Everyone else was a salesperson with a technical high school degree. In meetings, they spent much of the time looking nervously at one another and saw in Steve more to fear than to trust.

Certainly, one of the most difficult challenges for foreign startups in Japan is earning trust. Finding good employees is far from easy as well. Who would willingly put him or herself out for a Taiwanese boss?

Steve confidently stated that "We are fully committed to developing the antivirus software market and working in close partnership with Softbank. Our success is not in question." Softbank was, at that time, Japan's largest retail sales channel for IT products. Steve had taken his opening shot and calmly surveyed the situation. "In terms of technology," he noted, "we're already ahead of Jade (at the time, Japan's largest antivirus software provider). With continued research and development work in Taiwan and our strategic alliance with Intel, we will absolutely succeed as long as we earn the trust of our Japanese customers through good service." His ebullient confidence ever so gradually infected our Japanese colleagues. Eventually, they all participated wholeheartedly in this grand endeavor.

Earning our colleagues' trust was just the first hurdle. Earning the trust of customers required the focused effort of Trend Micro's local sales team.

Throughout those four years, I buried myself in my studies and invested myself in every aspect of our business. I had never been busier. Our children never got used to the climate. They developed asthma, and we made frequent visitors to the ER in the middle of the night. My eldest was coming into manhood and kept a busy social schedule. Steve, now heading an expanding worldwide operation, was often not home. I kept things going in Japan. I led Trend Micro's sales force and managed all communications between the Japan market and our R & D team in Taiwan.

Trend Micro's Japan office was not used to having a woman in charge. The discomfort was further sharpened by this particular woman's neither being Japanese nor wearing the practically mandatory business suit. She would sometimes even accompany them on customer calls. We thus decided to introduce me as Trend Micro's US-based vice president in order to give me an ostensible distance from day-to-day management and thus help our Japanese staff "save face." I did my best to fulfill the image required by that role. Although "face" little concerned me, I tried to maintain the façade because it was important to the team. After all, it was part of the "package deal" of doing business in Japan. I worked diligently to restrain the deep-set, no-nonsense business practices and habits we had learned in the United States and to adopt the restrained, roundabout style essential to getting things done in Tokyo. In the process, I helped translate Steve's ambitious vision for Trend Micro into a feasible plan that we could all work together to accomplish.

The first step to earning others' trust is often to demonstrate that you are willing to give your trust. Japan's ingrained cultural mores are highly subjective. They give high regard to tradition and precedent, are difficult to change, and are often defended with the conversation-stopping catchphrase: "This is Japanese way!" We framed many of our initial business decisions around the advice and suggestions of our local staff and then worked to nudge things in the direction we wanted to go. Taiwanese, after all, are the poster child of flexibility. With our eyes always on the goal, we remained ever ready to make necessary adjustments and changes along the way.

At the time, employees in Japan still enjoyed a high degree of job security, with stable salaries and good benefits part of the brick-and-mortar realities of the business landscape. Immediately after acquiring our Japan operation, we raised salaries across the board by 30 percent and then tied 30 percent of everyone's income to sales performance. This was the system we were familiar with in the United States. We gave everyone the 30 percent raise before factoring in performance, so this incentive program not only ensured no one lost out, it also offered a clear opportunity for them to earn significantly more than before. However, the instability it introduced to our employees' quarterly take-home pay made the system a regular target of gripes and groans. Dissenting voices were only quieted more than a year later, when staff saw their paychecks regularly increased. Mandatory, non-performance-based salary increases were also something very "Japanese." For example, when an employee married, it was expected that his or her salary would rise by a fixed percentage to help support new family expenses. We chose to retain this tradition in the fabric of the Trend Micro family, at least for the short-term.

In business, meetings play a central role in internal communications. Japanese companies typically use meetings as opportunities for managers to reprimand their staff, with staff either nodding deferentially or nodding off. We used meetings to canvass staff opinions and called on everyone in turn to speak his or her mind. It was an environment clearly outside their comfort zone. One staff member pulled me aside politely one day and said, "This is not Japanese way. You lose honor." Seeing an opportunity, I explained, "But I don't understand the Japanese way, so I must learn what you all think. If I cannot learn, then honor is useless." This explanation may have struck the right chord. The staff gradually became more open and willing to share after our brief talk.

There were some points on which we would not bend in deference to the "Japanese way." We remained singularly dedicated to continuous technological innovation, focused on antivirus software, and committed to using market research to guide our marketing and sales efforts. Basically, we insisted on integrating Japan into our global strategy rather than compromising to Japanese exceptionalism. At the time, many US companies did make these compromises and ran their Japanese operations separately from their normal international operations. We insisted that Japan keep firmly in step with our other operations around the world. This included supporting fully integrated operations and Trend Micro's global corporate culture and values.

In the arena of strategy, Steve's message was clear and to the point: "Think about what you should cut from your agenda. Do different, not just better."

The most difficult challenge was getting our Japanese colleagues to accept change. Reasoned justification, gradual implementation, and patience were all part of the equation. But the results were worth the wait, many times over!

We began launching Japanese versions of Trend Micro's product lineup a year and a half after our move into the market. We were all over Tokyo's Akihabara electronics district and took an impressive and growing share of national market sales. Jade KK, the one-time antivirus market leader, lost ground steadily as major market accounts switched over to Trend Micro. We switched gears to accommodate spiraling demand and grew our team from the initial eight to more than thirty employees.

Then, one night, while Steve was once again away in the United States, I was in the midst of a deep, exhausted sleep following a full day of meetings when the shrill, electronic ring of the bedside telephone dragged me unwillingly into groggy consciousness. I reluctantly picked up the handset, only to hear a cacophony of drunken male voices on the other end.

"Jenny-san. We have something to say to you ..." I immediately recognized that my callers were the half dozen or so Trend Micro colleagues from the meeting earlier that day. *Hadn't enough been said during the day?* I thought to myself. I crossly cleared the remaining fog from my head, sat up, and said, "Okay, I'm listening."

After initial courtesies, our engineer who spoke the best English came on the line. "You work very hard. We understand. We want to tell you— *arigato.* Please continue to work hard. We will *gambarimasu* (work hard) with you, too."

After more courtesies, he handed the phone around to the rest of the crew in turn. Each shared a short, personal message with me in simple Japanese they knew I would understand. I listened silently, unable to respond. At the end, unsure whether I was still there, one of them asked, "Jenny-san, *daijōbu?*"

They were asking if I was okay. The phone was wet with the tears flowing down my cheeks. I composed myself as best I could. "You guys are crazy, calling me in the middle of the night like this and making me cry. *Oyasuminasai ...*" I bade them a good night and put the receiver back. I was now fully awake and excitedly aware that Steve and I had finally tipped the scales. From here on out, the relationship with our Japanese colleagues would be one of mutual trust. We were now truly a team!

I was met with the typical detached greetings the next morning as I walked into the office. The *ohayō,* paired with a respectful nod, revealed nothing of our late-night conversation. Japanese take care not to wear their emotions on their sleeves and maintain a carefully refined air of dispassionate seriousness. Truths beneath the surface emerge only when lubricated with liberal doses of booze. I counted myself lucky that when the truth came out, I wasn't raked over the coals!

With internal trust secured, relationships of trust with external partners soon followed. Steve's partnering strategy with distributors, called Project Snowball, managed the rollout of Trend Micro's comprehensive national distributor network.

Trend Micro saw sales grow dramatically in the months and years that followed. By the time we launched our new windowing system, Trend Micro accounted for some three-quarters of all antivirus software sales in Japan. Trend Micro products were all productive cash cows for our distributors, which continued to include Softbank as well as the Otsuka Corporation, Fujitsu, NTT, and others. All became close Trend Micro partners.

Going to Market

After ten years in business, Trend Micro had nearly five hundred employees and thirty branch offices around the world.

We had venture-capital firms calling with cash ready to invest. Competitors were eyeing us with thoughts of mergers and acquisitions dancing in their heads. We turned them all down. We had a one-track mind that led straight to public listing.

The three of us obsessed over three possible options:

The first was to list on the New York Stock Exchange. This was the Holy Grail of high-tech company listings. A listing in the United States would make it easier to earn public recognition and attention. On the downside, however, the NYSE already had two antivirus software firms that had significantly more sales and market recognition than Trend Micro. A US listing would put us at a PR disadvantage that would be difficult, if not impossible to overcome.

The second option was a Taiwan listing. Taiwan was Trend Micro's birthplace and the home of our R & D operation. Furthermore, we already enjoyed excellent relationships with the market and the media there. Of course, all things being equal, Taiwan should be our first choice. Unfortunately, at that time, the Taiwan stock market was conspicuously devoid of software company listings.[1] Local laws mulishly recognized only physical assets such as factories and real estate properties. Our most important and valued assets comprised the expertise of our employees and our accumulated years of experience.

A Taiwan listing would also require our coming up with NT$200 million in capitalization (about US$6.25 million at the time)—quite a jump from the US$5,000 we'd needed in order to incorporate a decade earlier in California. A successful listing would thus require a major cash infusion. Several discussions in that direction wasted precious time with little result, and we became increasingly anxious that our optimal "launch window" would pass us by. We would need to go with another option, at least for now.

The third option we considered was the one on which we ultimately chose: a public listing on the Tokyo Stock Exchange (TSE). Japan was our largest market, and we had a recognized and respected brand name there. The TSE was also eager to add more software firms, especially foreign software firms, to its roster. There seemed to be just one major hurdle to cross: no foreign-incorporated firm had *ever* successfully listed on the TSE. Further complicating things was the fact that our proposed *kabushiki gaisha* (stock company) would be headed by a non-Japanese-speaking chairman.

Upon hearing of our plans for a TSE listing, Softbank founder Masayoshi Son offered to acquire a capital stake in Trend Micro. Softbank was a key Trend Micro distribution partner, so the investment worked on multiple levels. Masayoshi's involvement helped get all our ducks in order

---

[1] *The securities situation for software firms in Taiwan has changed significantly since then, and the Taiwan Stock Exchange now counts many successful software firms among its members. The success of Trend Micro's subsequent Tokyo listing and a desire to avoid the practical difficulties of maintaining the two accounts that would be necessary to support a concurrent Taiwan listing led us to abandon ambitions for an eventual public offering in Taiwan.*

and gave momentum to Trend Micro's ultimate listing on the Tokyo Stock Exchange.

Trend Micro formally joined the TSE on August 18, 1998. Our IPO garnered a demand-to-offer (DTO) ratio of 1 percent, and our initial stock price was twice what we expected. It was a memorable, heady milestone that was a long time in coming. We launched a secondary listing on the US NASDAQ exchange the following year. Softbank then sold off its share rights. Trend Micro had taken yet another substantial step forward toward internationalizing its capital.

Trend Micro's landing on the Nikkei 225 index in 2002 seemed a final affirmation of market acceptance and of confidence in the firm's prospects for future stable growth.

But if this was all I had to tell, it wouldn't make much of a story now, would it? For the true entrepreneur, seizing upon the next risk and returning to take up the next dance with danger provide the real thrills and rewards of entrepreneurism. Stopping to bask in victory would mean, "game over." Don't these rules apply to life as well? However much we might have looked forward to holding on to our achievements and settling into a "normal" business routine, the world that swirled around us would not have it. Our landscape was in a constant state of flux, change, and evolution, with only those willing and able to adapt and grow favored with success. In this game, today's leaders are fated to be usurped, while today's losers always have the chance to make a triumphant comeback. It is a never-ending cycle driven forward by the hard-and-fast rules of evolution.

Amid the unavoidable life-and-death struggle that defined the IT world, everything tangible seemed to fall by the wayside and disintegrate into nothingness. Perhaps, then, might intangibility be one of the essential facets of success?

CHAPTER 2

Trouble on Deck

Reform is sometimes required to inject the new cultural vibrancy necessary to strengthen a company's capacity to face up to current and future challenges. Such reform inevitably brings pain and confusion. I understood the hardships Steve faced in finding someone to succeed him as CEO of Trend Micro. I appreciated our colleagues for the discomfit they would face in a future transition. I knew that corporate culture in the software industry differed greatly from other industries. Nevertheless, I also realized the difficulties and frustrations that any ambitious industry executive would inevitably have in trying to saddle Trend Micro's entrepreneurial culture.

"I don't want to be CEO anymore!" Steve closed the cover of his laptop and gave me a serious look.

A proclamation like this would create quite a stir at an investors' meeting. However, I'd gotten rather used to outbursts like this from Steve over the past two or so years and was immune to their disconcerting sting. As I sat on the bed and folded the day's wash, I gave my pat response. "Right … once we find your successor and get everything else in place, we'll be free of all of this and able to arrange our lives as *we* want!"

Ignoring the sardonic barbs that were perhaps too well concealed in his wife's words, he continued with his stream of thought. "Ever since the public offering, I've kept thinking that investment strategy and day-to-day operations should be in two different hands. CEO and president shouldn't be the same person." I knew this was more than just grumbling. Steve's words gained the air of increasing conviction with each repetition. "It was ten years from Los Angeles to the Tokyo Stock Exchange. We have a stable, growing global business. The returns we've generated for our partners and founding shareholders have been exceptionally good." Steve was always concerned that those who took risks with him received their share of the benefits. "I'm the tip of the spear, but I can't manage everything. I'm not even interested in sorting things out and building organizations. There are lots of people who'd love to try their hand at being a CEO. There are many more capable than I of leading this company to the next level."

As Trend Micro's president for more than a decade, Steve had gone just about everywhere our business needed him. But this meant he frequently had to be Trend Micro's tip of the spear while pushing back against a haze brought on by jet lag, late nights, and continuous multitasking. While he and I both knew he couldn't maintain this pace over the long term, finding the right successor would be easier said than done. There had been precious few examples of smooth transitions of leadership in the high-tech sector.

"And who's going to fill your shoes? It's not like we haven't tried!" I picked up the folded clothes and headed for the doorway. I had made my point while purposely avoiding following my line of logic further down that rabbit hole.

The anxieties of our several experiences with transition still manage to send chills of dread up my spine.

When Bubbles Go "Pop"

Heady enthusiasm met Trend Micro's 1998 listing on the TSE, fueled by the fast-paced of growth of the World Wide Web and concurrent proliferation of Internet-borne viruses. Our stock price headed for the moon. It all seemed so unstoppable. Trend Micro attracted the industry's best and brightest talent, and within two years of going public, we had grown from several hundred to more than a thousand employees worldwide. Our boat was rising along with the fortunes of the new virtual world, and we were relishing the ride.

There is a saying that says, "Storms may burst from the clearest of skies." This easy-to-forget truism sums up an intuitive fact: what goes up must come down. Boats with the highest decks capsize first in the oncoming storm. During the year 2000, the Internet business model's reliance on steady streams of speculative cash brought the boom to a screeching halt. The sudden collapse of investor confidence in heavily hyped pets.com would be just the first of many high-profile bubbles to burst. It was followed by Enron, WorldCom, and America Online (AOL). In the end, few were spared from the newly re-found concern of investors for the true earning potential of the companies receiving their investments. The sound of bubbles popping reverberated across the marketplace. The change in investment climate was sudden and dramatic. It humbled even the market-hardened business leaders and ground-promising innovators into dust. Like a tsunami, the bad news just kept coming. The so-called "perfect storm"[2] savaged stock exchanges across the world, sparing none its callous wrath.

Trend Micro's consistently conservative approach to growth and investment and its solid revenue stream did not spare its stock from the general market flight from Internet-related securities. The market value of our stocks was halved. Of the many clients that canceled orders, the Japanese government's suspension of its comprehensive e-project was the most devastating. Trend Micro revenues failed to meet expectations by a significant margin. Clients in the United States and Europe also tightened their scrutiny of new purchases and dropped their investment in new network infrastructure.

It was under this cloud that we called a meeting of senior Trend Micro executives in Marina del Rey, California.

Trend Micro presidents from each region gave their abysmal prognoses in turn: "Revenues in Japan will fall short of expectations this year;" ""The outlook for US sales is not good;" "The situation in Europe isn't clear at this point in time;" "Our sales in China will not take off as anticipated."

---

[2] The term *perfect storm* originally referred only to storms of abnormally large size and force. It has been applied in the field of business and economics to describe a situation where numerous disparate factors converge to create an abnormally bad situation. Trend Micro has weathered three perfect storms so far: 1) the global economic crisis; 2) client delays in implementing e-digitalization plans; and 3) changes in accounting practices.

"Publication of the article 'IT Doesn't Matter'[3] spurred those CIOs who had not done so already to reevaluate their Internet-based productivity. Budgets tied to Internet activities were slashed across the industry." Trend Micro's CIO said, clearly appreciating the predicament in the IT industry at the time.

"To sustain our net profit margin," recalled Trend Micro's CFO, "we have only one choice: cut expenses."

"Our largest expense is human resources. I mean … would we really consider layoffs?" I said. Losing talent was my biggest concern. Once the bubble was gone, the stock options held by all our employees became empty promises. Quite a few employees were thinking seriously about quitting.

I told them "I'd prefer to cut sales and marketing expenditures first. I suggest canceling advertising for now." As head of Trend Micro marketing, I sacrificed a large percentage of my budget in order to give us a buffer that would hopefully be enough to protect HR. I was sacrificing our rooks to save the queen. But I was fully aware that it might only be a stopgap. I remained, along with everyone else in the company, deeply concerned for our future.

"No!" Steve insisted at every chance. "We are *no* bubble! PC sales continue to grow, and corporations will continue using computer networks. The burst of the Internet bubble had no effect on computer viruses, and digital security remains an important consideration." He remained indefatigable throughout and provided growing evidence to back up his claims. Confidence and investors gradually returned to Trend Micro as Steve's words began to reflect practical realities.

The CFO warned that lower investor expectations and the downward adjustment of anticipated returns could be expected to hit stock prices hard.

---

[3] HBR Chief Editor Nicholas G. Carr wrote and published "IT Doesn't Matter" in the May 2003 issue of *Harvard Business Review*. In the article, he likened IT infrastructure to a basic public utility and thus claimed that this infrastructure should not be factored into considerations of business competitiveness. Rather, he wrote, the most serious current threat to business was overinvestment in information technology. The issue once again drew heated discussion and debate when Carr published his follow-up book, *Does IT Matter?* a year later.

"Yes," Eva acknowledged. "But," she continued, taking the opportunity to yet again plug her idea of taking advantage of the ongoing market turmoil to enhance Trend Micro's R & D capabilities, "we should be *hiring* the best talent being let go by our competitors now."

"We've always needed more product managers. Perhaps now is a good time to hire some with good experience," I added. As the bridge between R & D and marketing, the product manager can have a decidedly accelerative impact on the software-production process.

"We'll weather this storm as long as we consolidate and intensify our core competitive strengths, and we'll be ready when demand picks up again." Steve always delivered such words with unwavering confidence. He knew that it was essential to keep all in the Trend Micro family positive and focused. One misstep might be all it took to send the organization back to square one.

Setting aside endemic concerns about the current business environment, we focused inward to pinpoint Trend Micro's core competitive advantages. We came up with five:

1) *Advanced virus-related technology and knowledge*: We clearly led all our competitors in this field. Our patented On the Fly[4] technology, invented by Eva, had already earned Trend Micro $125 million in settlements.

2) *Technology and market share for Internet gateway virus protection*: While Trend Micro was persistently second or third in the single-user license segment, we dominated the global market for virus-security products designed for servers and the Internet. Four out of every five Global 500 corporations were Trend Micro clients, and we owned close to 40 percent of the market.

3) *Balanced product innovation and product marketing capabilities*: Many companies founded by tech-savvy engineers are great at

---

[4] On the Fly is a technology that allows antivirus software resident on disparate network "nodes" to scan all handled files for viruses before forwarding them to their intended destination virus-free and cleaned, if needed. It is a four-step process, including file receipt, file caching to a proxy server, file scanning, and file forwarding. Trend Micro's On the Fly technology was awarded US patent no. 5623000 on April 22, 1997, under the title: *Virus detection and removal apparatus for computer networks*.

developing new technologies but lousy at turning those technologies into products that meet customer needs. Our business had successfully bridged these two aspects. We knew how to innovate and how to market our innovations to a worldwide audience.

4) *Comprehensive, well-respected global service network*: We had always treated antivirus as a service industry and were committed to constantly improving service quality. Trend Micro was the first to include a 24/7/365 service guarantee in its service contracts—a promise supported brilliantly by our three-shift service team in the Philippines. We were at one time the only software firm in the world to hold ISO9002 certification.[5] Service excellence translated into a strong upward growth trend for support-service revenues.

5) *Top-tier strategic alliances*: Focused solely on being the best in the antivirus segment, Trend Micro had no interest in acquiring businesses with unrelated products or services in order to boost corporate sales. We steered clear of the firewall sector, which already had its strong competitors. Like those of its competitors, Trend Micro's all-in-one Internet safety solution strategy benefited from strong alliance agreements with major industry players such as Cisco, Dell, and Intel. This was one component of our business strategy that Steve made sure did not change.

The soul-searching discussions and pep talks let us see more clearly the light at the end of the tunnel. Better appreciating our strengths gave the entire Trend Micro team new hope and fighting spirit.

Steve summed up our situation. "Our competitive strengths are our field weapons. But if we fail to change with changes in the overall environment, we will still face an unpleasant demise." With slightly threatening undertones, he continued, "In the face of danger, the only way

---

[5] The International Organization for Standardization (ISO) was founded in 1947 with its headquarters in Geneva, Switzerland. The founding mission of the ISO was to set appropriate product standards for products sold within the European Common Market (now superseded by the European Union) as well as to create standards that could be used worldwide to facilitate internationalization/globalization and reduce technical barriers to trade. The ISO 9002 standard establishes a quality assurance system for products of the manufacturing and service industries.

forward is 'change.' Change in organization, change in strategy, change in products, change in services … everything. We need to change how we market and sell, how we spend our funds, and how we operate. Everything must be reexamined and scrutinized. We can't afford not to change."

Everyone accepted with little surprise his announcement of Trend Micro's new cultural emphasis on "change." However, what followed was truly an unanticipated bombshell. "I need to change as well. I will be giving serious thought as to the appropriateness of my continuing as president." It was the first that any had heard of Steve's thoughts about stepping down and the first that any had seriously pondered the thought of a Trend Micro without Steve at the helm.

While it was certainly startling, many chose to interpret this first shot across the bow as Steve's way of underscoring the seriousness of his commitment to fundamentally change Trend Micro—even if that change meant turning the reigns over to someone else.

Trend Micro's helmsman never again mentioned in public his thoughts about stepping down. He returned to the urgent task of implementing those changes he saw as necessary not only to successfully weather the current storm but also to be ready to catch the favorable winds on the other side. Eventually, everyone forgot that Steve had once said he might one day remove himself from the Trend Micro picture.

CEO Search

But Steve didn't forget, and he made it a habit of reminding me of the fact.

Once the storm clouds that had dogged our industry for so long began to clear, Trend Micro's helmsman recognized that it was about time to return to our normal heading. In the relatively peaceful months after emerging from what seemed an interminably long time beneath well-battened hatches, Steve, in private, once more took up the idea of stepping down. He began taking some surreptitious shore leave to scope out potential candidates.

Steve and I had founded Trend Micro as a team, and I had always been officially in charge of the marketing and personnel ends of the business as well as countless other responsibilities that remained undignified by a proper department. My life had centered on our business and our family. There was precious little "me time" left. While I, too, yearned for the day when we could un-shoulder the burdens of running a business, honestly, if truth be told, I had gotten used to the frenetic pace; accustomed to working as part of a well-oiled operation; wrapped up in the adrenaline rush of the husband and wife team; and wholly comfortable with following Steve's lead forward. Thus, if a succession *was* truly in the cards, and if we were indeed suddenly lifted of our heavy professional responsibilities, I honestly had no clue as to how I would, or even *could*, handle it.

As for Eva Chen, the third partner in our entrepreneurial triumvirate, she had maintained a dedicated focus on the R & D end of the business. Steve had helped keep her mostly insulated from the front lines of sales and client relations as well as from the pressures of growing the bottom line. But she had recently fallen back into relying on some of her old bad habits. Also, with two young children, Eva was finding it increasingly difficult to juggle professional and family responsibilities. Thus, despite Steve's frequent overtures, Eva repeatedly refused to consider stepping into his shoes as the next president of Trend Micro Inc.

Stubborn once he had made up his mind and never one for empty words, Steve began looking outside of Trend Micro for an experienced senior manager. Intel's Internet Division, a longtime Trend Micro partner, was one of the places Steve naturally put out feelers.

Initially, it seemed an ideal match. Trend Micro hired away from Intel its highly experienced financial manager. He was honest and straightforward, and Steve appointed him to the long-vacant position of operations manager. Under his watch, he would help Trend Micro hire many more Internet Division managers away from Intel. However, these former Intel staff members, arriving with their own corporate culture, soon became a large enough minority within Trend Micro to begin pushing for changes in the way Trend Micro did business externally as well as internally. Fractious arguments simmered, and, ultimately, even our long-term R & D objectives fell to irreconcilable debate.

We had never considered that mere differences in corporate culture might ultimately impede Trend Micro's momentum forward. Intel's grounding in the world of IT hardware gave it a hard, no-nonsense approach to business, which it sharpened further with a business model that rewarded the "warriors"—those who upheld the stereotypically American ideal of "winner takes all." This was a culture diametrically opposed to Trend Micro's groundings in communication, compromise, collaboration, and cross-cultural values.

We had not overlooked the glaringly apparent differences in culture between our organizations. Rather, we hoped that they would somehow synthesize into something that would let Trend Micro retain its former advantages and strengthen its historical weaknesses. Perhaps Intel's high-strung corporate culture could offset Trend Micro's chronically introverted nature in order to increase competitiveness in our European and American markets. Our accommodative approach sometimes kept us from facing harsh realities and from challenging each other in order to optimize company growth. Intel's confrontational culture wasn't, after all, without its merits. Trend Micro's cooperative culture and its predilections against interdepartmental conflict perhaps reduced opportunities for employees to show personal initiative and leadership and, as a result, actually slowed our momentum forward. Moreover, in a transnational enterprise such as Trend Micro, finding equilibrium in terms of culture was orders of magnitude more difficult than in companies run on a cut-and-dried "American" model. After all, examples of true cross-cultural harmony on the international stage are preciously few and far between.

Thus, blending our two cultures was never intended as a short-term endeavor—especially because ours was the superficially "weaker" of the two. We had no idea how long it would take to work rigid steel into pliant putty. After all, who can be certain about the outcome of putting a boxer into the ring with a *taijiquan* martial-arts master or teaming a US cowboy up with a Zen Buddhist monk? Communications were always an interesting challenge. What passed as clear enough in the Asian mind seemed always in need of further clarification to the Westerner.

For the first time in its history, Trend Micro began seeing internal factional rivalries and indissoluble prejudices, with business proposals stopped dead in their tracks.

Change that recalibrates and rejuvenates corporate culture is essential to improving the entire organization. Pain necessarily accompanies this process. As head of human resources, I was Trend Micro's "first responder." It was up to me to handle as judiciously as possible the torrent of thorny HR problems that crossed my desk. On the one hand, I empathized with Steve's difficult search for a successor, sympathized with the adjustment troubles faced by our long-time colleagues, and understood the quirky culture that made the software industry special. However, on the other hand, I had to make accommodations for Trend Micro's new, highly experienced colleagues. When two worlds collide, when aggressive entrepreneurialism meets collaborative conservatism, troubles and frustrations are to be expected—in spades.

I set my sights invariably on a win-win result. I encouraged our long-time colleagues by saying, "They bring advantages that we need in order to grow in our weakest market, the United States. While they may be overly direct and place less value on relationships, they may indeed help us better accept and face up to harsh marketplace realities." I continued with a plea, "Let's all allow a bit more time both for them to acclimate to our culture and for us to recalibrate our own attitudes and learn to communicate with them better! After all, isn't communication a central facet of the Trend Micro way?"

On the other side, I counseled our new business warriors, "We've seen steady growth in business every year so far and already rank among the largest antivirus software firms in the world. We naturally have our own strengths and well-established corporate culture. I urge you all to hold your horses. Watch and learn. Learn to do business our way first before you start proposing necessary changes."

My explanations were oft repeated, as were my appeals for dispassionate understanding from both sides. Although my detached, dichotomized messages often seemed to dissipate on frustratingly deaf ears, progress was being made, especially in our increasingly cohesive European and American organizations.

It was at this juncture that Trend Micro's helmsman began hinting more openly about stepping down. Those sensitive to such things quickly sensed Steve's intentions, and soon people were making overt and covert moves to ensure their place on the shortlist of possible successors. Speculation about Trend Micro's future ran rampant throughout the company. Some looked to take advantage of the situation, while others greeted the potential for change with anxiety about the unknown.

Wanting to test the capabilities of several successor candidates as well as to create a professional management structure at Trend Micro, Steve asked me to step down as head of global sales first and then quit as head of human resources. I also relinquished my position as the deputy business controller and asked that managers in all departments work to ensure that all leadership transitions went smoothly and successfully.

For her part, Eva refused to budge on her control of Trend Micro product R & D. She couldn't stomach the prospect of seeing the world's best, highly customized antivirus system becoming subject to a board-approved product strategy. She was also adamantly opposed to focusing on numbers of virus hits to the detriment of Trend Micro's ability to safeguard computer-memory storage. However, she saved her strongest words for the debate about whether to outsource and/or acquire new products instead of keeping new-product development a wholly in-house operation. Our Asia-based research and development team was a point of pride for all of us. This team had created our leading-edge products, developed groundbreaking technological innovations, and made Trend Micro products accessible to users worldwide. They now argued that "Made it Here" was a millstone that hampered further innovation and growth and were constantly on the lookout for opportunistic new business hookups. For someone like Eva, who had pulled the organization up by its bootstraps without outside support, these insinuations were abrasive and downright humiliating.

Eva had singlehandedly built Trend Micro's R & D team from the ground up. Although we hoped she might eventually release her jealously guarded authority over antivirus product strategy to Trend Micro's executive board, Eva remained naturally suspicious of centralized management systems and unconvinced of Steve's intentions to step down. While the gladiators in the anticipated race for succession prepared to do battle, the king continued to publicly deny any plans to step down while searching frantically for someone able to smooth just such an exit.

Numbers Don't Lie

The rules of the marketplace are clear and immutable. Strategy leads to implementation; marketing ends in a review of sales performance. Within the hallowed halls of capitalism's security exchanges, up is the only acceptable direction for a company's sales to go. In the harsh light of day, numbers don't lie.

Steve's prospective successor had brought a phalanx of top-flight, experienced professionals with him to Trend Micro from a major IT hardware firm. But their brazen charge into our competitive sea ended with the roiling waves depositing them, disheveled and disoriented, back where they started on the shore. Another key difference separating our new employees from entrepreneurs was attitudes about spending money. As entrepreneurs, we had started with nothing and thus knew how to squeeze the most out of limited funds. They, on the other hand, were accustomed to spending their share of generously funded budgets; every penny of the approved budgets had to be spent on the fight at hand. Ending the year under budget invariably reflects negatively on a department's ability to carry out its plans. Thus, budgetary allocations are regularly and enthusiastically cashed out. Their philosophy on spending is simple: invest, attack, and win market share in hopes of maximizing return on investment. This is the basic American corporate strategy. Many now well-known firms have prospered by following such principles. However, many more, quietly forgotten to history, followed the principles into failure and bankruptcy.

Trend Micro had always been an Asian company that valued living within its means. We had never taken a loan and had never been in the red. Although we frequently came in under budget, we still managed to see our sales and profits grow. It was an exceptional track record. We pursued innovation and change and sought business that was enjoyable and interesting. We never spent more than was absolutely necessary and studiously avoided investments on empty luxuries. Trend Micro's thrifty ethics were deeply rooted in time-tested ancestral traditions.

After three quarters under new management, Trend Micro had a greatly enlarged headcount, huge increases in expenditures across the board, and plummeting productivity. Most troubling of all was the sharp cut in profits—something shareholders simply would not accept for long. External sales pressures, product-effectiveness issues, and internal disaffection gradually dragged Trend Micro's new corporate managers to conclude that communications were failing, innovation was being inhibited, and change was not happening. They pinned the problems on the resistance of Trend Micro's stubbornly entrenched entrepreneurial culture to bend to the necessities of top-down corporatism.

Regardless of the underlying reasons, the numbers did not lie. The experiment was failing in the dispassionate eyes of American capitalism. We had given them three quarters. Even they themselves had to admit that we had given them full liberties to play their hand. They knew the rules of the game, and, one by one, many left for greener pastures. However, some of those MBA-trained professionals stuck it out, and after several more years of experience with Trend Micro's culture, they came to embrace our person-centered management principles. They chose to stay and fight as full-fledged members of the reinvigorated Trend Micro team.

Steve was crestfallen by the ignominious departure of his supposed successor. He swallowed the humiliation and once more shouldered his executive burdens and rallied the troops to press forward to victory. He worked tirelessly, filled vacated positions, and even personally negotiated client contracts. Miraculously, the quarter immediately following the departure of our warrior executives saw sales rise and our profit margin regain a healthful glow. Investors rewarded the change with a welcome bump in share price.

The Taste of Being Lost

Steve hadn't seen pressure like this since our first years in business. It was worse than the IT market crash because the problems were internal— caused, at least in part, by his desire to step down. Guilt kept him fearful of letting his guard down again and he spent the next two years buried in his work, more stressed and tired than ever.

During these intervening years, our two sons had grown up and left to find their own fortunes. One went to work in Beijing, while the other went off to school in Boston. Our reunions were few and far between. Steve's desires to be free to pursue his passions once again bubbled to the fore. His true desire was to find personal peace and explore his inner self in order to attain fulfillment. It was a path that necessarily diverged from that of the past dozen years we'd spent creating and building Trend Micro. Although the excitement and passion of his early entrepreneurial days had faded, he still was expected to inspire the team to move forward. Although he began to doubt the ability of numbers and rewards to manage the human character, he had to continue maintaining those systems and to allow the use of hard-and-fast numerical indices. Models of business that he once accepted without thinking became sources of internal consternation. The desire for "change" encoded in Steve's DNA began finding its voice once again: "I must change my life! I'm going to take a different path!"

But this time, he had learned his lesson. He would keep his thoughts of succession private until everything was already in place. He reserved his expressions of honesty for late-night pillow talk, when he invariably also faced my disparaging remarks and his own internal contradictions.

"We've turned a startup into a publicly traded company. We've had all manner of corporate-management experience. We've been to more than fifty countries and managed IT professionals of more than sixty nationalities. I think we've had enough business experience, don't you? Can't we just let it go?" Although he regularly directed this question to me, I knew he was really asking himself.

"Yes. There's so much else we could be doing," I would respond softly, not necessarily wanting to fan his flames, yet not willing to steer him back.

His dream had always been to create a new business, and he had fully invested more than two decades of his life to make it happen. So, was it time to wake up from this dream and begin another? Could we begin planning our next exciting journey? Would it indeed be possible to set Trend Micro aside, set down our halos, and embark on that lonely path to self-exploration and personal discovery?

For my part, I naturally took my cues from Steve. But was I ready for a change? If not the boss's wife, then what?

Founding a company was never my personal dream. I had wanted to write and maybe to go as far as professional editing or publishing. I had expected to remain within the cultured confines of the world of arts and letters. While I unfortunately lacked the requisite talent and studies, I had enough sense to turn my sights toward more achievable goals. My jump from literature into business happened to coincide with the publishing of my very first short story in the literary journal *Crown*. For me, it marked the hideous end to broken dreams. I tossed it aside. "The world mourns not the death of a third-rate writer!" Limited life experience made my writing lackluster, and Steve's ebullient dive into entrepreneurism was a party that was hard to resist.

"Experience something different," he would say. "Meet people you would never otherwise meet. Learn the taste of hardship and even failure. Who knows? It may add some texture and depth to your writing." At his encouragement, I stopped translating English-language books on business management and began translating Chinese-language instruction manuals into English. I made the dramatic leap from Chinese literature to English-language advertising. Once an aspiring author of romance novels, I ended up publishing the story of our startup experience in *@Trend Micro* and my thoughts on business management in *Unstoppably Trend Micro*. I would occasionally awake in the middle of the night, see the pile of English and Japanese-language Internet magazines on my nightstand, and believe that I was in some otherworldly nightmare in which I'd lost my way.

I followed him with unvarnished enthusiasm down his entrepreneurial path, and in doing so, I gradually lost my glow of literary pretense. I stepped outside the ivory tower, trained in the foreign arts of business warfare, and went into battle. This exciting, stimulating life bore little trace of my former ambitions, and I did not regret my decision to take this very different path. In fact, thoughts of again shifting gears were enough to evoke anxious chills. Could I possibly find my way back into the realm of literature after leaving Trend Micro? Would I be able to write or even to edit?

A cold sweat gripped me as I was stoked by memories of losing my way in a crowd as a child and of getting lost hopelessly in the winding Japanese alleys. Unable to escape my own doubts, I felt like curling up and crying.

CHAPTER 3

Culture—Alive and Kicking

The mathematical symbol for "infinite loop" is ∞.

Customer expectations are on the left, while system innovation is on the right.

Cycling endlessly in perpetual interaction, with innovation as the driving force.

The importance of treating the client as a core value is something we learned only gradually.

"If you get lost, the most important thing to remember is: don't panic!" Steve often reminded me. "The worst that can happen is you walk a bit longer. You'll find your way sooner or later."

Steve never once lost his nerve or his secure footing on his entrepreneurial path. He was like a hawk, always circling, always alert. Once he had a target in sight, he acted quickly and decisively. Steve rarely missed his target. Perhaps it was this attitude of his that helped us manage so well along our dangerous path forward. We saw much success, avoided most pitfalls, and crossed every hurdle. Our occasional sidesteps were additional opportunities to learn, and we made the most of every experience—good and bad.

The end of March one year found us again in Tokyo for Trend Micro's regular meeting with shareholders. Afterward, we took our usual side trip to enjoy the seasonal pleasures of cherry blossoms and hot spring baths. As it was only the two of us this time, we made no particular plans beforehand. The first website that popped up after a search using the keywords "cherry blossoms," "hot spring," and "golf" was Kitsuregawa in Tochigi Prefecture, a place neither of us had ever heard of. The name alone dripped deliciously off the tongue, so we needed no further convincing. We entered our destination into our Japanese GPS system and, chatting away, headed out in high spirits. Not long into our journey, we realized that a wrong turn or two had gotten us totally lost. We had no idea where we were, and I began to slip into another panic. Steve pulled over to the side of the road, opened the door, and said, "Let's walk! It's nothing to worry about."

He took my hand and we walked until we were well away from the beaten path. Suddenly, we found ourselves standing at the entrance to a footpath lined by cherry trees covered in beautiful blossoms. A slight breeze brought the festooned branches to dreamy, fluid life. Petals fell like delicate flakes of new-fallen snow on our hair and shoulders and on the ground all around our feet. We had lost our way but had found a landscape that I would savor in my memory forever. Why cling stubbornly to a preplanned course and objective? Occasionally straying off course can be the ticket to something so much more beautiful!

This experience helped abate a lifelong fear of getting lost. Taking a new road and anticipating its unfamiliar scenes was the perfect cure to the tiredly familiar, well-traveled route.

My epiphany in Japan triggered ripples that brushed all aspects of my life: Why not drink green tea in the morning instead of coffee? Why don't I try *not* touching the computer in the evening? How about not packaging our products? Can we delink work efficiency and increases in salary? I even took to challenging my perspectives on our firm's immutable, eternal core values.

"Change is the value that most clearly differentiates us from our competition," I challenged our president. "So, I ask you: Is changing *this* value a possibility?"

Steve's predilection to change Trend Micro's strategy often left me confused and disoriented as to our direction and goals at any given time. Although I knew I wasn't a good debater, I couldn't help but take the opportunity to give him a taste of his own medicine. Seeing blood, I sensed the chance to move in for a kill.

We face changes in everyday life; the Internet is constantly evolving and changing; companies grow and mature; strategies get adjusted and tuned to new realities. So why can't the behavior of a team change in response to new needs and situations?

From its earliest days, Trend Micro had projected the 3C culture of Change, Communication, and Creativity. But questions remained as to the elements that underpinned this impressive façade. Did these elements adequately express the moral fortitude that was essential to operating in the realm of Internet security? Did they adequately describe our distinctive corporate DNA? Moreover, were they adequate to support our future growth and evolution?

Constructing Culture

Our 3C culture had been with us for as long as any could remember. It reflected the fundamental nature of Eva, Steve, and me. It also captured the spirit of our nascent entrepreneurial endeavor. But, at what point in time and under what fortuitous conditions had this set of cultural statements become our set-in-stone cultural core and oft-repeated corporate mantra?

Thinking on this question releases the emotional floodgates, and I am soon awash in pleasant memories of those hopeful, exciting early years of Trend Micro.

It was 1990, our third year in business. The issue of computer viruses was slowly but steadily garnering public attention, and we were at the Comdex computer expo in Las Vegas for the worldwide launch of our flagship antivirus software product, PC-cillin. It was an instant hit, and we soon had distributors in thirty-three countries racking up impressive sales. Steve and I were actively developing US market channels, and Eva was in Taiwan leading our engineers into daily battle against digital viruses. At the time, from top to bottom, Trend Micro had fewer than thirty employees.

Always the visionary leader, Steve announced that Trend Micro would hold the company's first worldwide distributors' meeting in Taiwan at the magnificent Grand Hotel in Taipei City. Invitations were quickly confirmed, and more than a hundred Trend Micro representatives from around the world gathered for the event. They wanted to uncover the truth about this upstart company, to know more about its products and technology, and to meet members of the organization and its talent in order to assess the long-term sales and partnership prospects. Of course, everyone was more than happy about taking the chance for a vacation in Taiwan as well.

The responsibility for organizing the distributors' meeting alighted naturally onto my shoulders. My small team got to work on the daunting task of putting everything together. We arranged venue details, reserved hotel rooms and catering, set the meeting agenda, booked the entertainment and side trips, and even arranged the media interview schedule. While we made steady progress, I was plagued with nagging worries. I felt I had left something out.

"So, the goal of this meeting is to bring our worldwide distributors to us so that they can better understand who we are and we can have a stronger long-term relationship with them. Is that right?" I pointedly asked the meeting's author.

"Yep!" Steve replied distractedly. He was lying on our bed, reading a book. His wife's perfectionist proclivities were sometimes downright maddening.

"But we've got just one product, and it's easy to understand. We have less than thirty people in our organization, so introductions shouldn't last long. Do we really need a three-day meeting?" I feared we might quickly run out of things to do and say.

"Okay, then!" he chided. "Just start talking about your interests … Chinese culture, Confucius, Mencius, Laotzu … the lot!"

I smiled and took up his challenge. "Well, that would be a definite party killer." I thought more on Steve's words and said, mostly to myself, "If not Chinese culture, what if I talked about our company's culture? Would that be overly incongruous?" I was ready to drop the subject and return to the business at hand.

"That's an interesting idea." Steve finally sat up. "Think about it … when you want to really get to know someone, apart from learning where he went to school, what he studied, his background, you're also curious to know about his personality, morals, character, and so on, right?"

"Agreed," I said, ready to extend the analogy to Trend Micro. "A company's culture can be likened to its personality and character."

Steve brought the idea into even clearer focus and said, "It's the code of attitudes and behaviors we follow in working together."

"But is this something they talk about at distributors' meetings?" I asked skeptically.

"No," he quickly replied with a grin. "So we will." He reveled in being the trailblazer. "Those who really know us trust us. They come to know and believe in our technology and services. It's what builds good reputations, right?"

My interest was rekindled. "The way you say it, this is probably important, then. So, how should we best define Trend Micro's culture? What makes us tick?"

As far as I can remember now, that was the first time Steve and I had ever talked about corporate culture.

We had a small operation, and opinions were easy to canvass. I posed the questions and everyone gave me their immediate thoughts. I found we shared a lot in common as a team, and comments rarely strayed far from insights like: "Steve loves to push change. He even uses magic tricks to get his point across;" "Innovation is critical. We never make 'me too' products;" "We've got so many distributors in so many countries that we're constantly communicating throughout the day. Jenny, didn't you always say that there could never be *too much* communication?"

Thus, it seemed as if *Change*, *Creativity*, and *Communication* did indeed describe fairly well everyone's approach to working at Trend Micro. These three concepts seemed to encapsulate the team spirit and eloquently reflect our corporate ethos.

As to why we stopped at those three nouns, Steve explained: "No more than that. Nobody would remember them all, and it would dilute our true character." So potential additions such as the ubiquitous *integrity* and *diligence* were all dropped. Anyway, because these concepts belonged to the nuts and bolts, the very fundamentals, of the way we did business, they were almost overly obvious and thus nothing special. Therefore, only those elements that reflected our innermost ideals and instructed how we conducted ourselves in business would be considered worthy of a place on the mantle of Trend Micro culture.

As our three core values of Change, Communication, and Creativity fortuitously shared the same first letter, it seemed only natural to further huddle Trend Micro's essence under the umbrella of 3C. It wasn't long after that someone stumbled on another fortuitous coincidence. "Are you sure you didn't choose '3C' because of your last names? Steve Chang, Jenny Chang, and Eva Chen!"

While not planned that way, the three *C*s of Trend Micro did describe our three personalities quite nicely. Perhaps it is a truism that a company's culture inevitably bears the imprint of its founders. I know that sometimes that imprint can cast a heavy shadow that is difficult to extirpate. For me, corporate culture is not static. Instead, it is a dynamic concept that is open to growth and change over time, driven by new people, new elements, and new directions. This is fundamental to retaining a corporate culture that remains not only viable but also distinctly relevant over time. After all, Chinese culture itself is a melting pot of nationalities and philosophical perspectives where communication and accommodation are constant and pervasive facts of life. Isn't that what has kept us viable through the millennia?

Integration & Renewal—Trend Micro @ 10

I was curious ... after over a decade of growth and a greater than tenfold increase in personnel, how did the Trend Micro organization now interpret their 3C cultural legacy? Most employees by this time had little, if any, personal interaction with the founders, so I suspected they might perceive our influence quite differently from those who joined us at the start. While the core values we ensconced remained in place, had their substance changed? Perhaps they had taken on greater nuance and richness. Especially once Trend Micro had gone public and had taken on so many outside managers, was there a perceived need to review and perhaps update the company's culture?

Issues like this, nonquantifiable and amorphous, yet so critical to business operations, were the ones that had always piqued my greatest interest. Three years into our life as a public company, I looked forward to giving our core values a thorough review and tune-up at the next regular meeting of Trend Micro's senior executives.

To lay the groundwork, I hired a professional psychologist to help design a questionnaire that would help elucidate our cultural strengths and weaknesses. I sent the questionnaire out to Trend Micro employees, partners, and clients worldwide, asking qualitative questions like: "What do you think Trend Micro could be doing better?" and "When you have questions/concerns, who do you normally confide in first?"

We intentionally left the last field open with the question: "Do you have any additional thoughts or suggestions?" The critical deluge that followed winded me.

"Excessively technology focused. Lack of attention to management issues." Moreover, the response from partners and clients such as IBM, Cisco, and Intel, as well as our own employees, was similar. Trend Micro's "flexible" approach to business was almost universally criticized.

"Trend Micro's engineer-entrepreneur culture lacks market focus," was typical of the acerbic comments given by members of our growing sales team.

"Lots of passion, little stability!" Our major account clients appreciated our passions but saw us as immature—perhaps even hyperactive. They needed us to be more constant and dependable in our business relationships.

"Ignores practical customer needs. Singularly focused on innovation!" Even our innovativeness was getting raked over the coals!

Despite my deep disappointment, the responses were there in undeniable black and white. As planned, I glumly shared my findings with our senior executives.

"Should we be discussing ideas on how to best overhaul or at least strengthen our corporate culture?" I asked them. I couldn't do this unilaterally. I would need the support of our executive team.

We three founders were Taiwanese, so it had only been natural that our cultural mores and values had definitely influenced the Trend Micro culture. However, while it was high time that we absorbed more Western corporate cultural traits, the process had to be executed artfully in order to avoid unwanted friction and a potential backlash.

Experience has taught me that the best way to implement a plan is to start off low-key and bring department managers into the discussion. Afterward, the issue can be opened up gradually to the entire organization, with everyone having the opportunity to get his or her opinion heard and incorporated, or at the very least, acknowledged.

"We may be at another critical turning point!" I said, "and this change may be nothing short of 'nation-building.'"

Trend Micro's fourteen senior executives launched into fervid discussion of the topic at hand. Some were clearly concerned: "Changing our core values will change our policy reference points and how we make decisions!" Others, however, were pleased: "Nothing should be 'unchangeable.' Change is part of our fundamental nature."

While discussion and debate continued, we had a difficult time delimiting the scope of the issue. Culture was a different animal from issues like sales and product development, which had clearly defined sets of measurable, indisputable results and indicators. The subjective assertions such as "I think" and "I believe" that habitually precede statements about "culture" and "spirit" often pin discussions in these realms to the wings of unrestricted imagination.

Finally, our COO, well read on management theory and highly credentialed through previous positions in major multinationals, cut to the chase. "Before discussing corporate culture, we have to define our vision and our mission." He concluded with a sober observation: "Maintaining Internet security has been the primary motivation for many to join Trend Micro."

Honestly speaking, I'd never considered that the slogan beneath Trend Micro's trademark might influence Trend Micro's recruitment efforts.

Another of our highly experienced executives added: "Vision encapsulates a company's *raison d'être*, the collective ideal of the whole organization. Our vision shapes our customer commitments, our product development strategy, the direction of technology innovation work, and, ultimately, determines our core competitive strengths." We had truly hit on an issue fundamental to Trend Micro and to its future viability as a business.

"As a company, we have control over data receipt and transmission. Beyond protecting systems from viruses, we are also ideally placed to filter or block access to potentially harmful and inappropriate websites," said Eva Chen, Trend Micro's longstanding chief technology officer. "We have an effective role to play every single time data is exchanged. We're not limited to virus protection. We're not even limited to security issues."

Again showing his ability to take things to their ultimate and logical conclusion, Steve stepped into the ring and said, "Right! The Internet is ubiquitous today. We're doing much more than just looking after Internet security; we are a key player in *global security*!"

With that settled, our executives from English-speaking countries worked to translate the concept into a fitting, suitably punchy new tagline for Trend Micro's corporate vision. We came up with a consensus on the phrase: "A world safe for exchanging information."

Our focus would be on creating a user-safe environment free of viruses, data theft, and data loss. Teetering at wits' end, we had finally forged a concept and a slogan approved by most executives.

But multiple readings of our new slogan raised a new question in my mind: *So, suppose we print this slogan and use it in our advertising. Does that make us practically responsible for all of types of security issues?*

"You and your nitpicking!" Steve snapped back. He was never overly concerned about words and wanted to stop my taking the issue further.

However, our English-language experts smiled and conceded the point. "Good thinking," they said. "We don't want to take responsibility for anything that happens outside of the Internet. We can fix that with the word *digital*."

A world safe for exchanging digital information! Heads nodded all around as everyone at the table tried the phrase out for size. The more we said it, the more it seemed the right elixir for our future business ambitions.

Soon afterward, on a business trip to the UK, our COO was asked by the immigration officer what business he was in. He straightened up and blurted, "A world safe for exchanging digital information!" His colleagues gave him a good ribbing for "drinking a bit too much of the Trend Micro 'Kool-Aid.'"

With the issue of vision settled, we turned our attention to discussing Trend Micro's mission, i.e., the actions necessary to realize the vision.

We all came to quick agreement that Trend Micro would broaden its scope beyond virus protection to the general safeguarding of digital information. Furthermore, we agreed that our control of data nodes gave us the added responsibility to secure the entire framework by using the best comprehensive Internet-security strategy possible. We would no longer focus on symptoms. We had our sights set on the fundamentals.

We would indeed become the content-security expert that best fits into network information flow.

Perhaps only fully appreciated within Trend Micro, this sentence expressed a goal that all knew would be extremely difficult to accomplish. Even so, it won quick consensus. After all, something easily done wouldn't be worth its salt as a mission statement, right? This mission statement would become the goal for everyone working at Trend Micro.

Time to Change the Menu - 4 Entrées and a Soup

Discussions on our vision and mission had consumed an entire morning. After lunch, we pushed on to tackle a more metaphysical topic: Trend Micro's core values. It was time to shift gears and ask our executives to give their left (logical) brain a rest and turn the ignition on their right (intuitive) brain. When I look back on that day, it was probably remarkable to have senior executives representing eight nationalities spending an entire day discussing culture—an issue superficially unrelated to the battles fought every day in the business "trenches."

Should we change our 3C culture? Is there something missing or something that needs to be strengthened? What key issues have we overlooked so far?

I chaired the discussion, so I did my best to hold back my own thoughts on issues. I focused on keeping the questions flowing. In fact, I even took some provocative pot shots in hopes of adding more fuel to the debate. "Why not eliminate 'change' as one of our values? We've changed enough!" "Communication is outmoded; we should shift to something new and more effective;" "Can't we innovate on innovation?"

Perhaps out of stubborn willfulness, perhaps out of fatigue, no one at the table could come up with anything better to replace 3C. "We cannot sacrifice change, because change is our most important motivational asset. Take out change and you tarnish Trend Micro's brilliance."

"Communication ... we should work to improve on this point, not eliminate it."

"Creativity is central to our success in rising to the top of the software industry. It is a value that cannot be replaced and that we should make sure always gets enough attention."

But there must be room for improvement, I thought. I turned to Steve. As the father of Trend Micro's 3C culture, I thought he might hold the key to its successful upgrade. "3C is here to stay," he said. "So, if we're going to add to it, what two facets of our business need the most help?"

Once Steve had framed the issue, the discussion flowed fast and free. Those eager to see Trend Micro focus more on market demand pointed to issues highlighted in my questionnaire. They raised Trend Micro's "engineer-entrepreneur culture" and asked whether we should continue prioritizing technical innovation over our customers' practical problems; if Trend Micro could make the transition from a product-oriented to a service-oriented enterprise; and which corporate characteristics would be most valued and desired by our customers.

Honestly speaking, our product R & D had never *really* taken the interests of the general user to heart. We were in a race for innovation, and our "customers of concern" were all high-end users. Everyone was a techie, and there was little need for explanations or user manuals. The only thing limiting innovation was our own knowledge and technical capabilities. This approach was certainly effective during our early years. We won over the "early adopter" segment. In turn, early adopters were trusted sources of advice for general users, so we rode the word-of-mouth wave into a steadily increasing share of the market. Product upgrades and a steady stream of updates and new versions tweaked our products so that they became accessible and "friendly" to general users.

However, the explosive growth of the World Wide Web, the exponential growth in data-transfer volumes and speed, and the increasingly diverse nature of corporate networks was ultimately too much even for the creative capacities of our in-house technical team. Now, true innovation was a two-way street nourished by customer feedback and refocused on meeting the practical needs of our customers. We urgently needed to decouple our R & D work from the now-outdated "innovation for innovation's sake" attitude. Trend Micro's "innovation culture" had to be reinterpreted for the times.

As a young student at Fu Jen University, I learned the importance of social responsibility. Trend Micro had learned to run using technology that was more advanced than its competitors and had ensconced "innovation" as a core value. In this new phase, it would be necessary to retool and reorient our business for the needs of general consumers worldwide—particularly those in the critical sectors of government and business. With the Internet becoming an increasingly central facet of life, Internet security was no longer an issue that affected just personal productivity or data protection. It was now intimately tied to group productivity and touched every aspect of life. A compromised bank network could deprive millions of people access to their accounts, and a crashed airline system could immediately endanger all air travel. Breaches in the security of medical-record systems and national defense networks presented the prospect of even more complex and frightening problems. We all appreciated both the immediate urgency and difficulty of safeguarding Internet networks. It was also now plainly clear that upholding our end of the bargain could only be accomplished through close partnership with our customers. A unilateral, in-house solution no longer held water.

Steve drew the mathematical symbol for the infinite loop (∞) on the blackboard. He said, "We start here on the left with customer insight, then move to the right with systematic innovation. It is a continuous exchange, an unending feedback loop, with innovation the key to sustaining the flow between the two sides."

From then on, the symbol featured prominently at internal Trend Micro meetings. We had found our innovative totem.

Our core values were further enriched through statements that required us to understand fully the needs of our customers, to cooperate closely with our customers, and to ensure that growth in service paralleled growth in product development. Development was intimately tied to the needs and expectations of Trend Micro customers. It was clear that "the customer" had to be incorporated into our core values. It was an addition that was long overdue.

Our fourth *C* (Customer) changed the dynamics of the original three (Change, Communication, and Creativity). The original three now "orbited" the fourth, giving Trend Micro operations an entirely new tone.

Further discussions identified trustworthiness as fundamental to Trend Micro's four Cs. As guarantors of Internet data security, what could be more important than our customers' trust? And how should we go about getting it? There was only one way: we had to earn it through trustworthiness!

The back-and-forth discussion converged on a new consensus. Our original 3C menu would grow to "four plus one." Trend Micro would continue to embody change, communication, and creativity, but from here on out, the customer rather than the technology would direct decision-making in order to build Trend Micro's trustworthiness with its current and future customers.

This 4C+T concept (with the *T* standing for *trustworthiness*) was particularly attractive within the Chinese cultural context. Menus in Chinese restaurants frequently had a page dedicated to set banquet meals, so our 4C+T equated easily with a 4 entrées + soup meal. It was a witty and fortuitous abbreviation that was easy to remember and easy to rally around.

Learning for Life

Although this 4C+T "banquet" emerged from the kitchen somewhat hastily and was perhaps still a bit under-baked, the day spent in earnest discussion had given everyone a new and broader perspective on our collective potential. We had laid the groundwork necessary to develop the new policies and actions essential for Trend Micro to move to the "next level" of Internet security.

The slogans and few lines of text that emerged from that day's work may not have looked like much, but they fundamentally changed my role at Trend Micro. I shed my chief marketing officer position and dedicated myself to my duties as Trend Micro's chief human resources officer; I also laid the groundwork for our company's reinvigorated corporate culture. I packaged the rollout of our upgraded ethos in exciting activities under the "Paramount Culture" banner and invited everyone in our global organization to join in on the fun. The team activities and events highlighted the key elements of our culture. Everybody who participated received a special personalized gift, each with its own special meaning. *T*hats asked the recipient to change perspectives in order to innovate; the cell phone holder shaped like two outstretched arms reminded the recipient to "embrace change;" the fashionable earphones reminded users that listening was half of communicating; the name-card holders embossed with the words *Customer Insight* requested that the recipient always work with the customers in mind; and the measuring tape conveyed the message that what can be measured is deemed trustworthy.

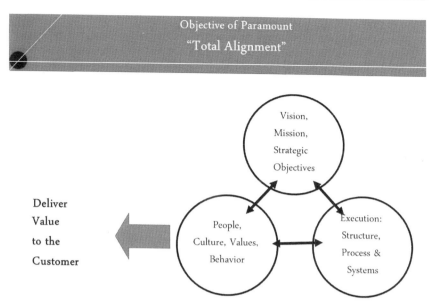

During that period, Steve and I called on our branch offices around the world once a year to promote Trend Micro vision and strategy and to exchange ideas and insights. Steve, reveling in the limelight, did his magic tricks, brought games, called lunch meetings, sang, danced … it often seemed as if we were a rock band on the road doing a world tour. We were exhausted, but *oh,* the adrenaline rush! When I look back, it was probably the high point of my professional career. I enjoyed a close rapport with all of our colleagues, felt the heartbeat of our corporate culture, and experienced the thrill of working with a cohesive and dynamic organization. However, I also learned that all parties must end. Even before the excitement and noise had slipped into happy memories, I began work on the nuts and bolts of implementing Trend Micro's cultural upgrade. I wrote new rules governing incentives and rewards, evaluations, and departmental responsibilities in hopes of fundamentally reshaping the way all Trend Micro employees thought about and conducted their business.

For any cultural initiative to take root and grow, it is critical that managers step up as "first adopters." Management provides the example to follow, and any transgression of core values is almost sure to raise doubts among staff and erode confidence. Although such transgressions are practically inevitable in an expanding, transnational operation like

Trend Micro, I did my best to keep the organization on the straight and narrow by stepping up communications with middle managers.

It was only later that we launched the Trend Learning Circle, a curriculum that Steve personally designed and built from the bottom up. With little theoretical pretense, courses in this series helped raise awareness of key issues. Experiential units led staff to better understand their own motivations, unlock their potential, and develop empathetic concern for the welfare and needs of others.

Trend Micro had launched a long-term program to accompany its employees on one of life's most difficult journeys: the journey to introspective self-awareness.

SECTION TWO: BUILDING THE FOUNDATIONS OF CULTURE

SUCCESSION & REORGANIZATION

CHAPTER 4

The Will of Heaven

The loss of family plucked us from the frantic pace of life. It gave us precious time to tally past joys and sorrows, assess our meteoric rise, and soberly consider heretofore-unimagined possibilities. Ultimately, it also gave us the opportunity to face our innermost selves honestly and to make decisions that had long awaited resolution.

Prodded forward in time, the number of tasks that we travelers will complete along our shared path invariably pales in the face of those many technology, marketing, customer, and cultural tasks that will remain unfinished. Plans seem never to keep up with inevitable change. Known to heaven alone, the secrets of the future remain frustratingly opaque to us mere mortals.

Steve was once again clearly in charge after clearing the air of discomfiting thoughts about succession and overseeing the departure of those executives unable to acclimate to Trend Micro's cultural ethos. Eva remained firmly in charge of product strategy, while I shifted gears to focus on corporate culture. All three of us threw ourselves into honing our respective crafts and fused our distinctive advantages into a formidable organization ready to take on all comers. Eva was in California's Silicon Valley, I kept a careful watch over our Asian markets, and Steve continued to lead the Trend Micro fight wherever in the world he was needed. We turned the tide, rallied the troops, and restored customer confidence. Sales and profits once again regained their buoyant, healthy blush. Trend Micro was back!

I have always regretted that family responsibilities so often took a backseat to Trend Micro's myriad demands. Fortunately, however, Steve and I always made a point to be there for the highlights: the birthdays, concerts, parent-teacher meetings, graduations, and the like. We faithfully cleared our schedules to make sure we were there. Our family made an annual ritual of going to the United States over Chinese New Year, when the children would visit with the grandparents and we would continue working. The Christmas holidays were always spent working in Taiwan. We had an uncanny knack for escaping holidays, finding somewhere where it was still "business as usual," and taking personal time in the fragments left over.

As for our parents, I could only beg their understanding. While Steve and I tacitly agreed that it wouldn't be right for us to go on long foreign holidays while our parents were still with us, the needs of Trend Micro regularly had us traveling to the four corners of the globe. Fortunately, we found a unique solution to keeping our parents happy and content.

Because Steve's parents lived in Los Angeles, we moved Trend Micro's headquarters every summer to the United States and, of course, made the most of the opportunity to spend time with his parents. On Eva's and my side, Mom and Dad and our brothers were founding shareholders of Trend Micro. Thus, annual shareholders' meetings in Tokyo were celebrated like family reunions. Of course, this ensured that Steve was applauded each time he took the stage and that an enthusiastic response inevitably greeted his proposals. With the formalities of the meeting over, everyone would then head out together for a much-anticipated spring holiday, with picnics beneath flowering cherry trees and days spent savoring the cultured airs of Japan's rightfully famous hot-spring districts.

I naively believed at the time that it would continue like this forever. As long as we continued investing ourselves in our business and our families, this annual cycle of family gathering could continue indefinitely.

When a new shareholders' meeting and a new cherry-blossom season hove into view, I never truly appreciated that another year had disappeared below the horizon. While I greeted familiar scenes with a comforting sense of déjà vu, it was simply an illusion. Time once spent was gone forever. Age, illness, and death bend to no one's control.

The Meaning of Life

Steve's father had worked for years to regain a normal life following his stroke. He enjoyed traveling and always found time to express fondness for his two grandsons.

We received an urgent call during a meeting of senior Trend Micro executives in Japan at the end of 2001. It was Steve's oldest sister. "Please come quickly. Dad's had another stroke. It doesn't look good." It was the first time I saw Steve panic. "I have to leave for Los Angeles, immediately," he announced abruptly at the meeting. He didn't even think to ask me to go with him. He dropped everything on the agenda and left for the airport. "I'll pick up our son and meet you there," I said as quickly as I could to make sure he heard before he left the room. Our oldest son was in California for school, so he arrived at the hospital before Steve to comfort his grandmother and aunt.

By the time Steve arrived, his father's condition had deteriorated beyond hope of recovery. The attending physician asked in a clinical, detached voice, "Do you wish to continue using the respirator?" Steve fell to his knees, grasping his father's still-warm hand. Between his tears, he spoke to his unconscious father. "Dad ... pass in peace!"

Steve was never one to flout the laws of nature. It was his father who admonished him to always accept fate and live within its dictates. However, the practical difficulties of doing so remain hidden until he was faced with heart-rending decisions such as this. Still holding his father's hand as it was gradually drained of life's warmth, he shook his head. No, his father would not need the respirator. Steve then heard a sound unfamiliar to his ears: the sound of his own weeping.

I arrived with our youngest son to find Steve an emotional wreck, with a face that had been unshaven for days. He made arrangements for a church funeral and solemnly accepted the condolences of family, friends, and colleagues who attended. Back home and safely behind familiar walls, he surrendered to the emotional agony and broke down in tears. "My father's life ... my life ... what does it all mean?"

No level of success, no amount of knowledge could answer that question. Steve had just recently begun exploring the tenets of Jungian philosophy and had already accepted that a key motivator fueling his entrepreneurial ambitions was the desire to earn his father's respect. "See! This classroom failure of a son made something of himself after all. Moreover, he did it in Japan—the country *you* admire most!" Steve stood proud. He had dissipated this dark cloud that had weighed so heavily for so long and was ready to build a new, positive relationship with his father. But his father had left the world just as Steve was ready for new beginnings. This sudden, tragic event thus naturally planted deep, almost unavoidable misgivings. What did it all mean? The business, the struggle and competition, and the hectic pace of life; what did it mean to his father, to himself, and to our sons? The questions sat like burning embers on his heart.

Steve moved mechanically through his daily responsibilities for a long time afterward. Unable to focus on the business at hand and deprived of his normally sharp senses, he was hovering on autopilot with no landing pad in sight.

My mood followed the contours of Steve's. We returned to Taiwan and to Trend Micro. Although not really up to the task, I had little choice but to put up a brave front. I took up many pending policy problems and chaired meetings dealing with finance, technology, and inter-departmental issues. Steve was there in body but not in spirit. I was not unfamiliar with these tasks, but without Steve's clear, focused, and purpose-filled existence, it was much more difficult. While Eva stepped up and took over key product-development responsibilities, she still remained unwilling to take full executive responsibility for Trend Micro. "Don't worry," Eva tried to comfort me in my physical and emotional exhaustion, "Steve will come back once he's seen enough of the mess. He won't abandon us."

Perhaps Eva really did understand him in that he simply could not let his own business and his hard-won accomplishments flounder for long. Three months later, Steve shaved his unkempt beard and took his place once again at Trend Micro's helm.

He told me what he wanted was a "graceful exit." He wouldn't, he promised, shirk his responsibilities. "Before I step down, I'll turn the company over to the right person and help them get going." I was naturally relieved. "Take your time," I said. "It will happen when it happens."

"Make Time for Yourself"

For all appearances, things at Trend Micro had returned to normal. Steve continued giving long-winded presentations and animatedly getting his points across. He even managed to come up with a few new magic tricks.

But the recent succession fiasco and the sudden loss of Steve's father had made us contemplate the true value of life. We began skeptically examining even some of our most cherished truisms.

Two years later found us again in Japan in late March for the 2004 shareholders' meeting. Sales were up, and we were able to complement the continued rise in our share price with the announcement of a cash dividend of ¥70 per share. Spirits were high. The future for Trend Micro looked better than ever.

After the meeting, Steve and I flew to Beijing for some time off. We visited our oldest son, who was now a university graduate and working at China Netcom. We savored the chance to relax after a particularly hectic several months.

Late that first evening, I was finishing up a yoga routine before joining Steve in sweet slumber when my Nokia phone suddenly began ringing, breaking the tranquility in our room. *Another major virus outbreak?* I prepared myself for the news, turned myself over, and hit the answer button. I was surprised to hear my oldest brother at the other end. "Jenny. Dad saw the doctor. They think he has liver cancer and are considering surgery. Please, come home as soon as you can!"

The years we spent building Trend Micro and traveling abroad on business could not have been possible if it were not for my brothers and sisters looking after the family and our parents. But I lived in fear of receiving late-night phone calls such as this. The last time, I learned that my father had suffered a stroke. The time before, I learned that my beloved aunt had passed away. Nothing sent a chill down my spine more than hearing my oldest brother's voice on the line. I would leave as soon as I could the next day.

Steve had an important meeting scheduled in the city that morning, so only our son and I took the early flight back to Taichung. My father, the man who only a month or so ago was happily passing around red envelope New Years' money to his grandchildren, was lying tired and frail on a hospital bed. I rushed forward, took his hand, smiled, and said, "It'll be okay, Dad. You'll get better." I had inherited my inveterate optimism from him. He said, "I dreamed of your great-grandfather and Guanyin Bodhisattva. They will look after me."

Optimism may fuel hope, but it stands powerless in the face of harsh, inevitable realities such as old age and death. Despite multiple treatments and Mom's reverent offerings of incense and prayers, Dad's condition only worsened with the passing days and months. We decided to bring him home for however long he had left and to stop all further debilitating treatments.

As much as possible, I stayed by my father's bedside through that difficult, painful time. I remained in Taiwan for more than two months—something I hadn't done since before our wedding. I comforted my insomnia-stricken mother, stayed with my determined father, and shared solace and support with my siblings. Once happy to sit back and listen contentedly to his children's stories and jokes, Dad now wanted nothing more than to share himself with us. He would reminisce on stories from his past until the pain became too much and he stopped. Clenching his teeth, he would nod for me to keep the conversation going. I held back the tears and would pick up on some story that I hoped would lift spirits and bring smiles to my parents' faces.

One afternoon, while Mom was resting in the living room and my brothers and sisters were out, I slipped into Dad's bedroom. I asked the nurse to give us some time alone and I lay down on the bed next to him, quietly wiping away my tears as my father slept. After a while, Dad moved his IV-entangled hand over on top of mine. It was the firm, warm hand I had loved to hold as a child. It had always been a source of comfort and safety. He said, "For so many years, you've helped your husband in business. Your father understands! You were always such a lover of books and literature. Make time for yourself!" He was concerned that I might have lost myself somewhere along life's journey.

Dad had invested in Trend Micro from the very start. He had always encouraged his son-in-law and daughters to reach for the stars, and he never hesitated to let us know how proud of us he was. Nevertheless, his outlook on life and his degree in philosophy from National Taiwan

University provided regular reminders that he was less interested in fame and fortune than in his children fully realizing their personal potential. He knew all too well the softy that lay not far beneath my tough façade. He also knew that my carefree airs did not trump the basic conservatism I had learned as our family's eldest daughter. Family and husband came first and foremost, always. Dad knew well my lifelong passions for the liberal arts and knew that my IT career had left them unfulfilled.

"Make time for yourself!" That one sentence landed like a well-seasoned battering ram on a soul already deeply conflicted.

Of course, Dad knew very well that his other beloved daughter's amenably congenial façade concealed an ambitious and calculating personality. Every time Eva flew in from California, Dad greeted her with the same good-natured smile on his face. "So," he would ask, "what have you invented this time? I'm all ears!" Eva would then try to repackage the world's latest, most complicated Internet technologies into a simple, yet satisfying narrative that would sate Dad's curiosity about his talented daughter's work. She would unvaryingly also add exciting tidbits like, "And I won such and such award;" and, "We just signed so and so as a new client." Her enthusiasm swept the pall of illness from Dad's face and replaced it with the glow of pride. He was truly proud of Eva and hoped she would continue blazing her own trail in the IT arena. Our father knew that there was more to Eva than her innumerable new and creative ideas. She had the ambition needed to make those ideas live up to their true potential. Dad's encouragement and honest, unvarnished pride were the wind in Eva's sails, carrying her forward to ever-greater accomplishments.

Acceptance

Dad left us on a warm day in May. Throughout his illness, he never once cried out in pain or complained to the heavens or even to those around him about his deteriorating health. He wasn't even burdened about tying up his affairs. He remained as open and caring as ever, and he waited until the entire family had come together by his bedside before bidding farewell. He said, "With you all here, I've nothing to worry about."

Father's life here on earth was one of magnanimous generosity and acceptance of life's natural rhythms. He never had much use for fame or for fortune and held no such lofty ambitions for his children. He imposed upon them only his boundless warmth and loving protection. He had long made a habit of being a source of encouragement and inspiration to all around him. He gave us generous space in which we could explore ourselves and our potential. He gave us opportunity without pressure. Dad's singular hope was that we *not* suppress our natural talents. While his life bore consistent testimony to his philosophy on life and attitudes toward education, it was only when he was ready to leave that we began to appreciate what we had in this man, that we finally began understanding how fortunate and loved we truly were.

Just one and a half years ago, it was the untimely death of his own father that had led Steve into unfamiliar territory—thinking deeply and philosophically on his past, present, and future. My father's natural acceptance of unavoidable fate heightened my own awareness and love of life. It rekindled my desire to explore further life's still-unrealized potentials. Steve had been steeped in the world of information technology since he graduated with his BS in applied mathematics more than twenty years ago. He had explored and tinkered with just about every aspect of the entrepreneurial experience. Now well into middle age, Steve should have been settling comfortably into his jaded years. But he continued longing for new experiences and untested waters. He still wished he could morph into the mythical roc and explore wherever the winds would take him.

At the sickbed of our loved ones, we three had ample time and space to introspectively examine and share our feelings, as well as to discuss plans for our runaway entrepreneurial success, Trend Micro.

Eva was finally convinced of Steve's honest desire to find a successor and my plans to follow his departure from the company. Dad's spirited encouragement had swept her remaining doubts about taking on greater responsibility. She was now willing to step up to the plate and out of Steve's shadow in order to give full play to her potential and still-unbridled enthusiasm. She agreed to take full responsibility for Trend Micro as CEO under conditions that she would receive the support of the board and the shareholders and that Steve and I would remain for a while in a support capacity.

It was thus the loss of family that plucked us from the frantic pace of everyday business and ultimately gave us the wherewithal to tally our joys and sorrows, assess our meteoric rise, and soberly consider heretofore-unimagined future potentials. Ultimately, it gave us the opportunity to face our innermost selves honestly and to make decisions that had long awaited resolution.

It was Dad's love and encouragement that finally extirpated Eva's final doubts, helped her accept her true career ambitions, and set her onto the path for which she was truly destined.

Streams of unstoppable tears belied my feigned strength and turned my attention toward my long-neglected dreams of youth. Psychologically, I was back to square one.

It was the sorrows of aging and death that had also awakened Steve to the emptiness of everyday existence. Years of entrepreneurial experience had slowly but steadily nourished the seeds of inner truth and given him the freedom to step away from ultimately barren ideals and make a gracious exit from the Trend Micro stage.

CHAPTER 5

The Fitness Plan

While we three felt that we had each arrived at our decisions both openly and democratically, we still were unclear as to how they would go down with our Trend Micro colleagues.

I thought that perhaps a one-time fitness checkup might help highlight the potential problems ahead. That, in combination with a so-called "goldfish bowl" discussion exercise designed to consolidate opinions, might help us identify and deal with a potential silent killer.

The three of us frequently took short-term intensive-training courses such as Peter M. Senge's *Learning Organization* course and the University of Chicago's intensive course on marketing.

The ceremonial forty-ninth day after Dad's death fell in mid-June of 2004. I was still in anguish, unable to sleep at night and certainly incapable of putting pen to paper. Days clumped together in a sorrowful blur. In an attempt to drag me out of my misery, Steve arranged for us to leave Taiwan. We went to Harvard University in Boston for an advanced one-week course on human resources management. It was designed specifically for experienced corporate managers, so applicants were carefully screened beforehand. The course fully leveraged Harvard's famous "case study" approach and proceeded at a fast and demanding pace. Students were required to stay on campus and were divided into discussion groups. Steve and I stayed in separate dorm rooms and, of course, were assigned to separate group discussions. Our normally interwoven lives were replaced temporarily by the realities of being classmates on different teams. We worked and reported on different cases, which naturally spurred a bit of contentious rivalry—something refreshingly new in our relationship!

Steve and Eva had only just finally struck a difficult consensus on succession. Although both agreed that Eva would take over as Trend Micro CEO the following year in 2005, the rocky experience with succession plans during the previous two years left me deeply anxious about how our colleagues might take this news.

Throughout Trend Micro's fifteen years in business, Steve had always been "command central." Eva and I had always been in key support roles outside of the limelight. Would people be okay with putting Eva in command and Steve and I in supporting roles? How would we even go about making such an announcement? How should we arrange the transition? How could we make the process as smooth as possible and help the new CEO settle easily into her position?

The Trend Micro culture had always been democratic and proactively participatory. Now, at this critical juncture in Trend Micro's history, we were especially eager to find some way to let everyone participate and have her or his say. We wanted to give people time to get used to the reality of succession and gradually acclimate to the idea of having Eva in charge.

Steve and I had come to Harvard two years previously as the focus of a business school case study on multicultural business management.[6] We were honored guests invited to answer sharp questions posed by Harvard students. This time, we were the students responsible to pore over case studies, participate in group discussions, debate issues, and focus all our mental energies on finding the most viable solutions. We fervently hoped that we might find ideas in our readings that would help smooth our upcoming internal communication issues.

With our case study published on Harvard Business School's website, our professors took the opportunity of our being at Harvard to chat with

---

[6] In their 2002 study on Trend Micro, Harvard Professors Lynn Sharp Paine and Kim Bettcher focused their interest and attention on the transnational nature of the firm's business culture. After a full year of honest and open discussion, the study was formally added to the Harvard Business School case-study materials library (N9-303-065) in March 2003. "Trend Micro has restructured the company to exploit every possible geographic advantage or resource around the world." Trend Micro was the first Chinese-managed IT brand in the world featured in a Harvard case study.

us in-depth about the inner workings of Trend Micro's global operations. While each had his or her unique field of expertise and academic perspective, they all shared in common a lack of practical management experience. Thus, they all were eager for the chance to put their ideas to the test in a practical business setting.

The ideas on organizational fitness of one of the team's lead professors were of particular interest to me. "Organizations have problems that, while known to all, are nonetheless allowed to inhibit operations because of fear of authority, the distraction of other responsibilities, or feelings of futility. This is the so-called 'silent killer.'" Steve agreed with the thesis of authors Michael Beer and Russell A. Eisenstat outlined in their paper "The Silent Killers of Strategy Implementation and Learning".[7] The problem, they wrote, is how to find these silent killers and encourage management to truly face up to the hidden dangers that threaten long-term corporate operations and sustainability.

I've always been a diligent student. "Listen to their words, to their ideas and suggestions. It's a system of delegation. Choose spokespersons for your various regions and departments, canvass opinions, organize the issues you identify, consolidate and distill, and then submit the refined, concentrated end product of this process to the highest levels of management. This approach sidesteps the general fear of voicing direct opinions while giving delegates a comprehensive, objective understanding of prevailing opinions," I suggested.

"Although we think we run a transparent and democratic organization, we don't really have a sense of how our colleagues really feel about this point," Steve added. "Perhaps if we did give it a try, it might really succeed in pinpointing the potential threats facing Trend Micro." Steve and I had a shared passion for rooting out problems. We feared being unaware, of *not* being called into action.

The thought of putting what I was learning to use got me excited, and I said to Steve, "Why don't we retain these Harvard professors as consultants and ask them to organize a fitness checkup for Trend Micro? We can use their 'goldfish bowl' technique to consolidate everyone's thoughts and flush our silent killers out of hiding! I think I could work with them to turn

---

[7] http://sloanreview.mit.edu/article/the-silent-killers-of-strategy-implementation-and-learning/

their theory into a workable plan that would let us thoroughly investigate and assess Trend Micro's potential internal issues. Because the professors will be impartial third-party participants, their opinions should carry quite a bit of weight!"

"When all is said and done," Steve said with a knowing wink my way, "I'm the one responsible for all of Trend Micro's problems."

"Understood," I chuckled and then returned to the subject at hand. "They've got the theory and we have the proving ground. Our cooperation has to be *mutually* beneficial. They mustn't just be given a free hand."

By the seventh and final day of the Harvard course, we had finalized with Professor Eisenstat's team the initial outline for our cooperation. They were eager to work with a transnational firm like Trend Micro and saw in this an opportunity to prove their theory across our many cultural settings worldwide. For our part, we were excited about the chance to meld our years of experience in human resources management and international communications with their theoretical framework. We all stood to benefit. We would plumb the inner psyche of our business organization and explore the thoughts and motivations that normally lay hidden and unreachable in the shadows.

Steve took this latest task as, if not more seriously as anything previous. He invested himself fully in this comprehensive checkup of Trend Micro's internal fitness because he saw it as laying the groundwork for his ultimate objective: succession.

Forged in Fire

A soft start was essential to avoid panic in the organization.

Since our earliest days, we had run a regular reading circle with our senior managers. We all would read a book or an article and then share thoughts and inspired insights in a follow-up meeting. After returning from the United States, I assigned an article by Professor Eisenstat published in the MIT Sloan Management Review for our next selection. The discussion afterward delivered a consensus opinion: "Our company undeniably has this kind of problem. It could be an issue of authority, perhaps not knowing whom to talk to, or just a reluctance to rock the boat, but there are certainly issues left unresolved at the core of the business that have been gradually bleeding motivation and strength from our organization."

Not long after that session, we invited Professor Eisenstat to give a talk at a Trend Micro senior managers' meeting. His presentation and the lively discussion that followed gradually sketched the outlines of an organizational-fitness plan that was tailor-made for Trend Micro's needs.

Nevertheless, the soft-sell approach wasn't enough to guarantee smooth sailing. Even after raising the plans for cooperating with Professor Eisenstat at our senior executives' meeting and setting the gears of the fitness plan into motion, we still encountered numerous obstacles and garnered feedback such as:

"To implement the process you're talking about will demand a lot of time and multiple meetings. We're scattered around the world and responsible for different aspects of the business. How do you propose we get everyone together for these regular meetings?"

"Goldfish bowl meetings? It sounds like you're preparing to call us for hearings at the Legislative Yuan (Taiwan's national representative assembly)! What you propose is quite unsettling!"

Our colleagues were all battle-hardened veterans of business and quickly realized the difficulties that implementing such a plan would entail. Moreover, they sensed that this road might lead to new and yet-unforeseen predicaments.

Despite the brevity of our "honest dialogue" objective, this would be a multifaceted project that spanned branch operations on five continents and involved every department and staff at every level.

Professor Eisenstat and I used his theory and my understanding of the Trend Micro organization and culture to formulate the following steps for our fitness checkup:

1) Have Trend Micro's fourteen senior executives draft a strategic plan for the company covering the next three years.
2) Create a validation task force with members drawn from managers in our various sales regions and the Trend Micro customer service organization. The task force will canvass the opinions of clients and partners about current Trend Micro products and services and about the firm's strategic planning ideas.

3) Create a fitness task force with members drawn from staffs within Trend Micro's regional R & D, administrative, and sales organizations known to be good listeners. Again using the strategic plan as its framework, this task force will interview colleagues at all levels to explore and identify the bottlenecks that are inhibiting policy implementation and progress. This step should encourage all colleagues to express their thoughts fully and to listen carefully to all complaints and criticisms in order to identify and target every potential "silent killer" issue within the organization.

4) Hold wrap-up meetings to discuss and enumerate each of the problems faced by Trend Micro—both internally and externally. After excluding issues of personal character and recasting emotional reactions in objective terms, the teams will produce a report that organizes the unvarnished words and insights generated during the interview process.

5) The Goldfish Bowl Meeting: With task-force members seated at a central conference table and Trend Micro's fourteen senior executives seated on their periphery, each task-force member will report to the executives in turn on the opinions, ideas, and experiences encountered during the interview process. While senior executives have the right to make comments to productively respond to and clarify issues in which they are cited, these comments should not be emotional or defensive. The role of an objective "third party" at this meeting is critical. Therefore, Professor Eisenstat will serve as meeting chairman to prevent discussions from devolving into emotional diatribes.

6) Once all reports have been heard, the senior executives will hold a separate series of meetings to discuss appropriate responses. These meetings must be productive, informative discussions that avoid dispute and conclude with a drafted list of practical improvement measures.

7) Task-force team members will meet again with senior executives to listen to the drafted improvement measures and provide the input and opinions necessary to ensure that all measures have consensus support for implementation.

8) Revise Trend Micro's overall strategic plan and draft a detailed plan for implementing the consensus-based improvement measures. Revisions may involve reorganizing the Trend Micro organizational structure, catalog of products, and internal management and external communication protocols. A final meeting between task-force team members and senior executives will hammer out the final draft of the new strategic plan.

9) Begin implementation. All implemented procedures and results will be announced so that the entire Trend Micro organization is clear not only about the results, but also about the reasons.

The importance of open and honest communication had been a pillar of our cultural ethos from day one. At international meetings and in annual corporate-culture activities, we consistently hit home the importance of facing issues directly and accepting challenges as they arose. But this time, the fixation on "silent killers," the mobilization of the entire Trend Micro organization, and the retention of a Harvard professor indicated that something was different this time. The more sensitive of the senior executives noted the difference right away. "Is the company in some kind of trouble? Are we sick? Otherwise, why the urgency about this 'fitness checkup?'"

Without missing a beat, Steve gave his confident reply. "No! Future prospects look *very* bright. That's precisely why it is imperative that we make sure we are as fit as possible *now*. So we'll be ready for future challenges. It's like any normal health checkup. Catch problems as early as possible and take preventive measures."

"Forged in Fire, Lived Happy" was the phrase I chose to capture the underlying purpose of this project. Several of our senior executives with Ivy League MBA degrees eagerly backed the plan to implement cutting-edge management theory at Trend Micro and began supporting the various elements necessary to implement the overall plan. Gradually, everyone accepted the general necessity of a fitness checkup, and discussions turned to the details necessary for implementation.

CHAPTER 6

Unvarnished Honesty –
the Goldfish Bowl

Trend Micro's democratic cultural ethos promoted nonhierarchical communications and a permissive style of management.

The friendly, familiar way I interacted with colleagues was free of any hierarchical considerations. It fostered the conviction that there was probably nothing we couldn't say to or share with one another.

I learned my limitations and the discomfort of true bluntness in Trend Micro's goldfish bowl meetings.

Even in the business world of today, effective "bottom up" communication is something not easily achieved.

"Listening" is the first rung on the fitness checkup ladder.

Although I am referring to corporate fitness here, the principle holds true for personal fitness as well. Taking stock of your own well-being requires carefully listening to your "inner voice." Why is fitness a good thing? What is my motivation? What are my goals? Where are the current problems? How much of a gap is there between current reality and my ideal? Only after these questions have been answered will you be able to tailor a fitness plan appropriate to your personal situation. Of course, being able to accomplish your planned goals is ultimately critical to the overall fitness process as well.

Listening and interpreting the "inner voice" are relatively easy for the individual. Not so for the group. What, one might ask, is the "inner voice" of a group? It has been said that public opinion is about as easy to get a hold of as flowing water. But, although flowing water may be impossible to catch, might there be a discernable rhythm within the torrent?

Those adept at listening are able to detach themselves from surrounding distractions and listen with empathy to what others have to say. They hear the rhythmic patterns in flowing water, distinguish static from noise, and hear how patterns interweave into a main "melody." Those needed for this task would thus necessarily be adept listeners. Most importantly, they would need to be people trusted by both general staff and management.

Just as the UK has its upper and lower houses of government and the United States has its Senate and House of Representatives, our all-important fitness plan adopted a two-delegate system: one for internal issues and one for external issues.

The Internal House vs. The External House

The work of Trend Micro's External House, named the Validation Task Force ("V-Force" for short), would focus on external communications. External validation had always been of critical strategic importance to Trend Micro. Thus, I made sure it featured prominently in our fitness plan.

Members of V-Force were primarily Trend Micro sales and customer service managers. It was their task to first explain Trend Micro's upcoming moves in line with the newly approved strategic plan to key customers and distributors and then to explore potential issues of concern and listen to feedback. Findings would be used at the senior executive level to make any necessary adjustments to plans and to confirm that plans were ultimately following the right course.

Up until this time, discussions during sales visits with clients had largely revolved around contract pricing, while visits from our customer-sales representatives addressed current product issues and their resolution. Now, we were taking things up a significant notch. The former myopic focus on prices and problems was replaced by shared thoughts on the direction of products and the business as well as overall business strategy. The "supplier – buyer" relationship was superseded by a partnership framed by Trend Micro's new strategic plan. Professor Eisenstat's original theoretical framework on corporate fitness had not considered the external communications dimension. However, the key role of customer insight in our corporate culture made sure that we gave our clients a suitably key role in the new strategic plan as the ultimate arbiters of the trueness of Trend Micro's course settings.

Later on, the members of V-Force shared how truly valuable the ongoing dialogue with clients' chief information officers (CIOs) had become. CIOs, they said, were the ultimate end users of software products. However, the CIOs shared that it had been only Trend Micro that was willing to spend the time necessary to discuss practical security-strategy issues with them and to listen to their opinions and perspectives. Trend Micro was viewed as a solid partner. Thus, through the medium of this fitness checkup, we had reconfirmed the position of "the client" at the center of Trend Micro corporate culture. Ultimately, client input influenced implemented product strategy in definitive ways, such as our policy statement: "Maintaining online productivity is sometimes more important than scanning for viruses." Client input helped sharpen the focus of our R & D efforts and embedded us more deeply into the user environment.

This exercise did more than just put organizational-fitness theory into practice. We took full advantage of the opportunity to further secure our corporate culture by injecting our core values into every facet of fitness plan implementation.

As to Trend Micro's Internal House, named the Fitness Task Force (a.k.a. "F-Force"), they were to handle internal communications, listen to the "inner voice" of the Trend Micro organization, and bring all silent killers into the limelight for open, frank discussion. One might be excused for presuming that interviewing colleagues would be a much easier exercise than interviewing clients. After all, they're all in the same uniforms and are comrades in arms fighting the same battles, right? In reality, the difficulties faced by F-Force were far and away more challenging than those of V-Force.

First and foremost, delegates had to be truly "representative" and had to include individuals from major markets such as China, Japan, and the United States as well as Europe, Greater Asia, and Central/South America, and had to bring a holistic picture of the Trend Micro business, including marketing, sales, R & D, customer service, and administration.

Still hoping to make this survey of internal opinion a covert operation and to minimize potential distress, we relied on personal recommendations rather than popular consensus to select F-Force's constituent members. The HR department and I decided to limit our recruitment to middle managers and developed a list of potential candidates known to exemplify Trend Micro's corporate-culture values. Candidates approved unanimously by the fourteen-member senior-executive board were shortlisted and then approached to encourage their participation. All task-force work was to be accomplished in addition to normal work responsibilities and would have to be pursued willingly and with passionate purpose. After a lengthy process, nine mid-level managers signed on to the Fitness Task Force, representing a healthy spectrum of geographic regions, department experience, and years of service.

F-Force delegates were transferred away from their home regions in order to allay misgivings and discomfort among their immediate colleagues, as well as to give them free reign to interview colleagues in other regions and departments. In terms of interviewees, local personnel departments were requested to nominate a group of twelve staff members deemed representative of the regional organization in terms of nationalities, departments, levels, and years of work experience.

Thus, Asia's delegates went to Trend Micro's European operation; those from Central and South America took the thirty-hour flight to Trend Micro's Philippines operation; European delegates went to China; US delegates went to Japan; Japanese delegates went to Central and South America; and so on. Their schedules were hectic and tightly packed. At each location, they arranged to meet with those chosen for the interview. The interview might take place in the office's meeting room or in a nearby coffee shop. None of the delegates had prior reporting experience. The first priority was to set the interviewee at ease to help ensure that the discussion that followed was as frank and open as possible. While kept within the narrow topic range we had set, actual discussions ran the gamut from cut-and-dry direct to downright circuitous. Delegates gave no hint of approval when interviewees said positive things about the company or their experience. If they complained about something, every effort was made to identify the underlying issue. Some of those interviewed asked that their session not be recorded, so delegates had to keep sharp mental or written notes, all while maintaining eye contact with the person talking. These were all critical interviewing points and techniques taught by Professor Eisenstat. All in all, it was a "baptism by fire" for our F-Force members.

Naturally, the expenses associated with this project mounted. However, the final result would justify the rationale for this groundbreaking endeavor.

Hernandez from Latin America said of his experience in the Philippines, "This special assignment has given me the opportunity to get to know my colleagues in many other regions and departments. It's opened my eyes. This has been for me exceptional training." It seems as an incidental bonus, the fitness plan was also a new training ground for Trend Micro's mid-level managers. In the years since his participation in F-Force, former Customer Service Manager Hernandez is now Trend Micro's managing director of sales for all of Central and South America.

Affable and well-liked, F-Force member Ai-mei Ma, an Asia marketing manager, was assigned to conduct interviews in the United States. Commenting on her experience, she shared, "Because these interviews didn't involve any conflicts of interest, I started off by just sharing with the interviewees the firm's good faith and interests in doing this project. The conversations really started flowing after their initial concerns were overcome. I got to hear a lot of explosively honest stories."

Japan-based Customer Service Manager Kutsuzawa had been with Trend Micro only three months when he was asked to join F-Force. "For me, it was 'shock training.' I'd never considered before about the stimulating effects that rooting out hidden problems might have on company growth." He admits now that the experience also helped him jettison old habits brought over from his former job and acclimate quickly to the Trend Micro mindset.

The three Harvard professors were duly impressed that we were able to fully implement their theory. For me, business management has to be practical. A theory yet to be tested lacks a firm footing, with no one quite sure where it might best fit. Moreover, companies without a firm cultural footing would find it particularly hard to establish the trust and consensus needed within implementation teams. This would truly make putting a yet-untested management theory into practice a risky exercise likely to end in failure.

Even with confidence in our solid cultural understructure and the solid backing of the board of senior executives, the fitness plan did entail a certain measure of risk. My insistence on making our plan even more open and comprehensive than originally intended only further added to the dangers if things were to go wrong. Professor Russell regularly cautioned that the actual results would be impossible to predict and may stray significantly from our expectations. "Are you absolutely sure about going ahead with this?" he would ask. Steve and I invariably responded with confident nods. How could we hope to achieve long-term fitness objectives if we made only a halfhearted effort?

The Barriers to "Bottom-up" Reporting

Our teams took three months to finish up all scheduled interviews. It was a generous outlay of time by Trend Micro standards. In the first meeting between the teams and our senior executives, the group cut to the heart of the matter and shared their key findings. Helped by the consulting team, identified issues were classified into the four principal categories of: product strategy, management practices, implementation efficiency, and organization and leadership. We distilled the general opinion, deliberated over the right words, appointed spokespersons for each designated issue, and made preparations for the next step: the much-anticipated "goldfish bowl" meeting.

As mentioned, I have always been on comfortable, familiar terms with my colleagues, largely overlooked hierarchical niceties, and felt comfortable giving as well as getting whatever comes to mind. I learned my limitations and the discomfort of true, unvarnished bluntness in our goldfish-bowl meeting sessions.

When the royal counselor Bigan in China's early Shang Dynasty advised King Zhou to rectify his errant ways, the angry king ordered that Bigan's heart be cut out. He did this even though Bigan was his flesh-and-blood uncle! The tale underscores the difficulty of delivering unpleasant news. We would certainly not be taking our cues from King Zhou, and we weren't living in feudal times. It was surprising, then, that the goldfish-bowl technique sprang from the world's "most democratic" country and from the school recognized as home to the most advanced business management theories. Clearly, "bottom-up" communications was still a difficult issue, even for modern twenty-first century businesses.

Trend Micro's democratic culture fostered nonhierarchical communications and a permissive style of management, with all matters handled based on good-faith principles. Despite this culture of openness, it was clear from the outset that our chosen delegates were choosing their words carefully when giving their presentations and stepping gingerly around many issues.

Cecilia was a young, ambitious team delegate from the Philippines. She was with Trend Micro for just one year when she was tapped for a middle-management position. She was selected to represent Trend Micro's Virus Center in the Philippines on F-Force. At the time, the center had more than five hundred employees and today has more than a thousand. She shared, "I was shaking. I was so nervous. How could I tell management about what I'd heard? Some of those people I interviewed were really direct!" She later reminded me of something I had shared with her at the time but had since forgotten. She recalled, "Jenny took me aside and said, 'You are not representing yourself here but all of your colleagues in the Philippines. Be brave and speak the truth. Don't be afraid.' Her words calmed me down. I went on to play my role and finished the job. Since then, I've lost my fear of speaking up and sharing my opinions at our international meetings."

Sincerely given interviews generated honest results that pointed to worrisome fractures beneath the surface. Some issues were longstanding, while others were more recent. Some were commonly known, while others came as surprises. Although some seemed best categorized as unlikely angst, some were clearly early warnings of potential future problems. Words came hot and heavy, and the air was thick with tense emotion. Among the senior executives, the president of our US operations was the first to stir from the awkward barrage and, in defense of his policies, begin explaining indignantly, "We have to do it that way because ..."

Steve sat through much of the session listening in silence with arms folded over his chest. I leaned forward in my chair and politely nodded and smiled as the occasion justified. Eva sat in stony silence throughout. Our CFO pulled out datasheets from time to time, believing he could find rational explanations for each issue raised. Our CIO let out sporadic chuckles that did little to hide his discomfort at the proceedings.

For their part, the delegates seemed to acclimate quickly to their authority and continued in their withering barrage. "Product R & D difficulties aren't evaluated before agreeing to client terms;" "Marketing activities are ineffective at targeting potential new customers;" "Our innovative products are out of sync with client needs." Our silent killers had been flushed into the open. No longer "silent," these issues were being put on notice by the collective, concerted efforts of the Trend Micro organization.

Throughout these meetings, Professor Russell was the impartial arbiter—a safety valve to keep tensions from boiling over. Sometimes, he used his authority to restrain the senior executives: "Just listen for now. No justifications or explanations necessary." Sometimes, he turned his attention on the delegates: "Please do not use phrases like 'I think' and 'I believe.' You are speaking on behalf of the general polity now—not on your own behalf." Under his deft mediation, the goldfish-bowl meeting plowed forward through two full days.

Our ashen-faced senior executives closed out one nervous meeting, only to begin another. When they were alone at last, their pent-up frustrations tumbled out in a jumble of self-justification. "That went far beyond what was necessary!" "Am I really that much of a micromanager?" "They don't know the true purpose of strategy." With the pep talks over, there were real issues to address. A response strategy needed to be discussed. Major problems on the agenda included Trend Micro's lack of a comprehensive set of rules and regulations, the inability of technology alone to meet customer needs, and frequent changes in strategic direction and the lack of related supporting measures. Another issue pointed the finger at Trend Micro's helmsman. "Today's Internet environment is vastly different from before. Is the current team of Trend Micro founders capable of leading us to the next level of competition?"

Problems came gradually into focus in the feverish discussions that followed and the myriad barriers to effective strategy implementation were unveiled one after another. At the end of the process, a knowing silence hung over us all. We knew that Trend Micro had arrived at yet another major turning point and that this time, we would need to fundamentally change our way of thinking.

At the appropriate time, Steve announced his determination to step down as CEO and recommended Eva to take his place. He said he felt that if Trend Micro were to rise to the next stage of competition, it would need a leader with the technological vision necessary to meet the Internet security needs of its customers. However, he continued, that leader would also need to be able to lead Trend Micro's global team forward within the framework of the firm's distinct culture. Eva, Trend Micro's chief technology officer, was a founding member of the Trend Micro team and experienced with all executive functions. Steve expressed his confidence that under Eva's leadership, she would ensure that the needs of the organization would be met while at the same time launching Trend Micro to the necessary next level of antivirus competition and technological breakthroughs.

Once again, the boardroom fell into an uncomfortable silence. No one was sure how to respond to Steve's proposal. Sure, Eva had long been a fixture in Trend Micro's executive decision-making processes, and they agreed that she was a good choice to succeed Steve, but hearing the words directly from Steve went down like a lump of cold oatmeal.

But Steve didn't stop there. He continued, "Administrative and investment functions should be separated. In the future, in my continuing role as board chairman, I will work with the board to keep a close watch over our business operations, while Eva will serve as CEO. Our roles and authorities will be distinct from one another. It's something we must do in the interests of our sustainability and growth over the long term." This new development was undeniably a step forward in giving Trend Micro a healthier corporate framework. Steve had for years served as both "principal" and "homeroom teacher." As Trend Micro CEO and board chairman, there were certainly times that Steve missed things. Moreover, seventeen years of being responsible for everything was tiring. Thus, everyone understood Steve's reasoning and had few concerns about Eva taking the helm as Trend Micro's next CEO.

"So what will your role be in day-to-day operations and management?" The senior executives were digesting the reality of succession and beginning to mull the implications.

"I'll be everyone's trainer! When needed, I'll join in on strategy discussions. Perhaps I'll organize critical skills-training courses for staff." Steve had been thinking about this for years.

"And how about Jenny?" Everyone knew that Steve and I always moved as a team.

"What difference would my not being here make?" I answered rhetorically. My role at Trend Micro had always been low-key, amorphous. Real operational authorities were in the hands of other, professionally trained executives. The toughest part of my job had always been serving as the interface between Steve and our executive management. Steve's departure as CEO would effectively obviate this need.

"Interpersonal and intraorganizational communications might not be as smooth with you gone," was the reply. "We've no one to replace you as Trend Micro's 'culture czar.'"

I knew early on that the advent of a new CEO would necessitate a comprehensive restructuring of Trend Micro's organization. As the managing director for global human resources, it was difficult to consider my own departure. I'd decided to ride the wave of change. "I will stay and continue in my current HR and cultural capacity." This temporarily assuaged some of the concerns rumbling through the group.

Everyone faced the future as a cauldron brimming with mixed emotions. With the main decision made, we were bracing ourselves for the changes those decisions would surely bring.

Reorganization

"Are we ready?" Professor Russell said, like a baseball coach looking to rouse his team for an imminent game. "Please, let's all move into the conference room so you can report to the delegates on your decisions."

The executives filed slowly into the room. They faced the nine respective delegates from V- and F-Force and the several HR managers on hand to facilitate the meeting. The air in the conference room hung heavy with eager anticipation for the coming news.

We had chosen the CFO as spokesman for the executive team. His implacable composure and rational approach to issues complemented his practiced use of humor at just the right time to relieve tensions. Attention first went to the strategies that would be used to address the various problems highlighted in delegates' presentations, followed by questions on these strategies, which would be fielded by the CFO.

Last but not least, the agenda turned to the issue of organization and leadership. At this point, the CFO gave a knowing glance at Steve and slowly sat down in his chair. Steve cleared his throat and began his prepared announcement. "It is imperative that the reorganization of Trend Micro start at the highest levels of management. As of next year, I will be only Trend Micro's chairman of the board, and Eva will be promoted as our new CEO."

This result came out of the blue for many employees. Ai-mei Ma later confided to me that, "We took it personally. We thought it was on our heads. We thought that maybe we'd been too harsh and that maybe the problems were so severe that we'd put even Steve on shaky ground."

Although the barrage of criticism didn't truly fit as a reason for Steve's decision, the goldfish-bowl meetings did bolster his conviction.

Next, Eva took the stage. The job ahead of her would be tougher than any she had yet faced. Taking up the gauntlet, she said, "What you all are expecting will take more than just a change in CEO. I hope to transform our regionally based organizational structure into a structure based on products." This set the audience into an uproar, with hurried conversations erupting throughout the conference room. Eva waited for a moment to let the news sink in before starting to describe the outlines of Trend Micro's future organization.

Throughout the past dozen years, Trend Micro had opened branch offices in more than thirty countries. We managed these offices under five regional offices: Japan, United States, Europe/Africa, Central/South America, and Asia. This latter office was responsible for all markets in Asia outside of Japan as well as for Australia and New Zealand. Regional offices were run by their respective presidents and were primarily responsible for marketing activities. Other key activities such as R & D, finances, human resources, and sales were managed directly by Trend Micro's home office (i.e., Trend Micro's senior executive board).

The review of internal and external delegate findings underlined the need for organizing our business around different client needs. The security needs of large corporate clients around the world are largely similar in that they want strong, centralized controls and regular, detailed activity reports. Small and medium-sized businesses generally want an "adequate" level of security that requires a minimal amount of manual control and is backed by comprehensive, effective customer service. Finally, individual users want something that provides security while being easy to use and backed by strong customer support. By contrast, differences among geographic regions are minimal. Small and medium businesses in Japan have the same Internet security requirements as their peers in North America and Europe. Even individual users are about the same around the world. If Trend Micro wanted to tailor its Internet security strategy even closer to the needs of its customers, reorganization of the business based on customer needs rather than geographic regions seemed the logical path forward.

This reorganization fundamentally changed how Trend Micro ran its business. Four new president positions were created for corporate clients, small/medium business clients, individual user clients, and innovative products, respectively. Each wore multiple hats that made them responsible for product strategy, R & D, and marketing planning in their respective client category. Each was responsible for a territory as big as the globe. Leadership in terms of geographic regions devolved to local Trend Micro organizations, which were responsible for achieving sales targets across all product lines.

Faced with the consensus and the preparation of senior executives, the delegates were gradually won over to the logic of restructuring the Trend Micro organization. It was the best way forward to creating a Trend Micro ready and able for future competitive pressures. Truthfully speaking, a decision to shift strategies without changing the organization would likely create paradoxes that would hamstring normal operations and ultimately prevent strategic initiatives from succeeding. Yes, change should best start at the top. It is a time-tested principle of business management.

Prolonged back-and-forth discussions eventually earned consensus for a top-down reorganization of the Trend Micro organization. Now it was the delegates who looked a bit overwrought. They had honestly reported on general opinion, braved the potential wrath of the "powers that be," and set in motion changes that were far bigger than expected. How would they reflect all this back to their constituencies? One delegate summarized her collective concerns: "Having gone through the entire experience, we understand how all the disparate pieces fit together to justify this huge reorganization. But we have a duty to answer to those we interviewed. How can we help them understand the actual process involved in making these decisions? Furthermore, how is the entire corporate organization going to be convinced of the honest intentions of these changes?"

One can spend a lifetime and still not fully master the art of communication and message delivery. All communications must be carefully planned and timed and presented in the proper order, and it must be taken into consideration how quickly news spreads via the Internet—especially among Trend Micro's social-network-savvy employees.

All eyes turned to me. At least until the upcoming change of guard, I was still the one everyone looked to for communication and information issues.

"I would like to ask you all to keep the discussions and decisions made here today confidential. I hope to hold back the speculation mill." I had rarely made such a seriously earnest request. "Human Resources and I will come up with a comprehensive communications plan, and after two weeks, at the managers' meeting in early November, we will confirm a plan to quickly and properly inform all Trend Micro colleagues about the reorganization decision." I made eye contact with everyone in the room to make sure they all understood and agreed.

The ball was in my court and it was my turn to feel the heat. However, this shouldn't be just my burden. I put my mind to work on a plan that would get everyone eager to pitch in and participate.

CHAPTER 7

The Chungshan Hall Summit

Everything here is out in the open. No one will be shortchanged. This is a cooperative endeavor for which we are all responsible. Our sincere objective is to build a healthy and enjoyable work environment that reflects our collective character and delivers the highest possible level of benefits.

Every change we make is a deliberate and necessary response to evolutionary change in our environment.

Yangmingshan's Chungshan Hall was built during Martial Law in the 1960s as an exclusive meeting venue for the ruling KMT political party. It is surrounded by exceptional natural beauty with its gurgling streams fed by natural sulfur springs, and there is an air of mystic, otherworldly charm. Despite its timeworn façade, Chungshan Hall and its Chinese aesthetics continue to weave an alluring spell over all who visit. With the passing of authoritarian rule, Chungshan Hall is now open to the public during visiting hours. However, few had embraced its potential beyond it being a sedate tourist destination.

I dove into preparations for Trend Micro's first global summit immediately following the conclusion of our goldfish-bowl meeting. Senior managers from around the world were invited to Taiwan for our formal announcement of the changes to come. As it would be the last time for Steve and me as hosts of an international meeting for Trend Micro, I wanted to break from tradition and hold the event somewhere more special than a hotel.

Steve came to the rescue with a snap decision. "Let's hold it at Chungshan Hall, then!" It was then up to Trend Micro's administrative team and I to get the ball rolling. We used our wiles to convince Hall administrators to open the venue up to the 150 Trend Micro senior international professionals who would be descending on Taiwan for the two-day summit. Next, we took up the challenge of getting the hall in order. We reconfigured seating, set up the audio system, installed the stage, ordered an appropriately large video-projection screen, hired caterers to prepare and serve the formal evening banquet, arranged for a cocktail party lunch on the roof, and organized exhibition space where country teams could highlight their national culture and products. We wanted to incorporate the building's scenic setting into the summit agenda as well, so we arranged to hold breakout team meetings outside on the grounds. Our careful preparations made full use of the building's multifaceted potential while highlighting Taiwan's exceptional natural and cultural appeal.

However, even knottier challenges lay ahead. We had to get the systems up and ready to simulcast the entire event via the Internet. Fortunately, of course, Trend Micro was an old hand at solving Internet problems. So, come hell or high water, we could still rest assured that we would have the fastest broadband connection permitted by current technology.

Above all else, we were doyens of "soft" ware, with a naturally strong bias toward content as opposed to the box it came in. Content would be the glue that held the global summit agenda together.

The Goldfish Bowl Takes Center Stage

Our next hurdle was to map out a strategy to win the full Trend Micro polity over to the idea of reorganization as well as to encourage their "buy in" of the tightly interwoven details necessary to realize its goals. If simulcast proceedings didn't pack sufficient punch, the attention of our audience would drift. They might leave altogether! What tricks did we have up our sleeve to help us keep our audience engaged, interested, and primed to absorb our core messages?

"Put the goldfish bowl onstage!" I said in a moment of inspiration.

My mind was still steeped in the events of the past few months, with my thoughts not infrequently stoked by the private urgings of our delegates. "It was so stimulating," they shared. "You really have to find a way to let everyone share this experience." They all stayed true to their oaths of secrecy and anxiously awaited the time and place when all would be revealed. During this calm before the storm, they all kept in regular contact and eagerly expressed their willingness to help in any way.

With the general idea in place, I began putting my mind to work on how to "stage" the goldfish-bowl experience. I abandoned thoughts of a slide presentation, but not before practicing various scripted talks until I was dry in the mouth. I then started thinking about the possibility of staging a theatrical reenactment. Staged highlights from our goldfish-bowl meetings might be broadcast worldwide to our colleagues. If done right, it could make everyone a virtual participant in the processes we had used to work through the problems and make each tough decision.

The responses to my idea were quick and unanimous: "You want us to act?"

I responded, "Not a play. We could do a documentary skit that would simply recreate the events at our meetings." Thanks to Trend Micro's annual Paramount Culture Tour, several of our senior executives already had stage experience, and they agreed to help out in this latest endeavor.

I happily dove into my new dual responsibilities as producer and announcer on this in-house theatrical effort. (*Who knows?* I thought. *This could be my first step onto a post-Trend Micro career path into a career as host of a culture and art TV or radio show!*)

Act 1 (scene brimming with positivity about the future):

Steve (introducing Trend Micro's famous Trend Performance Index (TPI) showing the trend over time for combined growth and profits): "We've experienced five solid years of growth in both sales and profits. Outstanding! You all deserve to give yourselves a round of applause."

CFO (playing the role of the contrarian, pulls out a chart showing our competitors' growth): "Steve. We've done well. But our competitors are doing better!"

Eva: "The Network Virus Wall product we launched last year in Texas won the exhibition's best new product award. They nicknamed it the 'Demo Queen!'"

CFO: "Sure. We've had good times! I like the newly redesigned look of the red box too. But just how many of these have we actually sold so far?"

Head of Japan Sales: "Six hundred units."

Head of US Sales: "Sixty sets."

Head of Asia Sales: "Six sets." (voices in room fade to a murmur)

(Lights in room fade; light pans over to the announcer)

Jenny: "We thought all was going great. Confidence ruled the day. But dangers lurked just out of sight, in the shadows." (explanation of the mortal danger posed by "silent killers" and a brief overview of the fitness plan follows)

Group discussion of the strategic plan followed by a slide presentation of the actual draft plan.

Act 2:

Jenny explains the importance of validation and then discusses the formation and responsibilities of V-Force.

Informal roundtable discussion with V-Force featuring individual members sharing insights learned in client interviews. Surprising findings are given special emphasis.

Act 3:

Jenny introduces the formation and responsibilities of F-Force.

Similarly, an informal roundtable discussion with F-Force features members sharing their experiences and detailing the problems they discovered during their internal interviews.

Act 4:

Group reenactment of highlight moments from goldfish-bowl meeting sessions

Act 5:

Steve: "We need to change. A new strategy calls for a new organization!" (Steve then describes reorganization plans and announces that he will continue as board chairman, with Eva stepping into the role of CEO.)

The spotlight turns to Eva, who formally announces her start as Trend Micro's new CEO as well as the plans to reorganize the company along product segment lines. She explains the importance of this reorganization and expected changes.

President of Sales (presentation focuses on calming concerns, describes what will be new/stay the same in future product strategy, and announces his new position as president for the SME business segment): "You may feel that our strategy is in a chronic state of flux. However, Trend Micro remains true to the vision and strategic theme set at the very beginning. The changes in strategy are necessary adjustments to keep us on course."

An Honest Dialogue under Taipei Skies

After the end of the skit, the majority of our live audience and those watching online reacted somewhat skeptically. Some even burst into applause, and we heard, "Good show!" However, the merriment was brief as everyone began taking notice of the serious expressions on the faces of the executives onstage. Clapping hands froze in mid-clap. "Really?" they one asked another, their faces cast in looks of confusion.

Of course, we never expected the news to go down particularly easy. Time was needed for all to talk among themselves and digest the news. The whistle sounded for lunch, and everyone filed out with his or her questions and concerns. The afternoon session was reserved for small-group breakout discussions.

On that delightful autumn day, amid the lush beauty of the Yangmingshan Mountains and the nostalgic airs of Chungshan Hall, attendees split off into groups of eight. Groups lighted wherever they felt comfortable—in stairways, around outdoor stone tables, and on the expansive lawn. Despite the relaxed setting, they all shared the same sense of anxiety about the unknown. Reorganization would affect everyone's work routine and professional responsibilities. Discussions ran hot and heavy with expressions running the gamut from concern to excitement … all the way to anger.

Small group discussions are the best format for getting people to express their true feelings and flushing otherwise suppressed opinions out into the open. The good weather, we hoped, might also help lubricate the candor. Steve and I visited each group. "Jenny," one employee asked, "aren't these changes happening a bit too fast?" Too fast? These plans had been on the front burner for nearly three years. "Aren't you concerned?" Concerned? Having Eva in charge made me more confident in our post-succession future than ever before. "What is Steve going to do?" *Weren't you listening to him?* "I'm not sure what I'll be doing," he said, "but I do know what I will not be doing!"

A pleasant evening breeze accompanied us as the sun gradually sank below the horizon and everyone filed into the main hall. Most still had burning questions and concerns about the coming reorganization.

We had each team select one representative, and, as we had done previously with our goldfish bowl/representative model, we asked each to come up on stage and grill our panel of senior executives with all the questions on his or her team's mind. For their part, the executives took their responsibility seriously. They carefully addressed each concern and responded to every suggestion. Issues that couldn't be addressed immediately were assigned on the spot for follow-up and resolution.

Those in the Trend Micro organization outside of East Asia who joined in online were doing so either early in their morning or long into their night. Many were determined not to miss out on this opportunity, and they submitted questions and participated virtually in ongoing discussions.

Thus, although we couldn't meet face-to-face with each one of our colleagues, we successfully established open, honest dialogue virtually over the Internet.

After the global summit had ended and managers had returned to their respective countries, we hoped they would use well the information and experience gained during these two days. We hoped they would be scrutinizing their own organizations with fitness checkups and perhaps even hold their own goldfish-bowl sessions as a catalyst to substantive bottom-up communications.

I'm sure there were a few "fish" that managed to escape our well-laid net and that were still swimming in pools of doubt and anxiety. Communication is, after all, a never-ending endeavor. The three of us hoped collectively that our careful efforts, coupled with Taipei's beautiful blue skies, might succeed in conveying the sincerity of our message and intentions. We laid everything on the table. We did our best to be fair, nonabrasive, noncontentious, and highly responsible on every key point.

We were looking to build a healthy and happy working environment that met the needs and priorities of all Trend Micro colleagues and provided the greatest benefit possible to all our stakeholders. The changes we made were *not* "changes of heart" but adjustments carefully made to keep us on the road to accomplishing our shared goals.

Surprise Party

As the skies darkened and stars poked through the fading embers of day, we shed our formal meeting setting for one better suited for celebration. With the day's responsibilities at an end, the time had come to let loose!

We were ready to once more trample across August tradition as we traveled the short distance from Chungshan Hall to Caoshan Lodge, one of ROC President Chiang Kai-shek's many official residences on Taiwan. We'd secretly planned a surprise party for Steve. Steve's forty-ninth birthday fell on the day after the summit. Although Chinese tradition shunned birthdays that ended in nine, I ploughed forward with covert planning on a Western-style birthday party for Steve, unbeknownst to Steve's mother or, of course, to Steve. It would be a celebration of his successful handover of executive authority over Trend Micro before his "half century" mark. From here on out, Steve would follow wherever fate and his fancy dared to take him.

Our eighteen-year-old son jumped up on the table and bellowed, "Dad! I've never told you this, but, although you think I blame you for never being home, you're wrong. I'm very proud of you! You're my role model! Happy birthday!" Although my son didn't know it, those words touched Steve deeply. While he had yearned for his father's acceptance, he needed his son's acceptance even more.

The party featured the best in traditional Taiwanese cuisine. Bowl after bowl of iconic *danzai* noodles emerged from the kitchen. Beyond reinforcing Trend Micro's unique cultural ethos, the global summit provided a rare opportunity to expose our international colleagues to the beautiful essence of Taiwanese culture.

Colleagues from around the world launched into performances they had prepared to wish Steve a happy birthday. It was incredible that they had time to prepare so well. Wasn't everyone busy with meetings? The Japanese team created a human pyramid. The American team performed a comedy talk-show skit. The team from Central and South America sang impassioned Spanish ballads. Even the normally reticent Taiwan team put their men in drag for a memorably hilarious performance of belly dancing.

Even after the performances were over and the laughter had faded, the party continued long into the night.

Cheng-tai Yin, older brother of well-known singer Johnny Yin, was at the time a manager in Trend Micro's Technical Division. He and his brother gave us their first public performance together since they had graduated from university. Nostalgic Western pop songs with guitar accompaniment came one after another. All were transfixed in the moment, unwilling to see the evening end.

Under the light of an argent moon, Steve and I held hands. Everything had turned out so wonderful. While all good things must come to an end, true friendships, once struck, *should* last a lifetime. Steve and I were a team on this entrepreneurial road. We'd seen our share of hardship as well as gleaned significant enjoyment and pleasure from the experience. The arguments along the way had left not a scratch on our mutual affinity and admiration. Our shared struggles had indeed brought us closer together than ever.

Starting from scratch, first with two people, then three and subsequently, more than two thousand, success and growth came suddenly. We'd jumped into the public consciousness with an out-of-the-blue stock listing, weathered the "perfect storm" inside a collapsing Internet bubble, and survived several hostile takeover attempts and a lawsuit filed by a former strategic alliance partner. Steve and I had traveled across five continents, had the pleasure of working closely with colleagues from more than thirty countries, and had made innumerable new friends. We'd seen it all—from the best to the worst. We had shepherded Trend Micro through each stage of corporate growth. We'd been there at every important moment. Our "baby" had grown up, and we were now prepared to see it continue on without our doting guidance. We were ready to move on to challenges yet to materialize, test our mettle on new experiences, and explore new facets of life's journey.

SECTION THREE: TESTING CULTURE

DANCING WITH DANGER

CHAPTER 8

Trend Micro's Nervous Leap Forward

Crises were no stranger to Trend Micro. I had handled each crisis personally, and Trend Micro had made it through each, unscathed.

But that was before Trend Micro went public. Our customer base was smaller and viruses were tamer.

This time was different. This time, it wasn't the threat of a virus but rather our own software program that threatened to destroy all we had built.

CEO transition in 2005

- Founded: United States in 1988
- Headquarters: Tokyo, Japan
- Employees: 2,500
- Operations in more tha 30 countries
- 2004 revenue: US$5XX Million
- 2004 Profits: US$1XX Million
- NASDAQ(TMIC) and Nikkei (4704)

CEO Eva Chen

$1,207,326
$1,085,348
$1,029,455
$985,062
$848,832
$718,718
$660,784
$600,000
$500,000
$400,000
$300,000
$200,000
$100,000

88 89 90 91 92 93 94 95 96 97 98 99 00 01 02 03 04 05 06 07 08 09 10 11

Annual Revenue

January 2, 2005, saw Eva officially assume the helm of the good ship Trend Micro. It was seventeen years since we'd founded the company together. We had 2,500 employees working for us in more than thirty countries around the world. Revenues were US$550 million, our net profit margin was an impressive 24 percent, and our market value was currently pegged at US$5 billion.

Reorganization was proceeding apace and Eva was showing that she indeed had the "right stuff" to propel Trend Micro forward into the future. Her attention to detail made all aware that she "had their backs" and saw everyone as a valuable member of the team. Two years of therapy and regular exercise had put her back in peak physical condition and given her new, impressive physical stamina. Trend Micro's rigorous schedule of meetings and travel that Steve and I once shared between us was now accomplished singlehandedly by our new "super CEO." She even made the time for a side trip to the National Aeronautic and Space Administration (NASA) in the United States to ride its Vertical Motion Simulator.

Eva kept regular lines of communication open with us. Steve, listening on the phone, made every effort to keep his advice to a minimum in order both to let Eva follow her instincts and to give her his encouragement. Although I still continued in my role as managing director for global human resources in order to help move the reorganization process forward, I deferred to the decisions of the new executive team and worked to implement their directives. Holding our tongues and letting others run with "our" ball was, at times, irritatingly unnatural. But it was an essential step toward Trend Micro making a clean break with ingrained habits.

Soon after the transition, I remember a colleague asking me what I'd like to eat at an upcoming lunch meeting. To everyone's amusement, I answered, "Ask Eva!" I even ominously declared at a senior international executives' meeting: "I am no longer the wife of the CEO!" It caught everyone off guard. They thought I might be making some new revelation about Steve and my personal relationship. I played my audience and, just as those words had sunk in, finished off with: "I've been promoted to *sister* of the CEO." The room burst into relieved laughter. The need for these purposeful pronouncements underlined that people still weren't used to the idea of Steve's not being the CEO and of my no longer being the CEO's wife. (However, even today, everyone at Trend Micro still respectfully refers to me as the boss's wife, while Steve has moved up in the unofficial title hierarchy to the "Big Boss").

More than thirty years of marriage produced two wonderful sons, as well as Trend Micro—our "third child." This rambunctious, impulsive offspring of ours had grown by leaps and bounds since the day we first registered and named it. It had galloped through our maiden launch of PC-cillin, our partnership with Intel, and the many other exciting changes of "adolescence" that culminated with our listing on the Tokyo Stock Exchange. The support and nurturing that Trend Micro required was in no way less (and, I regret to say, sometimes much more) than what we gave our sons.

Eva was as much of a founder as Steve and I. She joined in Trend Micro's second year and played a key role in giving the company its present breadth and depth. While none were more fit and able to take on the role of CEO, Eva still needed time to adjust professionally and emotionally to her new responsibilities.

Once a child leaves the nest to begin a new family and career, it is best for parents to allow him or her to forge ahead with minimal interference and constraint. Backseat driving is rarely the path to happiness for either the giver or the recipient of advice, no matter how well intentioned that advice may be.

Showing confidence is the best way to express trust. Letting go is the best way to express love. Tacit rapport is the best way to communicate.

While we three were acclimating to our new roles, the entire company was adjusting to the titanic shifts in leadership and business structure. Eva was learning to take charge of Trend Micro's frontlines, to handle clients, and to face the constant stream of new sales and shareholder issues. *She* navigated now from the captain's chair and needed to shift her perspective to a higher plane—beyond just product innovation and R & D. She also had to refashion her relationship with the Trend Micro senior executive team. No longer "one of the guys," she was now responsible to inspire and lead them forward to the next level of competitiveness and competition.

For my part, I had to stop being Eva's "big sister." Although she had long since stopped calling me *Jie* (big sister) in favor of my English name Jenny, Eva was still the regular "beneficiary" of my sisterly advice and protection. From now on, personnel and budgetary decisions were no longer mine to make. My intuitive whims would no longer be the deciding factor behind the organization of international meetings and motivational events. I needed to step into line with Trend Micro's new management. I was now part of Eva's team, responsible for global human resources and administration.

Adjusting to the new regime was an even bigger task for Steve. Learning to let go is invariably more difficult, as it requires stepping from the limelight into the shadows and letting others make decisions that are no longer yours. Stumbling through the transition risks not only frustration but also awkward irrelevance. I like thinking of a leader as Tarzan swinging purposefully forward through the forest. Sharp eyes focused ever forward are needed to spy out the next vine that will keep the forward momentum going. A jungle king that is unwilling to let go of his familiar vine for the promises of the next is doomed to swinging on a pendulum that ends back where he started. However, the time between the last and the next vine is invariably a moment of pure, tenuous inertia and a time of utter isolation. All energy and hope must be leveled at the untested vine ahead. Overthinking the problem is out of the question, as self-doubt is the quickest route to a mouthful of dirt. This analogy transfers well to the business world. After all, we had heard about and seen many corporate leaders who had swung out hopefully on the vine of succession, only to falter at the moment necessary to continue forward. They retained their grip on the familiar and ended up being pulled back in, largely to the detriment of themselves and their companies.

We wanted to be different. We wanted to escape Trend Micro's comfortable gravitational pull and proceed on to new adventures. For this, everyone in the company was working hard to acclimate and learn. There were, of course, mistakes made, the inevitable dead ends, and nervous tension. I liked to think of Trend Micro as a jumbo jet that could never land. It needed to be refueled in flight and could never let its fuel run too low. However, while performing these hazardous airborne refuelings, it still needed to maintain its steady course forward.

Turbulence was inevitable, as was grumbling and even the occasional backlash. But Trend Micro didn't waste a drop of precious "fuel" during the process. We surely lost a few employees to the transition, but that didn't detract from the success of the overall process. The fitness checkup had systematically changed the way that Trend Micro communicated, while it also redefined our roles within the company. With all eyes kept firmly on the "ball" of Trend Micro's future growth and success, our succession experience was truly an overall success.

The Chairman's Club

The yew year saw us firmly attached to our next vine forward. Steve and I now rarely participated in strategic or business-review meetings. We had stepped, at least for the moment, into our new roles as Trend Micro "guiding lights." We also began selectively participating in internal awards ceremonies, dividend distributions, pep rallies, and charitable events.

However, we continued giving Eva all the support she asked for. Eva created The Chairman's Club as a step forward into her new leadership role. Her prior focus on leading Trend Micro's R & D team meant that she was less familiar with the company's sales executives. The Chairman's Club was her vehicle for demonstrating that she both understood and appreciated the hard work of the Trend Micro sales team. Through this club, Eva developed an annual awards recognition program for Trend Micro's top sales achievers as well as top promoters of Trend Micro's corporate culture. The program feted award recipients and their families at a different exotic vacation destination each year.

Issuing awards in the name of Trend Micro's new CEO helped further increase the honor of award recognition. As our new highest recognition for culture, I naturally got involved in the process with my "F4" dream team (my so-called Fantastic Four, comprising my personal secretary, project manager, art director, and an IT engineer). Trend Micro had a proud tradition (sometimes better described as self-inflicted pain) of self-organizing and managing all of our international events and activities. We did everything ourselves rather than subcontracting out to a public relations agency, as a way of making sure every aspect reflected our core cultural identity and values. As a side benefit, this model also gave us the chance to work internationally with our partners, which brought us closer together and fostered mutual growth and development.

As everyone loves a good vacation, no one was short of ideas where the first Chairman's Club awards ceremony might be held. We set the budget, canvassed opinions, and tabulated the votes from our regional offices. The name Punta Cana came in as the surprise winner.

My initial reaction at hearing for the first time the name of our awards destination was, "Where's that?" Wherever it was, it sounded rather romantic.

"It's on the coast of the Dominican Republic. Supposedly has one of the finest, most beautiful white-sand beaches anywhere in the world. It's popular with American and European vacationers." I was pleased that my secretary Eileen Liu had already done her homework. "There are direct flights there from Europe and the United States. Of course, getting there from Central and South America is no problem. It's just a bit far removed from Asia. We'll have to make two transfers, and total travel time will be about thirty hours."

I then recalled a university classmate I had known from the Dominican Republic. "The Dominican Republic?" I chimed in. "It is one of Taiwan's diplomatic allies. We used to have an agricultural assistance team there helping set up rice farms in the country. I've heard that Columbus first stepped foot in America on what is now the capital of the country, Santo Domingo. I think he is buried there too. This could be interesting. Let's go!" I enjoyed Latin American culture and felt naturally drawn to places I'd never been. This was doubly true of places I'd not previously heard about. The stories of Punta Cana's scenic beauty, wealth of historic sites, good food, and cheap lodgings meant that we could have fun and keep things within budget. The only drawback was the relatively poor state of telecommunications in that part of the country. Getting in touch with the office and people back home might not be so easy. But, we thought, it was meant to be a vacation and award winners' family members would be along for the fun, so slow communications might not be such a bad thing. In fact, it just might be the lubricant needed to get everyone into an appropriately relaxed groove!

That was that! We descended from around the world on the recently "discovered" paradise of Punta Cana in the midst of a sunny and hot April. Days were spent having fun on the beach and splashing in the inviting waters of the Caribbean. We all changed into our formal best for the evening awards ceremony. Award winners accompanied by their spouses, and some even by their children, took the stage one by one on a carpet strewn with red rose petals under the cozy glow of candlelight. Pictures of their families were projected on the main screen, while the national anthem of each award winner was played in turn. Steve presented the specially designed trophies, I presented bouquets of flowers, and Eva emotively related the story behind each award decision.

We have always felt it important to share recognition for the achievements made by our colleagues with their family and friends. Success never happens in a vacuum, but, to varying degrees, owes much to the support and encouragement of family. Thus, we always made sure to include employees' families in our seasonal company banquets, our celebrations, and even our overseas incentive trips and always made sure they received their own gifts to show our appreciation. I knew from personal experience the sacrifices that families had to make in order to support their Trend Micro fathers, mothers, sons, and daughters.

The wife of a manager who had joined Trend Micro from Intel shared, "Trend Micro doesn't take for granted the sacrifices made by families. At least you take the effort to express your gratitude."

Affections kept warm mature into passion and loyalty. The awards ceremony in Punta Cana ended on a high note with romantic live Latin music and a buffet meal with an open bar. A dazzling light show and a revolving dance floor and ceiling transformed the room into an ever-changing, electric spectacle. Everyone gleefully let loose with toes tapping and bodies swaying to the rhythm as, two by two, they stepped onto the dance floor. Eva was the "dance queen" of the evening, with dance moves that had no problem earning everyone's attention.

Steve and I slipped out early for a moonlit stroll on the hotel's sandy-white shoreline—away from dance-floor lights, party music, and the continued merriment.

Lesson in Balance

The time had come to pilot my priorities back into orbit around family and loved ones. During those years invested in starting and growing Trend Micro, I had failed to leave enough time for our sons. I still carry a deep and abiding regret for this failing. Learning to find and keep proper balance is a hard challenge (perhaps the hardest) faced by women who juggle a family and a full-fledged career.

Steve and I flew from the Dominican Republic to the East Coast of the United States to see our oldest son. This "first love" of my life (yes, I still see my firstborn as my first love) was to be married just three months from then, launching him into the next phase of life's journey. While people thought of me as the woman behind my husband Steve, I thought of my oldest son as the man behind me. He had been smart and thoughtful from a young age. He was buoyant, lively, and always ready to help out with household chores. We regularly exercised together, he always listened patiently to my complaints and troubles, and, most importantly, he took an instrumental role in helping me raise his brother, six years his younger. He made every effort to fill the shoes of the oft-absent Steve.

More than love, I relied on him. So much so that I sometimes worried I might need him more than he needed me. Now he was getting ready to join the girlfriend he loved in matrimony, begin a family of his own, and become another's son-in-law. I can't honestly say whether my happiness at the time for this joyous event yet outweighed my own jealous reluctance to see my son leave me for another—this despite my liking of this quick-witted, intelligent girl my son had found and my confidence in their happy life ahead.

It was yet another lesson in letting events take their intended course. No one may "own" another person, even if you were the one responsible for bringing him into this world! I took solace in the fact that, while I couldn't keep him forever, I could make the most of his last few months as a bachelor. I looked forward to heartfelt conversations. Steve even more wanted to use the time to make up for his earlier absences. Our sons both looked up to their father. Not interested in being second-generation leaders of Dad's company, both nurtured entrepreneurial ambitions of their own. Steve finally saw his chance to "pass the torch" to his offspring and share his secrets of success. He booked our oldest son and himself for a five-day intensive Internet marketing seminar being held at Northwestern University in Chicago.

Eva's son and daughter were still young, and she was in the midst of the juggling act necessary to balance professional and family responsibilities. She smartly worked to arrange meetings close to home whenever possible.

After Punta Cana, she flew directly to Los Angeles for a global product managers' meeting. The contrast in tenor between this meeting, attended by some forty key product R & D executives, and the just-finished Chairman's Club event couldn't have been starker. The professionals gathered in Los Angeles came ready to discuss the future direction of Trend Micro product development and tackle the plethora of associated technical minutiae.

Eva was in her element. It was one of the things that set her apart from Steve as CEO. Steve was great at seeing the big picture and planning for the future. He has a keen eye for spotting and exploiting blue-ocean opportunities and then turning them into well-oiled, brilliantly efficient operations. As Trend Micro's helmsman, he took the high ground and left the details to others. It was this quality of his that let us work together as an effective business team. He set the course and made the big strategic decisions. It was me who, after mutual discussion, worked out the parameters and policy procedures. He gave me full authority and didn't interfere in my executive decisions. The same was true for the other members of the senior executive board, including Eva. In the absence of major problems, Steve left the details to his executive team and avoided micromanagement.

Eva had a more cautious and holistic approach than Steve and rarely let a detail pass unnoticed. At university, she was a star of her school's debate team. I had more than a passing familiarity with her talents because, even as children, I rarely won an argument against her. "Right" somehow seemed always to be on her side. Most in the company had learned not to wade carelessly into a debate with Eva, and when colleagues did challenge her ideas, they most often ended up ceding to her arguments. I once admonished her, as older sister to younger, that winning an argument doesn't necessarily win sympathy or support, nor does it mean you have the corner on truth. Every issue has two sides.

The truism held true for our CEO succession as well. The succession process had its advantages and its drawbacks. The two CEOs each had his and her own distinct style, strengths, and weaknesses. It was something people would simply have to learn to get used to.

Eva was already deep into the product managers' meeting when she received a telephone call from a Japanese product manager currently stationed in the United States. He reported that V.594, a new virus signature, was causing unexpected problems. There had already been complaints from some clients in the United States, and he was unsure whether the problem might also affect clients in Japan.

The call came in at 5:00 in the afternoon on Friday, April 22. In Asia, it was already the morning of the twenty-third, the following day.

V.594

To the man on the street, V.594 probably holds little meaning beyond being a difficult-to-remember code number. For Trend Micro, however, it will always recall a disaster of company-crashing proportions.

Antivirus firms must remain on constant, global alert to detect and stop threats to computer security wherever and whenever they might emerge. The line or lines of code unique to a particular virus is extracted and used to design software that will correctly identify and "clean" virus damage from computer systems. Software updates critical to keeping client systems clean and virus free must be provided as quickly as possible. A unique code accompanies each new virus software update (or version, designated by the prefix *V*), assigned on a cycle running from 001 to 999. V.594 was the latest update for Trend Micro antivirus software, which was uploaded on April 22.

All software updates are subject to meticulous scrutiny prior to public release. Even small problems have the potential to mess with a client's Internet environment and lead to unpredictable results—perhaps slightly slower data transmission speeds ... perhaps a hole in the virus net.

The V.594 debacle was something worse—something that would be much harder to forgive and forget.

A hardworking Philippine virus engineer had been working overtime through the weekend to resolve the threat of a new virus known as a "zombie." The zombie virus inserted itself into OS software, made changes to server codes, and launched attacks that struck deep into the heart of the global Internet infrastructure. It was proving a hard virus to control. The engineer analyzed the virus code, created an antidote program, and, after standard testing procedures, uploaded the necessary update to the Internet for global download. Two hours later, a customer service colleague in the United States discovered that the latest update had a problem. When run in Windows XP, the update ran a loop command that created an unending stream of copies of the virus code, which gradually filled up the host computer's hard drive and crashed the system. It was a disastrous development, and the update was immediately taken down from the update queue, with plans to analyze the problem and issue a new, clean update.

However, in those two hours, the instantaneous nature of the Internet had unleashed a global disaster.

On the surface, the timing might have seemed fortuitous. It was already the weekend in Asia and late at night in Europe and the Americas. Few companies would have their Internet security people still at work downloading updates, right? Actually, off-time hours, when demand on computer systems is lowest, are when most companies schedule automatic software updates and backups.

The installation of the update caused an immediate spike in Internet demand, slowed the World Wide Web to a crawl, and crashed affected systems. Even those who managed to get their systems back up and running were saddled with computers riddled with problems.

Our customer service engineers normally worked in shifts around the clock, 24-7, to address the emergency needs of clients. Most client issues were resolved quickly without further problem. However, a string of calls came in on April 22 that all described the same problem: a system crash after installing the latest Trend Micro update. Trend Micro's standard operating procedure requires issuing a global "red alert" immediately upon receiving three customer calls on the same virus issue. VP for US Customer Service and Sales Mitchell sensed immediately that something was not right and contacted the company's senior executive team.

This time, it wasn't a virus but our own software that was the threat source. Fortunately, President Oscar Chang and Trend Micro's other top technical experts were all present at the meeting. Eva cut the strategy meeting short and launched into an emergency meeting on the problem code and an appropriate response.

Noninterference Policy

The Trend Micro team was still loath to see Steve and I as "out of the loop." We were notified immediately and asked to add our authority to Trend Micro's response. After all, we couldn't, they said hopefully, just stand by during such a crisis, could we?

Steve had just relinquished the CEO baton and, like a leopard, was intently watching events unfold from the shadows nearby. He was keenly aware that this was an abnormally dangerous situation. "Will you go back in?" I asked. He answered, "Let's let Eva handle things on her own. We'll help out if she really needs us."

If the root cause was a technical problem, we had every confidence that Eva could resolve things herself. But this time, the problem seemed to involve issues on the client side as well. Japan was our largest market, and Steve had been in direct charge of our Japanese operations for many years. He had handled the client side there, while I had handled marketing and administration. It was a successful formula that had made us number-one. When Steve stepped down as CEO, Japan sales still accounted for around 40 percent of overall Trend Micro sales by value. Prior to taking over as CEO, Eva had little contact with our Japanese operation, and she was still in the early stages of learning the ropes in our biggest market. I couldn't suppress a nagging anxiousness. "But if we have problems in Japan," I asked Steve, "the media, customers, investors … they only know you. Is it even possible for you not to step up on this one?"

He struggled with his own trepidations for a while, but in the end still decided to keep for the moment above the fray. "Eva has been CEO for less than six months. She needs room to make a name for herself and win the confidence of the Trend Micro organization. If I come to the rescue at the first sign of trouble, wouldn't I be telling everyone that Eva doesn't have our full trust and confidence?" True to form, Steve was thinking of the future, while I was concerned with my sister's problem in the here and now as well as about the immediate fate of our Japan team. I had pulled Trend Micro Japan up by its bootstraps and been with them through good times and bad. The camaraderie I shared with Trend Micro Japan was special. I was their "mother" and "big sister." They were in trouble now, and it wasn't natural for me to sit by and just watch things unfold.

But at the same time, I wanted even more to enjoy my real role as Mom and spend quality time with my son. I had sacrificed much for my career and been off-kilter with my priorities for quite some time. I deserved time for myself!

Appealing to "noninterference," we let Eva and the senior executive board know that they were in full charge. "No problem," Steve said. "You guys can handle it!"

Despite pretenses, I remained deeply troubled—afraid for the company, our colleagues, and Eva; unwilling to stay away; and feeling more than a little guilty for setting our "entrepreneurial baby" aside. It was the first time we wouldn't be dropping everything to come to Trend Micro's aid. My thoughts wandered to more speculative concerns. Could this be a punishment for our taking a vacation? Might this be a test tailor-made for the new CEO?

There had certainly been other disasters throughout our seventeen years in business. Spec differences between PC286 generation microprocessors and the succeeding PC386 generation had made Trend Micro's latest PC-cillin updates incompatible with PC286-based systems. A problem with extended memory had also once caused Trend Micro's latest products to be uninstallable and required a 100 percent recall. Another time, a coding flaw caused the deletion of every instance of the letter p in documents—a mistake that made us the butt of industry jokes for longer than I care to remember. The one that shook us to our core was the politically motivated response to our honest description of the Beijing/Bloody! virus in Trend Micro's Threat Encyclopedia, which emerged in 1990, soon after China's violent crackdown on protesters in Tiananmen Square. Our competitor in the China market turned our honesty against us and informed the Chinese government. Chinese officials forced us to remove our products from the shelves, and our distributors demanded compensation. After hastening to China to handle the issue, Steve came just short of being arrested by Chinese public security.

Actually, the history of Trend Micro is riddled with unexpected disasters. We nevertheless managed to muddle through each, emerging frazzled but otherwise no worse for the wear on the other side. But most of our worst threats had come before going public. Our customer base had been smaller, and viruses were, in retrospect, much tamer back then. The storm at hand seemed one that had the punch to do major, potentially fatal, damage. Eva was only newly installed. Did she really have what it took to captain Trend Micro through the storm and back into calmer waters?

Yesterday, everything had seemed smooth for Trend Micro on the Internet ocean. Today, a squall had come out of nowhere that threatened our very seaworthiness. The danger reflected the unpredictable nature of computer viruses and the underlying fragility of the information superhighway. The "laurels" in this business were few and far between—offering precious little chance for rest.

CHAPTER 9

Staring Disaster in the Face

The hastily assembled SWAT team of senior Trend Micro executives on the thirty-third floor struck a consensus as to how Trend Micro would prioritize its response:

1) *Customer needs would come first. Trend Micro would prioritize the recovery and restoration of client systems.*

2) *All of the company's actions and communications would reflect a consistent, united front.*

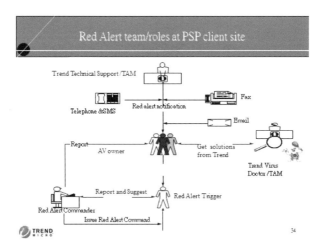

At companies like Trend Micro, emergency calls received in the middle of the night are certainly not unusual. Any new virus outbreak sent our global operation into action, regardless of the hour of day or day of the week. The duty officer responded to Internet troubles by implementing the Trend Micro Red Alert Procedure. First-line departments, including Customer Service, Technical Service, Virus Engineering, and Public Relations, were called to action, and users were immediately notified of the threat. Relatively serious problems brought second-line departments, including R & D, Systems Engineering, Product Management, and Marketing, in to assist. This system, in place for many years, had successfully addressed every problem we had faced.

United States
Friday, April 22, 2005, 5:00 p.m. PST

President Oscar Chang and Eva had been colleagues and close comrades for many years. They had both been with Trend Micro from its earliest days and had been responsible for building and leading the firm's world-class R & D organization. They enjoyed a natural rapport and enviable professional synergy. With Eva's promotion to CEO, President Oscar Chang continued to head Trend Micro's virus R & D center in the Philippines while assuming additional responsibilities as the new head of Trend Micro product R & D. More than anyone else in the Trend Micro organization, President Oscar Chang was Eva's "right-hand man."

After Punta Cana, Eva and President Oscar Chang took the same flight on to Los Angeles for the product managers' meeting.

A US account manager reported to the assembled team that V.594 was causing client computers to crash under certain circumstances. President Oscar Chang immediately called the program up. After a quick and careful examination, his extensive Internet systems knowledge told him that this was a problem that could, indeed, cause major problems.

As suspected, different from our usual threats, this danger had its origins in our own software program rather than in an external virus. He briefed Eva on the technical issues involved and then concluded, with unexpected solemnity, "This oversight may prove disastrous. The blame falls squarely on my team's shoulders. As such, I have no choice but to tender my resignation."

Eva had never seen him so despondent. Her first thought was to get him to calm down. "I'm as much responsible for this as you," she said. "This is no time to consider resigning. Please return to Asia immediately. I'll watch things from here and convene a meeting of global executives every two hours and update you on the current status and response measures. Keep in touch!"

President Oscar Chang trusted Eva. There wasn't a hint of reprobation in her voice. How she would resolve her customers' problems occupied her full attention. This singularity of purpose helped President Oscar Chang recover his composure and return his thoughts to his pressing responsibilities. His colleagues in the Philippines, he thought, would likely be even more distraught about this disaster than he. He was duty-bound to lead his team through the crisis. He had to get back to work in the Philippines.

From then on forward, Eva convened web conferences every two hours on the hour. She stayed on post day and night as Trend Micro's supreme commander.

Late in the afternoon on that California Friday, the sun was still shining over azure Pacific waters as offices around the city disgorged their workers, off for an early start to the weekend. At the same time and three hours ahead of California on the East Coast, TGIF celebrations were already in full swing.

My longstanding appreciation of the importance that Americans place on leisure and recreation redoubled as we learned that, in fact, most of our major clients had not yet downloaded and installed V.594, the latest, trouble-ridden update of our antivirus software. News of troubles originating from the United States came in a mercifully slow trickle.

Japan
Saturday, April 23rd, 2005, 4:00 a.m.

The ringing of his office cell phone startled Kutsuzawa out of a peaceful slumber. VP Mitchell was on the other end of the line. "V.594 has a glitch in the code. We're already getting intelligence about the scope of the disaster here. You need to get going and take care of things on your end."

105

Kutsuzawa had come over from Hewlett-Packard just a year earlier and wore critical customer service and technical service hats at Trend Micro's Japan operations. He managed a groggy reply: "How serious? Does the Philippines Virus Center have an antidote yet?" At this point, a hint of concern escaped from behind Mitchell's famously calm and collected demeanor. "We're not sure of the cause at this point. Reports of scattered damage have been coming in—mostly crashed systems that we can't repair yet."

Now fully awake, Kutsuzawa began to take action. He knew his Japanese customers valued safe operations above all else and were quick to download each new update. Japan would need an antidote, quickly. He logged into the company's Intranet and reviewed developments. At dawn, he roused his customer-service colleagues from bed and told them to get to the office as fast as possible. He threw on a shirt and jeans and rushed to Trend Micro's Japan headquarters under a dark cloud of anxiety.

The clamor of telephones ringing met his arrival at the thirtieth-floor office. Staff members were busy answering the flood of anxious, often angry customers. "*Sumimasen*, we'll get an antidote to you as quickly as possible." It was the standard answer provided by frontline responders. Kutsuzawa added the latest technical advice to the standard message. Customers would be asked to shut their computers down temporarily to prevent the problem from spreading further. Next, he called all Japan managers into headquarters for a meeting to discuss next steps.

Shimizu, a test-engineering manager in Japan's R & D division who regularly worked with Trend Micro's R & D team in the Philippines, was one of the first to receive a late-night call from Kutsuzawa. He made hasty preparations to fly out to Manila the same morning to sound out the situation. How could the normally cautious and exceedingly professional Philippines Virus Center let such a serious error slip by? Were normal procedures compromised to release updates ahead of the competition? While dozens of possible scenarios swirled through his head as he made his way south, he knew his most important role now was as the key facilitator of communications between Japan and the Philippines. He would have to fully suss out the problem and deliver an antidote as quickly as possible to his customer service colleagues. Even though he didn't have to deal with customers directly, he was highly sensitive to the importance of his mission.

9:00 a.m.

Under Kutsuzawa, Sekiguchi was in charge of Trend Micro's Japan customer service team. He had scheduled an early Saturday appointment to fix a chronic toothache that had dogged him for months. He was halfway into the procedure with a mouth limp from the heavy dose of Novocain when the cell phone in his pocket burst to life. "Don't move. Keep still!" the dentist insisted. If it were his wife, she would have given up after a couple of tries. But the phone kept buzzing incessantly. Who was it, and what was it about? The repeated calls made the dentist anxious as well, and he finished up the procedure as quickly as possible. Half an hour later, the Novocain had worn off enough that he could talk. He realized then it was his supervisor calling. Sekiguchi returned the call and received the curt message: "Get to the office now! Your department staff is already here answering calls. Make the necessary arrangements to install additional service phone lines. Get on the line also to our contractors to get them to give us more staffing support."

Takada, Trend Micro Japan's head of marketing and public relations, was floored by Kutsuzawa's sudden Saturday morning call. "We've got reporters here in the office asking our people what's going on. What should we do?" Reporters had never come uninvited. What was happening? Takada lived several hours distant from the office, so he asked that Trend Micro's female colleagues who normally helped out at investor conferences be called in to ask reporters to regroup in the twenty-seventh floor conference room and wait for a formal statement. The reporters should be treated to breakfast and drinks but politely prevented from wandering around and asking questions.

Cognizant of the seriousness of this sudden development, Takada donned his best suit and prepared for battle. He arrived at the office at 10:00 and was again surprised. Apart from the familiar faces of IT reporters from major news outlets such as Nihon Keizai, Asahi, Yomiuri, NHK, and Kyoto Shimbun, he saw plenty of unfamiliar current-affairs reporters. Their expressions were combative and unfriendly. One well-known journalist spied Takada walking in and shouted sarcastically, "Hey! Thank you, Trend Micro, for bringing the 'good news!' Because, as you are patently aware, no news is good news. Our agency Internet servers have all crashed. We can't receive overseas newswire reports and can't send anything out. We can't do much of anything except hang around here for updates on your getting the problem fixed!" So, Japan's news agencies were all Trend Micro clients, and now they had no way of sending or receiving news reports. No wonder they were so angry. They each had a dog in this fight. Normally suspicious competitors, the news outlets now rallied around their common grievance with Trend Micro and were out for blood.

Provoking the media was something we'd always avoided like the plague. But Trend Micro had somehow put the media at the receiving end of this disastrous blunder. Working hard to control his nerves, Takada stuck to his well-scripted principles: apologize first and then update the press on preliminary findings. The priorities for the reporters were, in order of importance: 1) What was the extent and severity of the disaster? 2) How did Trend Micro plan to resolve the problem? 3) How could Trend Micro have let this happen? and 4) What were the plans for compensation?

Despite his youth, Takada had significant career experience in public relations. Quickly finding his composure, he announced, "Our senior executives are all upstairs right now in an emergency meeting. We will let you know about the extent of the damage in a timely manner. We are currently working on a fix and investigating the underlying cause of the problem. We will make a formal, public statement addressing your concerns today. I ask only for your patience."

11:00 a.m.

Next on Takada's contact list was Omikawa Akihiko, general manager of Trend Micro Japan. He had just touched down in Japan. "Put on a black, formal suit and come to the office quickly." As he was heading out the door, another call from Takada came in. "White shirt, black tie!" Takada blurted. Akihiko wondered if it could really be that serious. Black and white were the only colors appropriate for solemn occasions. He was responsible for national sales and marketing and a veteran business warrior. After leading his delegation to Punta Cana, Akihiko had flown them all to New York to cheer on Japanese baseball legend Hideki Matsui in a game at Yankee Stadium. When disaster struck, they were in the air between New York and Tokyo and still blissfully unaware of the mess quickly unfolding back home.

Akihiko quickened his pace and sprinted the remaining distance from the subway station to Trend Micro's headquarters in Shinjuku. Before his hands touched the lobby door, he received another urgent call from Takada. "General Manager, do not go to the twenty-seventh floor! It is imperative that reporters don't see you yet. Take the service lift straight to the thirty-third floor and come right away to the meeting room. We're all here." With a career spanning Microsoft and Trend Micro, GM Akihiko was a seasoned business warrior, but sneaking around to avoid reporters was a new experience for him. His optimism and easygoing personality had won him high regard from colleagues and customers alike, and despite the still-confused state of affairs, his appearance in the meeting room had an immediate calming effect on everyone present.

Amateur photography enthusiast Kuroki, familiar to all with his shoulder-length mane of silver hair, had just signed up for an advanced photography weekend course. He was naturally reluctant to miss any minute of his expensive lessons—and then his phone rang. The urgency of the request left him no choice but to abandon his photography plans for now and prepare quickly to meet the battle ahead. Kuroki, an exceptionally talented systems engineer, was a former product manager and now the head of corporate client technical services in Japan. His refined appearance, honesty, clear thinking, and knack for getting ideas across made Kuroki GM Akihiko's first choice for company spokesman during this crisis. He knew that, for technical issues, mere apologies would not suffice. Satisfactorily answering reporters' questions would require someone exceptionally able to give careful, clear explanations.

Okazawa had recently turned forty-two years of age when V.594 unleashed its fury. Forty-two for Japanese men was supposed to be an ill-starred age—akin to Chinese superstitions regarding all ages ending in the number nine. His wife, a firm believer in such things, had made the necessary arrangements for prayers and blessings at a local temple. Just as the Saturday morning ceremony was finishing up, Okazawa received a call from his friend and direct-line supervisor, Akihiko. His first thought was to wonder if he was being invited out for another round of drinking or a game of golf. "Okazawa-san, we've got a big problem on our hands. I'm afraid we need to mobilize everyone, even the head of human resources!" After getting a quick briefing on the problem, he left his wife and son at the temple and sped to the office, thinking all the way about whether he should arrange for a ceremonial blessing of Trend Micro as well.

Okazawa was responsible for managing the human resource affairs of Trend Micro Japan's more than five hundred employees. He was an expert at conciliation and had earned interdepartmental trust. While Akihiko was confident in his ability to help calm frayed nerves, he had no idea how quickly Okazawa could bring results.

An anxious chorus greeted his entry into the meeting room. "Great! You're here. They shut the AC in the building off over the weekend. How can we get some air in here?" He looked across the room and saw a small sea of heads moving busily about against a backdrop of incessantly ringing phones. Everyone's forehead was dripping with perspiration. The mood was clearly not good. Letting out an exasperated huff, Okazawa-san walked over to the room's temperature-control panel and pressed down hard on one of the buttons. Air-conditioning fans churned to life and a cool breeze quickly banished the stale, humid air from the room. While continuing to fight the fire at hand, everyone burst into a spontaneous display of "thumbs up" to show appreciation to the hero of the hour. Actually, the building did keep the air conditioners on over the weekend. It was just that they all were too deeply immersed in the tasks at hand to think of actually trying to turn on the switch.

It was inevitable that the issue of compensation would soon be part of the discussion, so Trend Micro's CFO was naturally on the call-in list as well. Mahendra Negi, an Indian national, had married into Japan and joined Trend Micro as chief financial officer just a year after we took the company public. He managed the company's budget and served as corporate spokesperson on all public and shareholder issues. Mahendra was also a heavyweight on the global senior executive board, with significant authority and influence. Trend Micro would rely on his levelheadedness to see it through these choppy waters. He, too, had just returned from Punta Cana and was in the middle of his regular Saturday morning jog when he got the call. He rushed back home, changed into his white shirt and charcoal-black suit, stuffed a black tie into his pocket, and headed into the office. He knew there would be plenty of anxious investors and fund managers. He had to prepare briefing sheets necessary to answer the imminent volley of questions. Responses had to be consistent worldwide.

Trend Micro had a global investment base, and financial analysts would surely scrutinize any and all official statements with a fine-tooth comb.

Innovation Takes a Disastrous Turn

Thus, a hastily assembled SWAT team was formed comprising key members of the Trend Micro senior executive board like Akihiko and Mahendra and key members of Trend Micro Japan management like Kutsuzawa, Sekiguchi, Takada, Kuroki, and Okazawa. All were cloistered in the thirty-third floor meeting room, making phone calls and trying desperately to bring a semblance of order to the chaos. From the outset, they struck a consensus as to how they would prioritize their response:

1) Trend Micro's customer-first commitment mandated that they prioritize the recovery and restoration of client systems and the resolution of customer problems in a proper and timely manner.
2) In the interests of the company, all actions and communications would necessarily reflect a united front, and every decision would be backed by systematic, rational justification.

The SWAT team thus framed the company's response with Trend Micro customers as the top priority. Kutsuzawa, head of Trend Micro's customer service department, stepped up to the plate. Picking up a thick, felt-tip marker, he wrote the slogan: "For the Customer, For the Company!" in English on a sheet of paper and taped it to the wall in a spot that was visible to everyone in the room.

Although Akihiko was general manager, he acceded to Kutsuzawa taking the lead on this issue. Kutsuzawa would be the clearinghouse and filter for all information used in external communications. Meanwhile, the CFO kept a frenetic pace consulting the company's lawyers on issues related to compensation, communicating with company PR managers and spokespersons in Europe and the United States to ensure everyone was on the same page in terms of public communications, and maintaining a persistent dialogue with Eva, who was still in the United States awaiting expedited approval of her Japan visa.

Shimizu was in constant communication with the R & D organization in the Philippines. Philippine manager Cyril was acting head of that organization, pending President Oscar Chang's arrival in Manila.

Because the update was only crashing systems that were running Windows XP, initial suspicions focused on the possibility that V.594 hadn't been adequately tested on that operating system (OS) prior to release. If this line of inquiry held out, gaining control of the problem should be fairly easy. But as time went on, it became clear that other OS platforms were also affected. There was little doubt that the problem would continue getting worse before things started to get better.

The root of the problem seemed to lie in how this particular zombie virus began mutating after becoming embedded within an OS. Attempts to extract its code triggered further mutations, and the cycle continued. Always up for a good challenge, Trend Micro's engineers fought pitched, running battles with the virus that ended in victories but that invariably fell frustratingly short of winning the war. They sought desperately for the magic bullet that would penetrate its armor, reveal its secrets, and open the way to halting all further mutations. As with the climax of *The Matrix*, they were hoping for the one shot that would send the entire virus corpus into oblivion.

And they succeeded! They developed an antiviral program that was foolproof against zombie mutations. It had passed all standard testing procedures and was approved for upload as the latest PC-cillin update.

Where we went wrong was in failing to implement appropriate new testing procedures for this new, abnormally aggressive virus. The lack of a controlled field test was where the process fell on its face. Installing the update in the Microsoft XP environment put the system in an infinite loop that quickly occupied all available system resources and forced the shutdown of all other operations. It was only later that we learned that a key reason for the relatively limited damage in our European and American markets was because this "infinite loop" actually completed its cycle in just less than eight hours. Trend Micro clients who returned to the office on Monday thus found their systems operating normally. Thus, it was primarily factories with weekend operations that suffered system shutdowns and lost productivity.

In virus attacks, as in other poisonings, it is vital to quickly administer the right antidote. After the problem was discovered, we fixed it and designed and tested a new antiviral program that successfully eliminated the zombie virus without the computer crash. But it had been another two hours! Computers already damaged by V.594 had to be shut down, rebooted in safe mode, cleaned of the problem code, installed with the new antiviral program, and then (and only then) restarted as normal. It was a process that was both labor- and time-consuming. Our major clients had tens of thousands of computers that would need to be cleaned, one by painful one!

Adding further oil to the bonfire was our use of global web IT service provider Akamai as a third-party download source for updates. Many major Trend Micro clients had contracts with Akamai to regularly download and install antivirus updates to their systems from Akamai servers worldwide.

While the problem update had been removed from our servers and replaced with the antidote program within two hours, doing the same through Akamai was an entirely different problem. It wasn't that they were unwilling to do so but rather that wiping their worldwide system clean of V.594 and its buggy code required their running a system-wide diagnostic. During this extended period of time, customers unaware of the problems would be updating as normal. The disaster would continue cascading forward.

Soldier On!

President Oscar Chang had even more to be anxious about than most. Their doctor had confirmed that his wife was pregnant, and he had insisted on first returning to Taiwan to make sure that all was going well. However, his smiles on seeing her came against a background stream of phone calls that let her know his priorities lay elsewhere for the moment. "Go," she said. "Go back to the Philippines and do what you need to do. You'd be distracted if you stayed here now."

Aggressive and detail-oriented, President Oscar Chang was ever up for a challenge. But the overwhelming scale of this challenge was more than even his capacious confidence was willing to contemplate. He returned to the Philippines under a cloud of worry to take charge of the chaos that had overcome his normally smooth-running, convivial office. "We can't fail. We must pull this together!" he told himself and his team, who continued working feverishly for the root cause of the problem. After getting updates on progress, he walked into the center's conference room and joined the emergency video meeting already underway with Eva and other senior executives. The circle was now complete. All worked as one to see Trend Micro resolve the problems at hand.

Trend Micro Japan was pinned down under heavy fire coming from all sides. But despite its critical state, no hint of anxiety could be allowed to show. Headquarters had to remain stable to give confidence to those working on the frontlines. The company had trumped innumerable challenges and accomplished herculean tasks before. But those experiences offered little comfort in the current crisis. All looked inward for new strength to carry themselves and the company forward.

Everyone invested everything in the task at hand. They soldiered on against the monumental, and still-growing, challenges ahead.

Through the continued pain of his just-finished dental work, Sekiguchi led his customer service team in handling the flood of calls from angry users. He requisitioned additional internal office lines to increase the number of lines available to his customer service team. But it still wasn't enough. "We can't afford to keep anyone on hold for too long. They've enough to worry about with their inoperable computer." Sekiguchi arranged to open additional customer service lines through a third-party contractor and assigned staff to train the temporary operators. In addition to phoning in, customers soon began arriving at Trend Micro offices with their computers in tow. Some demanded on-the-spot repairs, while others demanded compensation. Many were emotionally distraught and some even threatened violence. The flurry of activity had pushed thoughts of his aching tooth into the background. Sekiguchi had advanced to "expert" level in the art of multitasking.

Just as things seemed on the brink of collapse, Sekiguchi heard a friendly voice from behind. "Sekiguchi-san. We're here to help. Just tell us what to do." The staff from other departments was arriving spontaneously to the customer service floor. Hearing that his department had been overwhelmed, they came from everywhere—from personnel, from administration, from marketing & sales ... even from the normally cloistered corridors of R & D. They had not been called in to work but were nonetheless sacrificing their weekends to stand with colleagues in their time of need.

Human Resources Chief Okazawa gave Sekiguchi a pat on the shoulder and volunteered to take over for a while. "Okay, human resources staff ... team up with a customer service colleague and listen carefully to how they're handling calls. Once you're up to speed, start taking calls yourself." Okazawa then took charge of the larger volunteer army. "R & D staff, please report to the head of key account customer services. You'll be communicating directly with client IT people on technical issues." He continued, "All other male colleagues, please come with me. We'll handle customers who come here to the office. Remember! No matter how angry our customers are, you must maintain a strict, apologetic attitude, uphold our 'customer first' principle, and do your utmost to resolve their concerns." He ended with, "Finally ... administrative secretaries, please make sure your colleagues are supplied with sufficient food and drink. This looks like it will be a long struggle."

Meanwhile, the reporters and media teams had reconvened as requested in the conference room on the twenty-seventh floor. All anxiously awaited the promised press conference.

As head of marketing and public relations, Takada shuttled back and forth between the SWAT team, where he got the latest updates, and the twenty-seventh floor conference room, where he briefed the media. On unresolved issues, Takada trod a precarious tightrope between giving too much and giving too little information to the press. It was a task made all the more difficult in light of the caliber of assembled reporters. Takada made regular, official statements on issues cleared for release and asked the media to hold their other questions for the impending press conference where, he guaranteed, all their issues would be addressed. The beads of sweat streaming down his forehead belied his congenial, relaxed smile. *Keep steady*, he encouraged himself. *I have to give my colleagues time to collect the information necessary to provide comprehensive answers to everyone's questions.* He knew that somehow, everyone would make it through the day's extreme challenge.

CHAPTER 10

Media Feeding Frenzy

During those critical hours with the press, any break from a unified front by any member of the team, any hint of nondisclosure, any fabrication of an answer to a reporter's question would surely have been eagerly exploited.

Those critical hours, if improperly handled, held the potential not only to topple Trend Micro from its perch but also to eliminate it from competition altogether.

In Japan, Trend Micro had long been a darling of the media, with a squeaky-clean corporate reputation. We were seen as guardians of Internet security waging a continuous and impressively effective battle against viruses, Trojan horses, and hackers. Trend Micro's stock was on a steady climb, its Taiwanese CEO seemed always up for another award or major speaking engagement, and its reputation as an industry model seemed all but unassailable.

But on the April 23, 2005, Trend Micro's lofty reputation had taken a nosedive. Its impressive resume of accomplishments, awards, and accolades counted for naught in the aftermath of V.594. Angry reporters, also among those directly affected by the disaster, were staked out in Trend Micro's largest meeting facility, waiting for the promised press conference, waiting to hear the company's plans for setting everything right again.

Saturday, April 23, 2005, 5:30 p.m.

"Everyone ready?" GM Akihiko asked gravely. "All right. Let's head downstairs." He walked down the stairway and into the broiling cauldron in the company's main conference room at the head of a handpicked delegation that included CFO Negi, Customer Service Director Kutsuzawa, and designated spokesperson Kuroki.

In the office and working feverishly on multiple fronts since they had received their early-morning urgent call-in, these senior executives had been running on an adrenaline-infused rush all day.

The virus analysis report finally issued by the Philippines Virus Center at 3:30 in the afternoon framed the focus of Trend Micro's response. Since then, the topic of discussion had centered on the myriad potential problems that still lay ahead. However, in line with Trend Micro's cultural ethos, all knew almost instinctively that complete honesty would be the rule in meeting with the press. Everything would be reported as it truly is. Nothing would be concealed. We would leave no half truths that might be exposed later.

Everyone walked with heavy footsteps toward the room. The door opened and Akihiko entered first, greeted by the incessant flash of cameras. He was surrounded immediately by reporters. They were not only from the print media but from NHK and other broadcast news outlets as well. Although well used to facing the media, General Manager Akihiko was taken aback by the size and mood of this gathering.

Scanning the room, he spied Takada in the crowd holding a microphone and nodding confidently to his group. Takada's steady demeanor had an immediate calming effect on the team, and they proceeded as planned onto the stage. They stood in formation and, in unison, made a deep, respectful, long bow to their audience.

The solemn row of men clad uniformly in black suits, starched white shirts, and black ties, differentiated largely by hair color that ranged from jet black to distinguished gray, made for an impressive, silent expression of apology. It was only later, when we revisited photographs of the event, that we noticed how much Kutsuzawa, on the line's extreme left, stood out in his deep-green shirt and jeans. He had rushed into the office in the morning in his day clothes, and no one particularly noticed the oversight during the chaos of the day. When the pictures were published, we all felt his awkward attire simply added to the sense of earnestness in Trend Micro's official apology.

With the long bow over and cameras silent for the moment, the team slowly stood erect, their eyes red from both exhaustion and emotion, to face their inquisitors.

Akihiko started the next phase of the press conference off by reading Trend Micro's formal statement of apology. Next, spokesperson Kuroki explained the cause of the problem, Trend Micro's plan for resolution, and the current status of progress.

The press, uninterested in following the preplanned script, began shooting off questions to those on stage in rapid succession. Takada held his ground as the designated moderator for the press conference. "Please, let's take things one at a time! We will answer all of your questions today. We've nothing to hide and will provide regular reports on the latest developments."

Takada separated the problem into its subcomponent issues and assigned different parts of the room for each issue, where reporters could go and ask all their related questions. Akihiko took the lead on issues related to operations and compensation, Mahendra Negi fielded questions on finance and stock issues, Kuroki took charge of questions on technical issues, Kutsuzawa handled questions on the scope of the problem and current progress toward its resolution, and Takada handled arrangements for follow-up interviews and issues not covered by the others.

The ordered handling of procedures, our not using Trend Micro's spokesperson as a protective shield, the willingness of senior executives to personally handle questions in their respective areas of responsibility, and the insistence on facing all problems directly gradually diffused the initial, emotionally charged atmosphere. The executives successfully steered discussions toward company plans for meeting the needs of its customers and away from unproductive debates over guilt and retribution.

During those critical hours with the press, any break from a unified front by any member of the team, any hint of nondisclosure, any fabrication of an answer to a reporter's question would surely have been eagerly exploited by the press. The resulting articles would have had a ruinous impact on the company both internally and externally. Those critical hours, if improperly handled, held the potential not only to topple Trend Micro from its perch but also to eliminate it from competition altogether.

Long afterward, I asked those who took the stage that day, "So, did you practice beforehand? How did you handle it?"

Takada said, "Not at all. What time did we have to practice? However, what we had was consensus. We all operated according to the principles of honesty, based our responses on data prepared beforehand, and refused to hide or be protective of information. But at the same time, we wouldn't let reporters make guesses or follow unfounded hypotheses. We told it like it was and made corrections on the fly as needed."

For his part, Kutsuzawa shared, "We all shared an abiding faith in Trend Micro as a good company. We still had the same commitment to customer service. It was only that we'd suffered this unexpected, major setback. But it didn't mean we were bad. There was no ill intent involved. This was something that people needed to understand. I think that this level of honesty and confidence was appreciated even by the angriest of reporters there that day."

That Trend Micro was indeed a "good" company was picked up not only by reporters but by employees companywide as well. Overt expressions of self-love were rare and generally not encouraged, as Trend Micro had always valued substance over appearance. However, in the company's darkest hour, employees closed ranks and were eager to highlight their commitment to Trend Micro's core values. There was no hint of recrimination, ridicule, or finger-pointing. There was also no hesitation, doubt, or fearful withdrawal. Instead, everyone stood up to be counted, to be a part of the solution—even if that just meant helping out with monotonous copying, making sure everyone had enough water in his or her cup, or making the run out to bring lunch in for everyone. There was a comforting sense of solidarity and willing sacrifice to ensure everyone made it through okay. Employees volunteered throughout to work longer hours, extra shifts, and over weekends to make sure Trend Micro always had enough people on duty.

This is genuine love, volunteered from the heart by those who knew themselves to be "part of the family."

A Midnight Repast

Needing to meet their deadlines, the television reporters had largely left the room by 7:00. Those from the press media continued pressing their questions to the executives. As head of Trend Micro's all-critical customer relations, Kutsuzawa asked for the reporters' understanding and returned to the thirty-third floor. The others remained and answered the continued flow of questions from the media.

From one end of the room, Takada gestured to General Manager Akihiko that he wanted to speak to him in the hall outside. Akihiko made his way to the door, worriedly thinking, *Oh, no! What's happened now?*

Takada met him and said, "One of the news services missed taking a picture of our group bow. They asked if you would be willing to do it once more for their photographer now, in another room." Akihiko breathed a sigh of relief and couldn't help but let the hint of a smile sneak out from his otherwise serious façade. A picture? Of course. It was the easiest thing he had been asked the whole day. "Of course," he said. "Let's do it!"

So, in an adjacent small meeting room, and unbeknownst to the other reporters there, Akihiko gave one of the press agencies an exclusive bow to photograph and include in their article. One pleasant result was that their article was one of the most generous to Trend Micro published the next day.

As midnight approached, the last of the reporters packed up and left, and the phones finally stopped ringing. Akihiko suddenly realized he'd gone the day without eating a meal and that his stomach was clamoring for something more than a snack. He pulled Human Resources Chief Okazawa away from his duties at the head of Trend Micro's volunteer army, and they headed out together into the streets near the office to find something good to eat. Seeing only a Taiwanese-run noodle restaurant open amid a neighborhood of darkened shops, they walked in and settled in at a corner table.

"Hey, I've seen you! You're the one I saw on TV today, right? Your company is in big trouble." They hadn't anticipated that the owner might actually recognize Trend Micro's general manager. All heads in the restaurant turned to look at Akihiko. *Aiyo*, he thought. This was not the way he'd hoped to earn his fame.

"General Manager," the worldly Okazawa said in a low voice, "I suggest you don't go out drinking or be seen playing golf for the next three months."

The Trains Grind to a Halt

How could an unassumingly small viral code and a testing oversight make such big headlines? Why had this seemingly small slip-up attracted so much attention?

Apart from the damage to the media's Internet access, problems related to V.594 multiplied and touched the daily lives of tens of millions of ordinary Japanese citizens.

Japan Railway (JR) was a longtime Trend Micro client. Not only did the JR trains in Tokyo not close on Saturday and Sunday; ticket sales were always highest on weekends. When JR's automatic ticketing machines crashed on Saturday April 23, the company had to quickly mobilize additional staff to man the overwhelmed ticketing windows. It wasn't enough, and many passengers couldn't pick up their pre-booked tickets. They missed their train and their weekend plans. The reaction was, of course, incendiary. Used to their automated, computer-managed lifestyle, the Japanese had little tolerance for problems like this.

This incident sullied JR's proud reputation and exposed the entire organization to the enmity of innumerable passengers. The anger leveled by Japan Railway at Trend Micro, amplified by the ready condemnation of its passengers, added fuel to the already red-hot media fire.

At the eye of the storm, Trend Micro's software guru President Oscar Chang struggled to get a grip on the problem in Manila. Burdened by the knowledge that his center was the cause of the debacle and knowing that precious time had been lost while he was traveling, he remembers feeling at the time, "I'd never before imagined that the social responsibility of a software engineer could be so vast, or that a single oversight could have such far-ranging implications and do such harm. After all, we all just worked in our lab writing software code and battling viruses. At times, it even seemed unreal, like we were video-gaming. How could we and our work have spawned a disaster of such global proportions?"

121

Trend Micro's Director for Taiwan Sales Pao-cheng Hung remembers, "In Taiwan, the problem hit automated production lines in manufacturing plants the hardest. Factories typically work weekends to get product out. When their computers went, things started to pile up, shipments were delayed ... everyone was livid. My 'apology itinerary' lasted for over a month before it was finished. We were being chewed out all day every day. We could only apologize profusely and try to explain the technical issues involved. Honestly, I was really worried. Our customers were describing losses in the tens of millions of NT dollars. Our antivirus software retailed at only a few thousand NT dollars. How in the world would we ever be able to make up for those kind of losses?" It was a terrifying time, made worse because there was nowhere to turn and vent this anxiety.

The position of VP for US Customer Service and Sales Mitchell was even stickier. Americans stand much less on ceremony than Asians and are quick to let you know what they truly think. He recalls, "It was fortunate that we work directly with our key accounts. We notified them immediately once the problem was detected. They also do their own in-house testing of software prior to installation, so they don't simply download and install. Thus, losses in this segment were negligible. However," his tone changes abruptly, "we were in a different situation altogether with our SME customers. Most in this segment purchase our software through systems integrators, who bundle their sales with technical support. Each of these systems integrators has a large customer base spread out across the United States. There was no way they could have contacted each of their customers individually about the problem, and pretty much all with factories working that weekend were affected. Afterward, one IC design house that specializes in television chipsets insisted on a meeting. Four of their senior executives showed up to chew us out. My sales rep in the meeting with me was speechless, and I could only continue with the apologies and listen patiently as they listed their grievances and losses. It went on for a solid two hours!"

Mitchell gave a self-deprecating chuckle. "You know, it was the worst verbal flogging I'd ever been through. But on the upside, I learned a lot more about the IC chip-design process and about their needs. The experience was instrumental in helping us design better service support packages." Afterward, the VP did take the reprimands of his customers to heart and retooled Trend Micro's standard service contract to better support clients.

The impact of the V.594 bombshell took a rather interesting turn in China. Trend Micro's China clients were mostly government bureaus and financial organizations. Thus, most were closed for business and unaffected by the update program. One customer, however, insisted that we make a personal apology despite the lack of damage. He even threatened a lawsuit if we failed to do so. Adhering to the firm's customer-first principle, Trend Micro China's Manager for Customer Service Pang Cai took the request with due seriousness and arrived at the client's offices with gift in hand after a five-hour drive. He made his profuse apologies to the lineup of senior company officials and then listened attentively to two hours of merciless scolding.

After that, their senior IT manager told Pang he wanted still more. He demanded that Pang Cai take him out for drinks to clear the air. "You owe me!" he said. The whole story began coming out an hour later, after quite a few rounds had already been downed. It turned out that the manager's boss had turned the news of the V.594 debacle in Japan into an opportunity to humiliate him for his original decision to use Trend Micro. "Why did you reject the antivirus software I recommended?" his boss demanded. "Why did you insist that we go with Trend Micro?" His professional integrity was attacked and his motives were questioned. He had suffered incalculably because of his trust in the Trend Micro brand. Taking him out for a drink and listening to his troubles was the least we could do to help make things better.

The V.594 disaster unfolded differently in our different markets. Customers in each of these markets also had different ways of relaying their anger and expectations regarding compensation. Trend Micro could offer no excuses. We could only apologize profusely, listen patiently, and promise change. Would we be forgiven? That was something no one had the time or the stomach to consider ...

CHAPTER 11

The Warmhearted Dragon

Throughout the past four months, they had naturally nurtured concerns that Eva may not be the equal of Steve in terms of courage and charisma.

They wondered whether she could move Trend Micro forward in a Japanese business world still dominated by men.

Her speech, however, had won them all over. They knew now that, while her style was very different from Steve's, it had the sharp edge necessary to take Trend Micro into the next Internet era.

When she first learned about the problem, Eva knew the crisis presented a tough challenge. However, she was confident in Trend Micro's ability to see things through after spending more than a decade building and nurturing the company's R & D team. Still, while she knew that her team had the technical skills to solve any problem, she had much less control over the reaction of Trend Micro's customers. Nevertheless, long-term, cross-departmental cooperation at the senior executive level gave Trend Micro critical synergy. Moreover, regional sales teams had deep-rooted experience in their markets and enjoyed good working relationships with customers. Thus, Eva felt that as long as the company stuck to its principles and let staff members do what they needed to do, they would weather the storm and make it through intact to the other side.

She wasn't yet fully cognizant that the problem at hand went far deeper than any previously encountered. Steve had made it clear that she was in charge and that, while he and I were ready to provide support as needed, we would work only behind the scenes and wouldn't be part of Trend Micro's public response. Eva had been CEO for less than a year. If Steve were to take charge again, even if only temporarily, it would not only severely undermine long-term confidence in Eva's capabilities as Trend Micro's leader but would also send mixed signals about Trend Micro's response to the crisis. Despite a thousand concerns, we bit the bullet and let Eva fly solo. We all accepted the risks and dangers in taking this path. Where the three of us had previously ridden out the rough patches, Eva was now alone at the helm. We were learning the hard lesson that relinquishing power is exponentially more difficult to accept than assuming it.

As part of Eva's response plan, she decided to call for regular videoconferences with key Trend Micro leaders every two hours during the crisis to ensure everyone was up on the latest status and developments. These leaders would include President Oscar Chang of the Philippines Virus Center along with the CTO, CFO, CLO, and all regional marketing, sales, and customer service managers. She realized that it would be especially critical to have the entire Trend Micro organization working together and from the same playbook.

Of course, Eva could no longer take a strict R & D perspective on the problem. She was responsible for the big picture and in charge of leading a comprehensive response. Trend Micro's problems were the worst in Japan where, fortunately, Trend Micro had the richly experienced and well-liked Akihiko in charge. Eva felt confident leaving Japan customer issues in his capable hands.

But President Oscar Chang at the Philippines Virus Center was proving less steady. He was slow in taming the chaos and had even offered to resign and accept blame for the disaster now engulfing the company. He and his team were the key to quickly creating an antidote program and starting to reverse the damage. President Oscar Chang shouldn't be expected to bear this burden alone. Thus, Eva decided to make the effort a partnership. She would work with him to resolve the technical issues relevant to the current crisis.

Eva made it clear at the first videoconference when she explained, "This is not the '594 Incident' but rather the '594 Project!' It is a project that we are investing in as a company, and I want every one of my managers in all departments to work cooperatively on achieving project success. This is neither a simple accident nor a sudden crisis. This is something that demands a long-term, full-scale review of our business practices and that will surely end in our changing for the better." While dropping *incident* for *project* may have seemed a superficial name change, it was crucial to redefining Trend Micro's response to the emergency. It took the effort to a higher level and encouraged everyone to see the problems at hand as part of a longer-term initiative. Transforming the crisis into a project had a palpable calming effect that permeated every corner of the organization.

Eva was anxious to fly either to Japan or to the Philippines. However, a practical problem stood in her way. Eva held a Taiwan passport; both countries required a valid visa for entry; and the application process couldn't even begin until Monday. There was little choice but to wait.

Developments from Japan continued to stream in, with the clip of Trend Micro Japan executives giving their deep, apologetic bows featuring prominently in NHK's national news broadcasts.

She knew Monday would be the earliest she could get her visa, which would put her in Japan only by late Tuesday—more than three days into the crisis! In Japan, it was already April 26. What to do? What could be done? Despite her wracked nerves, she knew she had to keep her spirits up and control her emotions. She remained glued to her computer for forty-eight hours. She held videoconferences every two hours, did research, and communicated constantly with her managers to make sure she knew everything that was going on, to make necessary executive decisions, and to keep everyone calm and focused on the tasks at hand.

Railway Disaster

Dawn arose over Japan on Monday, April 25. It was the first working day of the week, and by that time, Trend Micro had succeeded in helping most of its business customers restore and reboot their systems and return to normal operations. This included Japan Railway's automatic-ticketing system. While we still had an untold number of personal user issues and compensation claims still ahead, Trend Micro's team seemed to have closed out this first phase of the crisis. Everyone stood ready to face the certain challenges ahead in phase two, when Trend Micro would begin sorting out compensation claims.

It was still Sunday afternoon on the US West Coast when Akihiko hove into view onscreen. Visibly unnerved, he reported, "There has been an accident on the train, on the Fukuchiyama Line near Amagasaki in Hyogo Prefecture." Eva's face blanched white. Akihiko continued, "More than a hundred fatalities and more than five hundred injured." Silence fell over the online discussion. No one dared to ask the cause of the accident. No one dared even to breathe. Everyone broke out into a cold sweat. Akihiko added, "It's all breaking news … no details yet. I will let you know more soon." Eva ended the videoconference. She didn't dare go online to look at the news; she feared that things were already beyond hope of recovery.

"Have we killed people?" She sat silently, hugging her shoulders and shaking uncontrollably.

In the Philippines, President Oscar Chang ran remorsefully out of the office and into the street, yelling, "Run me over! Hit me; hit me! I can't bear this responsibility!" Men don't cry easily. But even tears failed to ease his regret and self-condemnation.

News of the crash continued to unfold. The train had always been a model of safety. Why this disaster? Why at this time? Although speculation ran rampant, no one outside of Trend Micro had thought to pin the blame on JR's antivirus software. It was unsayable! It was unthinkable! The maw of chaos and terror threatened to take everybody with it. Everyone shared the same thoughts but dared not speak them aloud. No one was detached enough even to make any gesture of hope or encouragement. Everyone just waited. They waited for the results of the JR investigation.

Four hours later, the situation had become clearer. The problem lay with the young engineer of the train. It wasn't the tracks, the train, or the crossroads, and it wasn't a problem with the antivirus software. The engineer was driving the train faster than permitted speed limits, attempting to get back on schedule. The train left the rails going around a corner, sacrificing many lives. Japanese corporate culture is often rigidly uncompromising. JR prioritized on-time service and demanded its engineers ensure their trains arrived and departed on schedule. Mandatory punishments were meted out even for slight delays. Verbal abuse was commonly practiced, as were punishments like janitorial duty, followed by the writing of a long essay expressing the offender's deep regret for whatever he happened to do. On realizing he was running behind schedule, the young, self-confident engineer at the head of this particular bullet train run picked up additional speed to make up time. He had already run several warning lights by the time his train careened around that fateful curve. The train flew off the tracks and into an apartment complex, compounding the tragedy with additional deaths and injuries.

Corporate culture wields tremendous, far-reaching influence. In this instance, it had gone so far as to lead a young employee to quash his better senses in an attempt to accomplish the impossible!

I was sorry to see our Trend Micro staff greeting the news in a manner totally out of step with the general public. "It wasn't us! It wasn't us!" Relief and a measure of celebration rippled through the organization. But our colleagues weren't reveling in the misfortunes of others. They were simply relieved to have dodged this potentially lethal bullet.

"Nothing weighs more than the weight of worry!" President Oscar Chang admonished. Thinking back on that longest of nights still brings tears of emotion.

After hearing the latest update from JR, Eva placed an urgent call to President Oscar Chang. She knew he had taken the train news harder than anyone else. "It's okay. Don't worry. No need to worry! You can get back to focusing on our technical issues, starting on the redesign, and strengthening our test environment and SOPs. I'm leaving for Japan tomorrow and will be in Manila as soon as possible to help you." Eva's calm, firm voice rekindled President Oscar Chang's fighting spirit. She paused for a moment, then asked in a less commanding tone, "There's something else I would like to discuss with you …"

Hearing the doubt in her voice, President Oscar Chang gave a crisp reply. "Anything. What is it?"

"I'm going to take a pay cut to acknowledge my responsibility for this crisis. I would like to ask you also to go on half pay for the duration. Would you agree to do this?"

President Oscar Chang chuckled. "Please! You know I'll agree to whatever you ask. Let's just get this problem fixed, and if you want me to work on no pay from here on out, I'm willing!" He was back! He had been spared the traffic and had survived unscathed. Now, he was back at his post for good. He asked only to be able to lead the team that would fix this mess. Talk of salary, reduced or removed, seemed awkwardly superfluous at that moment.

"Okay. Thank you." She had never issued an official reprimand or docked anyone's pay before. Having President Oscar Chang agree so readily to her request made things easier, especially at this juncture.

Sometimes, the appropriate meting of penalties greases the wheels of redemption.

The Pink Shirt

Eva was on the Monday afternoon flight to Tokyo. With her ties to the Internet temporarily severed, she could finally catch up on some sleep. She had always had a secret love for long flights. Far off the ground, she felt cocooned in her own personal space. This was where she had done some of her best work: coming up with new inventions, framing new proposals, putting new ideas to paper. But this time, she forced herself to shut the world out and get some well-deserved shut-eye. Once on the ground, she would have an itinerary packed with responsibilities. There would be press conferences and further formal apologies. She needed to look and be at her best for her colleagues, customers, the media, and the public. "We already have control of the situation," she said to herself. "All we need to do now is to finish it."

Secretary General Momoko met the plane personally at Narita Airport and used the time on the way into the city to brief her CEO on the most recent developments. They boarded the Narita Express and headed to Shinjuku Station. Momoko handed Eva the latest printouts and began her briefing. "You have a press conference at 2:00 this afternoon. You missed the press conference last week and journalists want to hear what you have to say."

Next, as requested by General Manager Akihiko, Momoko began updating Eva on key issues, advising her CEO on the questions the press would likely be asking, and suggesting how she should respond. She even asked Eva to commit to memory the formal apology prepared by the company's lawyers that she would be saying to reporters. Momoko had grown up in the United States and thus spoke English fluently. The pace of the discussion grew faster and more urgent as the Narita Express drew closer to Shinjuku Station. Momoko wanted to make sure Eva understood everything by the time they stepped out onto the station platform.

Eva listened intently to everything Momoko said. Nodding occasionally, her mind was absorbing while preparing for the task ahead.

On arrival at Trend Micro's Shinjuku headquarters, she set thoughts of the imminent press conference aside and called on Human Resources Chief Okazawa to take her to each floor in order to personally deliver her thanks and encouragement.

"*Otsukaresamadeshita.*" Eva plumbed her limited formal Japanese to thank her colleagues for their hard work and sacrifice. "Thank you all for sacrificing your weekend and for your dedication to our customers. Because of you, we will resolve our problems and emerge at the other end of this crisis." She continued, "I have a press conference this afternoon where I will deliver my personal apology to our clients and the public. But before I did that, I wanted to thank you all first. Let us all work together. *Gambate!*"

Later on, a Japanese colleague related to me the electric, emotive effect that Eva's visit and personal expressions of concern and thanks had on everyone that day. "She understood and appreciated our effort! She stood with us!" Her visit further rallied the Trend Micro "troops" to move as one, steadily toward the light at the end of the tunnel.

That afternoon was taken up by Trend Micro's second press conference. This time, we convened the event at the well-known Okura Hotel. An experienced translator was on hand to carefully deliver Eva's statements into Japanese. Momoko, thinking back on the tenor of that day, recalled, "It was the classiest press conference I'd ever seen our company hold. Fancier even than our investor meetings." Once everyone and everything was in its proper place, it was time to ask CEO Eva Chen to make her entrance. It was only then that our colleagues noticed she was still wearing the pink shirt she had worn on her flight from Los Angeles. It was the polo shirt we had special ordered for everyone attending the Punta Cana awards ceremony, with a bold, red *T* emblazoned across the front. It was an attractive design … but wholly inappropriate for the occasion at hand.

"Eva," Momoko said, "please change into a black suit before going out onstage!" The secretary general had been so busy with taking care of Eva's other preparations that she hadn't thought to mention this earlier.

"No!" Eva answered decisively. "The shirt represents Trend Micro. I'm proud of who and what we are." She continued, "Steve used to wear polo shirts with our logo to press conferences too. It's part of our image."

"But ..." Momoko wanted to explain that this time was different, but she also realized she wouldn't be able to talk her new CEO, who was unfamiliar with the intricacies of Japanese formality, out of her decision. She placed an urgent call to CFO Negi for help. "Please help me convince Eva! You're a foreigner. You may be the only one able to convince her."

While no one wanted to add to the tensions of the moment, it was nonetheless imperative that Eva conform to Japanese cultural expectations at this critical time. That's why Trend Micro's Japanese executives turned to Mahendra Negi.

CFO Negi had been at Steve's side through countless investor meetings and press conferences. He knew very well Steve's predilection for wearing polo shirts at such events and that this had been part of Steve's cultivated persona. It reflected his desire to convey a message of straightforwardness and honesty, that "what you see is what you get." While Mahendra didn't have any problems with the approach in general, he did recognize that, today, it would be important to conform to Japanese tradition. Erring on the conservative side would be the wisest choice. He walked over to the CEO and said as diplomatically and softly as he could, "Eva. You're here to convey an apology. It would be best to follow the traditional way. You don't want to risk spawning new problems, right?"

Time-Out for a Coffee

Eva gave a deflated huff and changed quickly into her black suit, a just-purchased pair of hose, and a pair of formal, black, high-heeled shoes—a suit of armor for the battle ahead. PR Chief Takada breathed a sigh of relief. He started to prep his CEO in a hushed voice. "Okay. You will first give a formal bow to the audience and then deliver the formal statement of apology prepared by our lawyers. That will be all. We've all prepared for the question and answer session afterward."

Eva smiled, seemingly lost in her own thoughts. "I need to use the restroom first. Can you get me a cup of coffee?"

Takada turned to Momoko. "The press conference begins at two exactly. Make sure there are no delays."

Momoko's heart raced. She had joined Trend Micro six years prior and had been an invaluable aide to Steve and me. While work had kept her busy, things had never been as nerve-wracking as they were now.

Eva came out of the restroom, and Momoko produced the coffee as requested. Cup in hand, to everyone's surprise, Eva stopped in her tracks and became lost in the moment, sipping slowly from the cup with a look of clear, relaxed relish.

"Eva, please move quickly to the hall. The reporters are waiting for you." The normally reticent secretary general was clearly flustered. She anxiously dropped the niceties and worked to herd her CEO down the corridor as quickly as possible.

Her coffee finished, Eva straightened her tight-fitting skirt and began walking toward the hall. She knew she was about to face one of her life's most difficult moments. She would walk into a room filled with people not particularly well disposed to her or to Trend Micro at the moment—a sea of reporters waiting for this foreigner female boss to make some laughable faux pas, to make her apologies in unfamiliar English, to try and make amends for her company's terrible blunder.

She had needed that "coffee moment" desperately to calm her nerves and instill emotional balance and courage. She instinctively realized the importance of distinguishing between what was important and what simply couldn't wait. Trend Micro provided the blueprint for a cultural ethos truly distinct from the mainstream. She had no intention of surrendering blindly, as Japan Railway did, to the dictates of a clock on the wall.

Another row of black suits appeared onstage. This time, Eva was in the middle, flanked by GM Akihiko on her right and CFO Negi on her left and other departmental managers beyond them. All stood up straight and looked out onto the reporters assembled in the room. "*Ichi, ni ... san.*" All took a formal ninety-degree bow in unison. They kept their eyes on the ground, looking neither right nor left. Silently counting to fifty, Akihiko gave a silent signal and the group stood up straight again.

Takada had advised those new to this Japanese custom that bowing was easy. The public statement afterward, he said, would be more difficult.

After the collective bow, they all took their seats and the host of that afternoon's press conference stepped up to the podium. He introduced Trend Micro's recently installed CEO and explained that her arrival in Tokyo had been delayed due to the necessity of applying for a visa.

Eva stood up and made another deep bow to the audience, alone. She took the microphone and in simple Japanese delivered her own short, prepared apology. Next, she delivered a sincere apology in fluid English to Trend Micro's customers and to the Japanese public. Only then did she turn to the apology and format prepared by her company's lawyers.

Afterward, she strayed from the prepared script. "I feel I must provide a more adequate explanation of the reason behind this mistake. It was caused by our pursuit of innovation ..." The lawyers beneath the stage looked at one another in disbelief, shaking their heads in consternation. Caught off guard, Tanaka shot a nervous glance to Akihiko seated onstage. Akihiko nodded back, signaling for calm. He had every confidence in Eva's ability to handle this matter well on her own.

Eva continued to describe the technical difficulties posed by the zombie virus, the creative measures taken by Trend Micro engineers to extirpate the problem at its roots, and the failure to run adequately comprehensive tests prior to the release of the V.594 update. She described her company's systematic response to the crisis both in the immediate and longer terms and promised that it was the first and would be the last crisis of its kind at Trend Micro. Trend Micro's new CEO ended by stating, "We are committed to fully solving all virus problems and upholding the comprehensive security of the Internet. However, in sustaining the innovation necessary to pursue these goals, we have made a serious mistake. Please, I ask that you give us another chance! Please do not doubt our service capabilities! Please do not lose your confidence in us!"

Her eyes stared confidently around the room. After a brief pause, she continued. "President Oscar Chang, the head of Trend Micro's Virus Center in the Philippines, is hard at work in Manila. Wanting to make a personal expression of apology for the error made by his team, President Oscar Chang has volunteered to cut his salary by half. For my part, from now until every single affected computer is once again running normally, my own salary will be cut to ¥594 a month."

Her sincerity left the audience visibly touched. The insights Eva gave them on the inherent difficulties of the antivirus software business made finger-pointing more difficult. The confidence and sincerity with which she delivered each of her points had a powerful effect, and a silence fell over the hall as she finished her last sentences. She slowly bowed once again. Camera flashes followed her as she walked back to her chair. Mahendra gave her a hearty "thumbs up" from below the podium.

CFO Negi later told me, "Japanese press conferences meant to deliver an apology are always serious. It is a ceremony, and speeches are rare. Actually, they are rather cookie-cutter. Most lack sincerity. Eva delivered her sincere apology, an explanation of the problems, a request for understanding, and a strong statement of self-deprecation in perfect English. It was very human of her, and a gesture that transformed fundamentally the press conference's atmosphere. It exceeded everyone's expectations and totally caught those menacing reporters off guard."

Her speech took her Japanese senior executive team off guard as well. They had naturally nurtured concerns over the past four months that Eva may not be the equal of Steve in terms of courage and charisma. They wondered whether she could move Trend Micro forward in a Japanese business world still dominated by men. This speech won all of them over. They knew now that, while her style was very different from Steve's, it had the sharp edge necessary to take Trend Micro into the next Internet era.

Of course, the changed mood in the audience did not preclude reporters asking their tough questions. They wouldn't let Trend Micro get off that easily. Seasoned journalists asked sharp questions, but they were clearly willing to accept the answers given by Eva and her executives onstage. They were no longer anxious to draw blood.

With the press conference over, Eva returned to her office. Jet lag now filled the gap left by the weighty responsibilities of the afternoon. She felt suddenly very hungry and tired. Eva lifted herself up and took the elevator alone down to the food court on the building's basement level. She had once jokingly remarked that she worked in order to eat. At that moment, that simple bowl of soba noodles in front of her was the best possible reward she could have imagined for the seventy-two hours of work she had just finished.

Her hunger pleasantly sated, Eva walked out of the noodle shop and toward one of her most favorite things about Japan: a vending machine. At the drop of a coin, she could choose from any of several dozen drinks on offer. She decided on a can of iced milk coffee. The one she'd had before the press conference had been too bitter!

"Let me, Chief Executive!" An unfamiliar man behind her (definitely not a Trend Micro employee) slipped a coin in the machine. "Your salary is now 594 yen. This coffee costs a fifth of this month's income."

No experience could have been more touchingly appropriate at that moment! Eva decided to accept without protest. She turned to the stranger and thanked him. *Arigato.*

The press conference had already made the news. She suspected that from this point forward, Trend Micro would have more sympathizers than detractors within Japan.

CHAPTER 12

High-Wire Act

Our core value had always been innovation, and Trend Micro staff was encouraged to take reasoned risks and to dare to make mistakes.

If we were to quash the person responsible for this initial blunder, wouldn't it be hypocritical? How could we ask our people to trust us from that point forward?

How could our team continue to test the limits of innovation and make the breakthroughs necessary to keep Trend Micro at the top of its game? The answer was that we couldn't shake our own foundations; we wouldn't lose the fear that would invariably undermine confidence and curtail organizational willingness to innovate. After all, innovation was our bread and butter!

Like I said, penalty sometimes paves the way to redemption. Philippines Virus Center Chief Oscar Chang's salary cut seemed the ticket to calming his overwrought nerves. Eva's temporary rehire at a symbolic ¥594 a month now seemed to have sold the public on Trend Micro's determination to set things right again. But, what about the colleague who had made that initial error? Should he be punished? Did he deserve redemption?

Eight years have passed since the dark days of the V.594 crisis. However, even today, few within the Trend Micro organization actually know who it was that uploaded the faulty virus code onto the Internet. Eva, Steve, and I have never asked or been told either. From what I've been told, no investigation was even made.

Was this perhaps an oversight in the heat of the moment? Did the singular focus on our customers cause everyone to think that there was someone out there who actually deserved to be punished for violating Trend Micro's core business principles? Throughout history and around the world, the first reaction to a problem has nearly always been to ask who was to blame, followed invariably by insinuations and vociferous denials of responsibility. Why was Trend Micro different? Why, in the face of outside accusations, did the Trend Micro organization, while launching a thorough assessment of its procedures, not drag the culprit out for a good public thrashing?

Trend Micro's response on this count continues even now to be a point of pride for me. It was an incredible accomplishment! It was a response rooted in our corporate culture, framed by our core values, and accomplished by thoughtful consensus. It certainly did not simply gloss over problems, nor was it blind paternalism.

On the day after the press conference, Akihiko led Eva and the "apology team" to the headquarters of Japan Railway. They had suffered the most from the V.594 crisis.

Their more recent calamity had not erased the memory of the mess caused by Trend Micro's buggy update from the mind of either JR's CEO or his IT chief. Despite their formerly good rapport with Steve and Akihiko, the dozen or so senior JR officials seated that day around the conference room table looked at the visiting Trend Micro team with only dour, unforgiving expressions. They were awaiting an explanation before deciding whether or not to pull Trend Micro software from their systems and replace it with another product.

After completing their obligatory bow of apology, Eva pulled out her notebook computer and asked for a hookup to JR's projector. She opened up a slide presentation that she had finished the night before with her R & D team entitled "Root Cause Analysis." She began detailing the seven points in current standard procedures where the crisis may have sprung and explained the actions her teams were taking to fix each in a timely manner. Trend Micro engineers, she said, were enhancing their emulation of customers' actual operating environments and improving emergency customer-contact capabilities. Moreover, new rules in place now required all testing be double-checked by a second engineer. Eva's insider knowledge and professional attitude allowed her to share honestly and openly the causes of the problem and to discuss what had been learned. Akihiko translated Eva's presentation in English into formal, polite Japanese.

JR's IT officials had, of course, suffered through system crashes before. After hearing Eva out, they were all pleasantly surprised. "This new lady CEO," they turned to one another and said, "she knows her technology." After deliberating a short while, they determined Trend Micro's response measures and service attitude to have been adequately swift and proper.

Responsible for domestic sales, General Manager Akihiko asked JR officials how his company might further improve their product and services. He concurrently suggested that Trend Micro unilaterally extend the validity of its JR service contract in compensation for JR's losses. The severe expressions across the face of their customers softened gradually, and the discussion turned to internal management issues. One of the questions raised by a JR official was: "What are your plans for punishing the employee who made the mistake?"

Eva and Akihiko exchanged furtive glances. Although this was an issue they'd not yet discussed, their perspectives were similar. "Multiple factors were at work in this problem. President Oscar Chang and I accept full responsibility, and any punishment shall be ours alone."

The reply evoked raised eyebrows across the conference table. "If it were our company, the culprits would be punished in order to maintain proper respect and order."

In the United States, clients affected by V.594 also asked the same question. "What's the punishment?" Finding and punishing those "most responsible" for the problem seemed to be something everyone expected of us.

The Weight of Culture

Every ethnic group, every country is defined by unique cultural traits. In general, the culture that defines a corporation is more specific and narrowly defined. In a nutshell, a business is created by a group of people driven to solve some problem. These people share a common goal and a consensus on how that goal might best be achieved. A specific line of thinking and attitude and approach to work thus emerges organically from how a business is structured, shaped by rules outlined in the corporate charter. "Maintaining a consistent work attitude even when no one is looking or is even able to know what you are doing"—this is what I perceive is the true essence and expression of corporate culture.

The various products and services that a company provides in order to resolve a specific problem or problems provide critical justification for that company's reason for existence. These naturally feed a cultural ethos that forms the unique "signature" of that company. Every element of that corporate ethos is retained or jettisoned based on the litmus test of its appropriateness to moving the business as a whole positively forward.

For example, there is a reason for a military culture's preference for strict discipline and top-down management. After all, holding a referendum while closing in on the enemy's guns likely won't deliver ideal results. Similarly, the reliance of government bureaucracies on taxpayer funding nurtures a natural emphasis on accountability and conservative cultural mores that value hierarchy and procedure. While often reviled, bureaucratic culture is justified by the core values held universally by government organizations. The corporate cultures of direct marketing and investment banks may find tremendous value in highlighting their "star players." They set high-performance employees up as role models to emulate and, perhaps, beat, with those failing to keep pace clearly cognizant that their days with the firm are numbered. As for accounting firms and legal firms, they foster cultures marked by a professionalism that sees the rational trump the emotional and lets evidence direct decision-making. Interesting potential outliers are the cultures that mark religious and volunteer organizations. They are held together by a shared ideal that often downplays hierarchies and the pursuit of reward and uses "love" and "hope" to focus members on achieving organizational goals.

Each cultural ethos generates behaviors that set it apart from all others and support the pursuit of distinct goals. While it may seem intangible, culture is marked by its own ineffable weight and profundity.

Although none of us had earned a formal MBA degree, Steve, Eva, and I had nonetheless built and led a successful multinational IT company that did business in more than thirty markets around the world. In Trend Micro, we had created an internationally respected and oft-cited model of "transnational business management." We'd gone beyond the principles of humanism to make sure that every major business decision reflected basic humanistic principles.

With the situation in Japan temporarily stabilized, Eva prepared to catch a flight to Manila. She would join President Oscar Chang and his Virus Center team to work on finding a technical solution to the problem at hand and establish the protocols necessary to turn this crisis into a positive, growth-oriented learning experience.

Before departing, she called Steve and me and then convened a quick videoconference with her senior executive board. The one-topic item of discussion earned a quick and decisive consensus: "no investigation and no punishment of the engineer whose action had led to this crisis."

Our core value had always been innovation. How often had I encouraged Trend Micro staff to take reasoned risks and to dare to make mistakes? If we were to quash the person responsible for this initial blunder, wouldn't it be hypocritical? How could we ask our people to trust us from that point forward? How could our team continue to test the limits of innovation and make the breakthroughs necessary to keep Trend Micro at the top of its game? The answer was that we couldn't shake our own foundations; we wouldn't lose the fear that would invariably undermine confidence and curtail organizational willingness to innovate. After all, innovation was our bread and butter!

Another argument for leniency was that the fault for the problem could not be entirely pinned on the engineer who posted V.594 for global download. Everyone along the chain, from development through testing and distribution, made mistakes. Old habits are blinders that obscure potential dangers. What would justify piling blame on the last man (or woman) holding the V.594 "hot potato"? Anyway, his or her motivation was clearly good: the complete elimination of the vexing problem of zombie viruses. There was no willful playing around with new, untested methodologies. Everything was done aboveboard and in the believed interest of Trend Micro customers.

But, of course, the flip side of this logic made it difficult to consider when, if ever, our employees could be called out and held accountable for their faults. Were we creating a "workers' paradise" where any infringement could be tolerated?

No. All actions are accountable to their motivations. Actions inspired by personal gain, such as accepting kickbacks, using one's official position for personal gain, inflating accounts, pushing unwanted sales to meet sales goals, or cutting corners to earn unwarranted efficiency awards reflect poorly on individual character and should and have been punished swiftly. Trend Micro had indeed previously fired employees for such infringements.

Problems that are not rooted in character issues but rather repeatedly poor judgment will still weigh heavily on employees at performance-review time. I like to use the anecdotal story "Yan Hui Never Makes the Same Mistake Twice" from the Confucian Analects to stress the importance of using mistakes to learn something new.

As for mistakes made willfully, while they may violate company rules and may reflect an unwillingness to conform to workplace expectations, they also may be rooted in the pursuit of breakthrough innovation and may be done in spite of the risk of ridicule and punishment. Thus, care should always be taken in deciding if and how to pursue punishment for mistakes that fall into this category. In general, problems within Trend Micro have always been handled on a case-by-case basis with due consideration made for normal behavior and underlying motivations.

Walking the Tightrope

Actually, it is very difficult to arrive at true "justice" through strict adherence to hard-and-fast rules. But, whatever we did, we owed it to everyone to explain our final decision on the issue of "to punish or not to punish."

After concerted deliberation, we went back to our roots ... back to our core values.

We would use the opportunity presented by the crisis to achieve something positive. Trend Micro would demonstrate the power of its culture and reaffirm its commitment to the path of innovation.

It was like walking a tightrope, trying to maintain a delicate balance between the extreme of either side. With eyes focused forward, the Trend Micro team made every effort to avoid any potentially game-ending misstep. Innovation requires the acceptance of mistakes. The leeway you give will naturally affect the severity of mistakes you may face. We were all walking that fine line through the air, balance pole quivering up and down, aware that we could fall at any moment. Only by staying centered was Trend Micro able to regain its footing and balance and to continue confidently forward.

Trend Micro shares shed 4 percent on the first day of trading after news of V.594 hit. Within one week, we had lost ¥60 billion in market capitalization. This was one tangible cost of innovation. Another was the incalculable damage to our reputation worldwide. We were headline news. As customers questioned their confidence in our products and services, our competitors rushed in to feast. Internally, morale was flagging as all looked in the mirror and saw themselves at least peripherally culpable for the problems now engulfing their company.

Our newly appointed chief technology officer, Raimund Genes, was a seasoned R & D professional from Germany. His unyielding expectations with regard for quality were made all the more intense by his similar demands for efficiency, speed, and perfection. He had regularly demanded more of our virus-testing procedures out of a desire to ensure Trend Micro was always a step ahead of its competition. Raimund sent an e-mail to President Oscar Chang immediately after news of V.594 broke.

Looking back on that day, President Oscar Chang recalls, "I was so not looking forward to opening that message! I let it sit there on my screen for a whole day before finally clicking on it. To my surprise, it said: 'I am sorry. I think corners were cut on testing procedures because I pushed too hard.' I went numb. My eyes welled up. Even Raimund wasn't pointing the finger at us!"

Eva arrived in Manila in the evening of April 27. This meeting of R & D comrades in arms shone much-needed light into President Oscar Chang's "darkest hour." Eva patted him on the shoulder, conveying that she understood his heavy burden. Resignation would have been an easier route to take, but he had chosen to stay and face up not only to the mistakes that he and his team had made but also to the censure of Trend Micro's clients and perhaps even of colleagues. This, Eva knew to be true leadership.

At the time, the Philippine Virus Center was in a state of panic. Like a child that had done wrong and was waiting for the punishment sure to come, our R & D colleagues now showed none of their trademark optimism and confidence. *Might doing more just make things worse?* they thought. Might it be better after all to follow the rules and avoid the potential pitfalls inherent in risk-taking?

Eva met deep into the night with key Virus Center managers. After carefully examining every step of the R & D process and procedures, they drafted strategies to be implemented over the short-, medium-, and long-term. Eva would stay by their side through the duration to help see things through.

Eva penned the following letter before leaving Los Angeles for Japan.

> *To my dear colleagues at the Philippines Virus Center and all members of scan engine and product development teams:*
>
> *I know that the V.594 crisis has put you all under tremendous pressure. We are the first line of defense against Internet threats. We are responsible for maintaining Internet security while pursuing excellence in everything we do. We have to strike a difficult balance between quality and speed in order to make sure that client systems always operate reliably and well. Our solitary road is littered with obstacles that we alone are responsible to identify and remove. It is thus not surprising if we falter and lose our footing on occasion.*
>
> *I am aware that the current crisis stems from our attempt to use an innovative approach to resolve permanently the problem of zombie viruses. The intent was clearly good, reflecting the innovation we both seek and need. I not only respect this spirit but also want to see it continue to flourish. I will not see future innovation compromised because of one failure. In fact, I wish the exact opposite. I want this problem to be a rallying point around which we all redouble our commitment to making innovation the increasingly reliable engine powering Trend Micro into the future!*
>
> *This crisis highlights that our product R & D and testing procedures remain overly focused on products and do not adequately consider the needs of customers.*
>
> *Together, we have developed an exceptional antivirus software platform. We developed V.594 and ran*

comprehensive tests to confirm that our software could again identify and remove all known viruses with an accuracy of 100%. We believed this adequate to end the testing process and release V.594 on the Internet.

But our procedures failed to adequately consider the differences between our test environment and the operating systems used by clients. Internal protocols ensure we test all updates on stand-alone computers running the latest OS versions. Clients, however, run a wide range of versions with differing specifications. Multitasking issues also affect some client systems. When a problem emerges, our engineers know that to clean the system you need to reboot in safe mode and eliminate the problem code. However, many of our customers do not know this.

We neglected to consider the differences inherent in our client environments. We forgot that clients don't know as much as we do about resolving virus problems. We failed to emulate the client environment in our testing procedures.

Okay then! We've now paid our tuition and learned a lesson of tremendous value. What is important now is that we learn this lesson well and make concrete changes for the better. In light of this, you will all incorporate the following into your work:

1) *Short-term: The virus code team will establish immediately a lab to allow the comprehensive testing of our software in simulated customer operating environments. We will invest the funds necessary to emulate various Internet computer models, operating systems and application software packages. While we won't be able to account for every customer situation, we will use interlacing to target an initial coverage rate of 80%.*

2) *Mid-term: Members of the product R & D team will begin to work on the same principles. The environments of existing, new, upgrade, and crossover clients will be*

emulated and used in our testing work. Consideration must be given to the knowledge and abilities of client IT managers.

3) *Mid/Long-term: The underlying philosophy of issuing virus updates shall be thoroughly considered and discussed. Does the number of virus updates equate linearly with level of client security? Is it our customers who are asking for updates or are we providing updates based on internal considerations? Should we be following different update protocols for different client environments or is our current "one size fits all" approach correct? Are updates formatted to optimize client security or for our own convenience? Finally and most importantly, how should we define our update protocol to ensure that it truly has the customer as its primary consideration?*

We learn; we change; we crawl incessantly forward. We cannot allow a single fall to sap our fighting spirit. I am well aware that every one of you is dedicated fully to your responsibilities and committed to realizing Trend Micro's long-term vision. We care deeply for the safety and security of our customers and wage a pitched battle against those who wish to launch their attacks over the Internet. Our distinctly high state of readiness, enthusiasm and professional commitment also created the conditions for V.594. Otherwise, why would we go to such trouble? Otherwise, why should we pursue with such passion new ways to win our battles?

Please continue as you always have. Continue taking risks; continue trying new ways of doing things; continue to learn. Do not feel discouraged. Definitely do not shrink from the many challenges still to come. In moving forward together as a team, we will achieve more than either we or our competitors have ever achieved before!

Remember always that Trend Micro is building and investing in an organization that is constantly learning and improving. We accept mistakes while making absolutely sure that we learn and improve as a result. Let's use the V.594 experience to learn the true value of innovation and use it to take us one step closer to excellence!

Straddling the Border between the Material and the Ideal

President Oscar Chang shared his opinion that, "If Eva hadn't hurried to Manila like she did, I would not have been able to carry on. Her remaining with us through that critical period carried a message not lost on any of us. I didn't shirk my responsibilities either and remained on the job for three months before I allowed myself to leave and see my wife in Taiwan." His failure to be with his recent bride through the first months of her pregnancy is something that President Oscar Chang says he will regret for the remainder of his days. It may indeed be the longest-lasting side effect of V.594. For better or for worse, he now lives firmly under the "thumb" of his better half.

The day after Eva landed in Manila, General Manager Akihiko made an unexpected visit to the Philippines Virus Center together with several of his managers. They came bearing gifts, weary from both their journey and the events of recent days.

After asking President Oscar Chang to gather all of the Center's nearly one thousand employees together, GM Akihiko opened a box filled with folded origami cranes, individually crafted from colorful sheets of paper. He announced, "Thank you all! I know you are working hard, as we are, to resolve the problems at hand. You probably haven't had a good rest in many days. Your colleagues in Japan made these cranes for you as a symbol of our shared cause. I know many of you like Japanese snack foods. We have brought a large selection of our favorites to share with you all. Please enjoy!"

Some in the assembly had already begun to tear up with emotion. Japan had been the epicenter of the crisis, and Akihiko had personally accepted much of the criticism leveled at Trend Micro Japan by its customers. Yet he had come to Manila not to ridicule but rather to convey the support and camaraderie of Trend Micro Japan. The general manager continued, his voice rising with emotion, "We will continue the fight on the frontlines.

No problem! You are our critical line of supply. Please keep us supplied with the weapons we need to continue taking the fight to those who want to undermine the safety and security of the Internet."

Back in the United States, Steve had wrapped up his intensive course with our son at Northwestern University. Returning to the East Coast, he told me, "Eva has already responded to the media and made apologies to our customers. I think the time is right for me to go to Japan and see whether she could use my help."

I was up to speed on the situation in Japan. Although still concerned, I decided to stay with my son as he made his wedding plans. "Go," I said. "I'm staying here, but please remember everything you do and see there and tell me about it when you get back! This is an experience surely worth remembering."

Steve arrived in Tokyo on the same day that Eva departed for Manila. Poor, frazzled Momoko had just waved her new boss off, only to greet her "Big Boss" back to Japan. Her eyes were dry and red from multiple nights of little sleep. Apart from asking her to schedule various internal meetings, the Big Boss gave her another, rather unusual request. "Get a video camera and record as much as you can of the company's response to this crisis … people answering phones, discussions with customers, tired colleagues … Also, you'll need to interview Akihiko, Kutsuzawa, Takada, Negi, Kuroki, and Okazawa. Ask them to give their perspectives and thoughts on the V.594 crisis."

It was a task new to Momoko, made all the more daunting because everyone was still caught up in the whirl of activity that surrounded the office. Navigating Trend Micro's headquarters with a camera in hand seemed wholly out of place. She would feel like an intruder gathering evidence for some future indictment. It may have been the days of sleep deprivation, but Momoko's face was writ large with embarrassment and discomfort. Steve, perceiving this, took her gently aside and explained, "I want to make a record of these events. It will be very valuable in the future." To underline his resolve, he added, "If you're not willing to do this, it's okay. But you know I will get somebody else to do it. I leave it up to you to decide whether or not you take part in this highly significant project."

She still held her reservations, but she knew someone else would indeed be drafted if she didn't take up the order. But wouldn't she be responsible for holding her colleagues' feet to the fire? Ignoring her many doubts, she took up the camera, learned all the buttons, and followed Steve as he weaved his way around Trend Micro's offices. She asked colleagues various questions. In the process, she earned her share of exasperated looks and offhand comments, such as, "What are you doing with a video camera in the middle of this mess?"

Years later, Momoko fessed up to me about her feelings at the time. "I really hated the Big Boss then. His ideas were so off the wall. It was ridiculous! Anyway, I followed his instructions, took a lot of video footage, then turned it all over together with clips from the news to a professional media company. They edited everything into a fifteen-minute documentary. We've since played that video at a lot of Trend Micro events. It never fails to have an emotional effect on those who see it. Some have even thanked us for preserving a visual record of that critical turning point in Trend Micro's history." She stops, gives a self-deprecating laugh, and picks up where she left off. "The things that the Big Boss asks us to do ... it's often only later that we understand why. I think that documenting everything on video was the most difficult and also most worthwhile and lasting thing I have done in my Trend Micro career!"

Even many years later, that documentary continues to convey the gripping emotions and tensions of that time and to portray the determination and strength of everyone involved. It also successfully provides an enticing glimpse into the kindness and humility that lay not far beneath the surface of Trend Micro's resolute response.

Businesses in the IT sector are uniformly portrayed as coldly impersonal. Our modern-day business model comes from a Western capitalist framework. It is firmly rooted in materialist principles, with preference given to the rational over the emotional. The "unquantifiable" is invariably considered unscientific and, more often than not, disparaged as valueless. The philosophical traditions of East Asia, however, draw sustenance from the individual. Emphasis is placed on humane concerns, with traits such as benevolence, honor, and duty held in high regard. For those steeped in Western thought, such concepts lie dangerously within the borders of the intangible, making them awkwardly fluid, capricious ... even absurdly impractical.

At the helm of a transnational high-technology firm, we have worked hard to strike and keep an appropriate balance between the extremes of cold materialism and impractical idealism. Operating as an Eastern organization internally and a Western organization externally allows Trend Micro to successfully achieve Western capitalist business objectives using a model of business management grounded in Eastern humanism.

It has not been easy. Our experience with V.594 was a valuable lesson. But was it a lesson well learned? At the time, that was a question still too early to answer. It would be another six months before other events would highlight the import of changes made. It is only now, many years later, that hindsight shows just how priceless the V.594 experience truly was. Lessons learned and changes made had a clear hand in creating the innovative leadership enjoyed by Trend Micro today.

CHAPTER 13

Picking Up and Moving Forward

It is certainly not a story of illustrious accomplishment, certainly nothing about which to boast. Nevertheless, I am indelibly proud.

Faith in innovation trumped the very natural urge to wither in the face of a mistake. Our prioritization of the needs and concerns of our customers won their trust while our open, honest discussion of the issues ultimately won their understanding.

In the end, it was willingness to change that pointed the way forward into the cloud.

The Threat to Market Capitalization

The value of publicly traded firms is reflected in their market capitalization. It is a cut-and-dry issue of money that directly affects investor earnings. All pretenses of idealism go out the window when market capitalization is being discussed.

After the Saturday press conference, CFO Negi prepared himself psychologically for the worst. Sure enough, from the opening bell on Monday, Trend Micro's once unassailable stock price started a precipitous tumble on the Tokyo Stock Exchange. Nikkei Indexed stock number 4704 dove immediately from its Friday close of ¥4,280 per share. Mahendra could only hug his shoulders and stare at the real-time updates scrolling across his computer screen. "Fall ... just fall. We're all over the news. It's inevitable that we'll fall the maximum amount allowed today." Unlike Taiwan's floor limit on stock price falls to 7 percent per trading day, the

Tokyo Stock Exchange permits daily fluctuations of up to 20 percent of a stock's absolute value.

CFO Negi was unshakably pessimistic about the situation. There seemed no reason to feel otherwise. Over the weekend, he had patiently answered countless questions fielded by financial journalists and stock analysts. Standard & Poor's response was uncomfortably immediate. They put TSE4704 onto their watch list, "due to the long-term effects of this incident."

But to the surprise of all, Trend Micro stock held firm after falling 5 percent in value, even gaining back some lost value on unexpectedly strong buying interest. Not believing his eyes, Mahendra sat up straight in his chair, tapped on the keyboard, and double-checked with other information. It was true. Trend Micro was holding steady … a true miracle!

Before joining Trend Micro, CFO Negi was a senior analyst at Merrill Lynch. Thus, he was naturally inundated by calls from former colleagues wanting updates from the source. "How are your clients reacting?" they asked. "What is the expected impact on contract renewals?" Mahendra replied, "We don't know yet. There's a lot of anger targeting us now. We'll make our apologies and explanations one by one." Despite the surprisingly mild drop in share price, Trend Micro's CFO was not yet ready to express any measure of confidence.

He never believed in stock-price manipulation and always took an honest, forthright approach to stock analysis. He also adamantly opposed making false pretenses for short-term company gain. For this, he enjoyed a spotless reputation in the financial sector that earned him nearly universal respect and trust. Thus, despite his six years as Trend Micro CFO and the industry experience it had given him, Mahendra Negi maintained the straight-laced ways and astute acumen of a stock analyst at the top of his game.

However, his insightful powers of analysis had failed him this time. At the closing bell, Trend Micro stock closed at ¥4,100—just 4 percent off its Friday close, a loss of around ¥180. The bottom was never tested, and trading volumes were seven times higher than normal. It was an indicator that investors hadn't quite lost confidence in Trend Micro's ability to make good of this crisis. In fact, not a few investors saw in the limited drop an opportunity to pick up additional shares.

The first day of trading after the crisis was marked by surprise instead of the expected plunge. The good ship Trend Micro remained high and dry and ready to fight another day.

The following week saw steady drops in its share price of between 2 and 3 percent. When it was all over, the value of the firm's market capitalization had shed about ¥60 billion. The half month that followed saw continued instability that ended in Trend Micro stock leveling off at around ¥3,200. This was a 20 percent deflation from pre-crisis levels.

Then, in mid-June, news began to spread that Trend Micro's key accounts were showing no sign of switching to other service providers. Conversely, Trend Micro was renewing and expanding its service contracts. Perceptive analysts upgraded their expectations, giving TSE4704 strong upward momentum once again. By the end of June, Trend Micro was trading at ¥4,000, a level just shy of the company's pre-crisis share price.

Trend Micro's strong third quarter report showed sales at 13 percent above the previous year. Despite a crisis-related 25 percent increase in operating costs, net profits had held steady at an impressive 38 percent.

By the close of that year, TSE4704 was testing new highs and holding steady at around ¥4,600—a rise of 9 percent above pre-crisis levels.

The Impact on Sales

While stock prices reflect investor confidence, sales reflect consumer support.

It was possible that those customers now accepting our apologies were doing so out of practical considerations. As they needed us to get their systems back to normal, many surely felt unable to immediately abandon Trend Micro for another antivirus solution provider. They thus stood back and watched us skeptically as we worked to get things right. "Your software error caused us to lose business," many said. "What are your plans for compensation?"

Compensation was the awkward elephant in the room. It was an issue raised incessantly and pursued with vigor. It was an issue of concern for our colleagues and partners, our customers, the media, and the software industry at large.

Microsoft's standard contract was the model that nearly all software providers used in their contractual dealings with customers: compensation for losses attributable to purchased software shall be compensated up to the value of the purchase price. Microsoft's executives really knew how to stack the deck in their favor!

There had been many prior examples of software-induced disasters, some even worse than the aftermath of V.594. Even so, there was no precedent for providing compensation above and beyond contracted obligations. The current situation thus set the global software industry on edge. Trend Micro's agreement to settle compensation claims would not only end in bankruptcy. It would be a dangerous precedent as well … a violation of established practice. Our software peers thus sat and watched nervously as events unfolded. At the time, the Internet landscape was complex and highly intertwined. A temblor anywhere could have a far-reaching, even game-changing, impact. Client computer systems were still a motley mix of OS standards and specifications, making comprehensive testing exceedingly difficult. This meant that any antivirus software provider might fall into the same trap as Trend Micro did with V.594. Furthermore, the larger the customer, the more herculean the task of cleaning up in its aftermath.

While not missing out on the chance to delight in the misfortunes of a competitor, antivirus software companies were well aware of their exposure to similar errors. Arai, Trend Micro Japan's current director of marketing, was working for the distributor of a Trend Micro competitor when the V.594 bomb exploded. He remembers that "at the time, our first reaction was of course eager anticipation at the prospect of watching this drama unfold. We'd take full advantage of the fallout. But also, the ferocity of the media attacks made us also feel sympathy. We were also afraid that if Trend Micro really did fall, it would be a hard lesson for all of us."

Steve studiously avoided interfering in how Eva was handling the crisis and neither made any public appearances nor communicated with any of Trend Micro's customers. He knew that under Eva's leadership, technical issues would be expertly handled and that General Manager Akihiko was exceptionally qualified to manage both customer and sales issues. Finance and legal affairs, however, were two areas in which Trend Micro had less experience. CFO Negi and Steve shared an excellent relationship and a long history of close and successful cooperation. While Mahendra was exceptionally good at handling the company's day-to-day financial affairs, the current situation was a different kettle of fish. Without Steve by his side, he wouldn't have the confidence necessary to move quickly and decisively.

Steve's attitude toward compensation was firm. Mahendra, Akihiko, and he hammered out a common position on the issue. "Trend Micro will handle matters in accordance with contractual obligations. System-restoration expenditures shall be separately reimbursable if customers provide proper receipts. We will make no promises regarding comprehensive rectification. All customers affected in the crises shall have their contracts automatically extended by three months. Business losses suffered by customers may be discussed and resolved bilaterally. However, compensation shall be limited to the actual price paid for the product." Service was a significant source of revenue for Trend Micro. Thus, offering three months of additional free service meant a significant short-term loss in sales income.

This was an uncomfortable course to take, particularly as we needed customers to renew their contracts with us. A report in the US media reported erroneously that Trend Micro had agreed to compensate for losses in business caused by the V.594 bug. We had no way of knowing whether it was an honest or willful mistake. At the order of the CFO, Trend Micro's finance division immediately issued a public statement to clarify the issue. Nevertheless, the aftershocks of the US news report lingered for an uncomfortably long time. There were, of course, many individual users who found Trend Micro's clarification hard to swallow. In all cases, as long as a customer presented valid receipts for computer repair and/or system restoration, we provided separate, individual compensation.

As for our corporate clients, most were clear on the business ground rules and did not argue for additional compensation. However, how many would actually renew their contracts when the time came? That was the real question on everyone's mind.

GM Akihiko announced, "In order to address the immediate needs of our existing customers, we are drastically cutting marketing expenditures. We are suspending all advertising, eliminating quarterly sales targets for sales staff, and temporarily halting new customer development activities.

Our objective in doing this is to focus our full attention on our customers to provide them with comprehensive recovery services."

Trend Micro had received gold-medal recognition from Japan's national service association only the year before. A number of months after the crisis hit, Akihiko was invited by the same association to present the gold-medal award to the current year's recipient. "I must confess that I am uncomfortable in taking up this responsibility. As all are certainly aware, we are in the midst of a crisis of our own making. What could I possibly say to those attending this event?" To his surprise, people he both knew and didn't know came vociferously to his defense. "Very good. Trend Micro handled the emergency exceptionally well. Good job!" The chairman of the association insisted he not only present the award but also share his experience during the crisis. "Recognizing a problem and changing; bravely facing up to your responsibilities … these are marks of truly exceptional service!"

At year's end, every one of our customers renewed their contracts. Some even upgraded to higher service levels. The year after the crisis, the value of Trend Micro services had more than doubled. Mitchell in the United States and Kutsuzawa in Japan had learned from the experience and launched service packages tailored to the different environment and service content needs of users. The spirit of service that Trend Micro upheld through the crisis had deeply impressed its customers, making it easier than ever before to re-up existing accounts and to attract new business.

"Not a single corporate client abandoned us because of V.594 … not a single one!" Akihiko remembers with conviction. His smile still evinces the hint of relief. Of course, he has long since returned to enjoying self-indulgent pleasures like visits to *izakayas* and weekend golfing.

Technology Reconsidered

Eva, once a star pupil in Cheng Chi University's philosophy department, loves sinking her teeth into a good problem.

The problems underlying V.594 highlighted that current virus-coding techniques were at an impasse. When Steve and I started Trend Micro in Los Angeles in 1988, there were a total of five computer viruses in the entire world. That number had since expanded to tens of millions, and the list was still growing larger by the day. Standard practice remained to list every known virus, old as well as new, on a file that was saved to the user's terminal and referenced during virus scans. Even with the rapid growth in computer storage capacity, the virus codes needed by antivirus software were occupying an overly generous portion of available computer resources. Virus scans invariably reduced computer performance speeds, making antivirus software at most a tolerated nuisance. The trouble of maintaining effective antivirus protection made some users loath to run scans regularly, which compromised their security.

The number of virus codes, the building blocks of virus protection, is on a continuous upward growth curve. The number has, in fact, gotten so large as to be practically unmanageable for most computer systems.

"Is there a feasible way," Eva asked her R & D engineers, "for us not to store virus codes on user computers? Could we rather store this list on a dedicated, large storage space and access it only when the antivirus program is launched?"

The engineers saw it as a stimulating concept and set to work. Trend Micro's R & D team is a group of intriguing intellects avidly interested in avoiding boredom. Their high salary is not enough to keep them. They crave to be fed a diet of challenging problems.

"Storing all virus codes to a large, dedicated database means that client computers can just run the software program along with a small agent program that will be responsible to identify and upload all suspicious code to the database for comparison work. The results can then be downloaded to the client, and the antivirus software will handle the suspicious code accordingly."

The further the engineers got into this task, the more excited they became. Although "cloud" computing was a concept still yet to be born, this team was engaged in developing some of its technical components and "big data" analysis applications. This project gave Trend Micro an industry-leading position in the arena of cloud technology and a leg up on tapping its virtually unlimited potentials. Today, many of the world's major corporations maintain comprehensive cloud security contracts with Trend Micro, with implications of these agreements going far beyond antivirus protection. Our mission has already expanded to helping "secure your journey to the cloud."

So, in the end, we successfully turned a serious loss into a major gain. We met our fall with a serious, introspective examination of our business practices and direction. We changed fundamentally, turned from death's door, and took to the clouds.

The innovative spirit must lead the rise from every fall, and mistakes are a near prerequisite to advancing to the next level. Thank you V.594! Thank you also to those customers and journalists who so unreservedly served up the criticism that we so richly deserved … and needed.

Keeping Talent

As head of Trend Micro's human resources, the prospect of a crisis in the business always loomed ominously in the background. Crises struck at the heart of a business's soul, shook confidence, and often led good employees to pull up and leave.

Trend Micro Japan's SWAT chief Kutsuzawa confided to me much later that, "Frankly speaking, it was not long after I moved to Trend Micro from HP that I began to seriously think I might have sailed with the wrong ship. This is a company that doesn't have a clear rulebook, doesn't respect hierarchy, and gives unclear instructions. I was often forced to figure out how to accomplish things myself. HP has a good corporate culture too, but there are rules there that must be followed. So, I thought, what is up with this TSE-listed Taiwanese company?"

He continued, "It was about half a year after joining Trend Micro that Jenny invited me to join the fishbowl meetings and to be a member of 'F-Force.' I interviewed colleagues in other countries on behalf of Japan and our customer service team on our corporate culture and strategy. It was a new experience for me. I don't believe I'd ever before heard of a company that actively encouraged criticism from its employees. It was then that I understood the difference in Trend Micro's culture. There was a method to the madness. A shared optimism was pushing everyone forward and achieving results." Kutsuzawa's first year at Trend Micro was a wild ride. "It wasn't long before Eva took over as CEO and Steve and Jenny withdrew behind the scenes. Then V.594 exploded and I was saddled with significant responsibility. I wasn't prepared for the outpouring of support from so many colleagues, who came to my assistance without being asked or ordered. No one complained or griped at all. Everyone simply worked as a team to see us all through the crisis at hand!" It is a memory that he still finds hard to believe.

Of course, Kutsuzawa did not leave. He has since completed his MBA at Hitotsubashi University and is now a manager in Trend Micro Japan's Marketing Department. He remains General Manager Akihiko's right-hand man and over his career has recruited many top-flight professionals into the Trend Micro family.

Cyril, a manager at the Philippines Virus Center, was the staff member on whom President Oscar Chang relied most through the V.594 crisis. The pressure she felt during those months was second only to his, and it was she who led the Virus Center through Trend Micro's darkest hour. She remembers, "The thing that most touched us then was that President Oscar Chang and Eva didn't speak a word about blame. They even gave us pink teddy bears and stayed with us through the crisis. Steve also sent our team an e-mail with just two words: 'Stay Cool.' He couldn't have imagined the comfort and confidence those two words gave us."

Thoughts about that time still bring tears to Cyril's eyes. "Our supervisor didn't blame us, but we volunteered to sacrifice our bonuses to show that we were all in this together. There were quite a few who couldn't stand the pressure and quit. Those who chose to stay now share an inexplicable bond. We have a new clarity about the meaning and importance of what we do and are more mature and aggressive about it." She says, "General Manager Akihiko led a team from Japan to encourage us. They reviewed test procedures together with us. They gave us presents of paper cranes and lots of different kinds of snack foods. Three months later, after we'd gotten back on our feet, we sent a gift of delicious dried mango from the Philippines in appreciation of their generosity and help." Having colleagues in other countries ready and willing to drop everything and assist in times of need helped Cyril feel she wasn't alone and kept her diligently focused on the all-important virus code work.

The team from Japan gave more than just paper cranes and tasty snacks. They left in Manila Trend Micro Japan's topmost expert in R & D and testing, Shimizu. He would stay for the next five full years, helping Virus Center staff continuously improve their testing procedures. Shimizu recalls, "No one ordered me or told me to do so. If Eva or Akihiko had said, 'Go. Move to the Philippines!' my natural reaction would have been to refuse outright. But they called me in and asked me, 'What do you think we should do to help our Philippine team upgrade quality?' I thought the matter over. I knew it would have to be a long-term effort. Nothing would be accomplished with anything less. It would require reflecting the high demands and expectations of our customers in Japan into our testing procedures. If a Japanese colleague wasn't a direct part of the process, communications would be exceedingly difficult. I don't quite remember how it happened, but I volunteered … enthusiastically. I was there for five years. By the end of my stay, my colleagues back in Japan pretty much took me for a native!" Now back in Japan, Shimizu heads Trend Micro's Emergency Management Center. There was no one more fit for the job than he.

Arai, the one previously mentioned as working for a competitor, joined Trend Micro within a year of the V.594 crisis. Meeting with him, I asked, "Weren't you afraid? After all, Trend Micro didn't have the best reputation then."

"My first reaction to the media attacks was as a fascinated bystander. Later, after watching the even-keeled, meticulously proper response of Trend Micro's managers, my attitude started turning toward respect. It got me thinking. The massive public response to a mistake by an antivirus software maker indicated to me both that this was a business with bright prospects and that Trend Micro carried quite a bit of weight. Later still, I learned that Trend Micro took the self-effacing step of asking an independent information-security firm to inspect its internal testing procedures. This told me that this was a company that knew how to look deeply into its own operations and that its future shouldn't be underestimated. So, when Akihiko asked, I immediately grabbed the opportunity and joined Trend Micro." Today a manager in the marketing department, Arai now persistently chips away at the customer bases of Trend Micro competitors.

Although I did not participate or contribute directly to resolving the V.594 crisis, I am gratified that the corporate culture that I had worked for so long and hard to build had taken root in Trend Micro colleagues around the world, congealed, passed muster, and played an active part in seeing the company successfully into the light again. Since then, I have presented at major Trend Micro meetings, sometimes at length, other times more succinctly, on the positive lessons learned from this failure experience using the documentary filmed by Secretary General Momoko under such difficult conditions. These presentations invariably evoke a stirring response from both those who had been part of Trend Micro's experience and those who had not.

Culture must adjust and mold itself into the tenor of changing times, and storytelling is still the best way to convey important lessons to new generations.

This concludes the most detailed description of the story of V.594 that I've ever written. It is certainly not a story of illustrious accomplishment, and there is certainly nothing here about which to boast. Nevertheless, I am indelibly proud. Faith in innovation trumped the very natural urge to wither in the face of a mistake. Our prioritization of the needs and concerns of our customers won their trust, while our open, honest discussion of the issues ultimately won their understanding. In the end, it was our willingness to change that pointed the way forward into the cloud.

Benevolence, honor, and duty are part of a spirit that crosses all international and ethnic boundaries. Culture rooted in humanistic values and principles can survive, and thrive, in the utilitarian corporate world!

SECTION FOUR: CULTURE IN PRACTICE

BUSINESS CLAD IN CULTURAL ARMOR

CHAPTER 14

I Am a CCO!

I remained uncertain about how I would play out my new role.

Despite its "metaphysical" nature, culture had to find practical expression in day-to-day operations.

Despite its "spiritual" nature, culture could not overlook the necessity of satisfying material needs.

While I was the captain of our (Trend Micro's) culture, I was incessantly drawn to cultural horizons beyond our corporate confines. I found myself invariably looking for practical ways to bridge the potentials and realities of our internal culture with those of external culture.

Confidence feeds on challenge. Eva continued to earn confidence and respect in her leadership even as the ominous clouds of V.594 dispersed and faded gradually into memory. Steve and I began making plans for a long-anticipated vacation. As Chairman, Steve was sticking admirably to the confines of his position. He no longer attended internal business or policy meetings. He even stopped responding to company e-mails.

The long process of reorganizing the company concluded in July 2005. Asia Human Resources Vice President Connie was the engine that led our entire global organization into the new era. She made the plans and made sure everything was in place so that Trend Micro's restructured organization continued to operate at the highest levels of fitness and efficiency. I had worked with her closely for three years and knew well her professional abilities and experience in this area as well as her purpose-driven yet warmly confident way of handling every task. I had no doubt she would work exceptionally well with Eva and be an effective part of the effort to take Trend Micro's global human resources organization to the next level.

I told Eva, "I've always put my trust in Connie. She will ensure you have full control over personnel matters, and I will be able to relinquish my responsibilities." Although I had for a while tried my best to work as a part of Eva's new administration, the results were not particularly efficacious. After all, I was still her big sister, and it was tough for either of us to change old habits. It was natural for me to be the one looking out for her. I instinctively wanted to share my experiences, stop her from making mistakes, and give her what she needed to succeed. However, this did little to facilitate Eva's becoming a seasoned CEO. Although Steve and my positions had been one of a superior and a subordinate, we were equals as husband and wife. I had the right to speak my mind, and Steve could take or ignore my ideas as he chose. The situation was somewhat different when the one speaking was an older sibling. I came to realize that my opinions not infrequently put Eva between a rock and a hard place and simply made doing her job more difficult.

Retreating in Order to Move Forward

My proposal to Eva and our senior management team to let Connie manage Trend Micro's global HR operation passed unanimously.

"And what about you?" I was asked. "Jenny, what will you be doing?"

I was ready for that one. "I would like to become Trend Micro's first chief cultural officer," I replied. Hearing my own words made me realize the need to provide additional details. "If you ask a hundred of our colleagues to name our core competitive advantages, I'm willing to bet that at least eight out of ten will mention our corporate culture. It's a key, intangible asset of Trend Micro that ties all of us together, no matter where we are in the world. However, we've got a president in charge of strategy, a CFO responsible for finance, a CMO to manage our brand, a CTO to handle research and innovation, a COO responsible for business operations … what we're missing is a CCO to handle the critical issues related to Trend Micro's corporate culture."

While the idea made perfect sense, defining the responsibilities of a CCO position would prove to be a challenge. A seasoned veteran of the business world at the meeting turned a skeptical eye toward me after hearing out my enthusiastic ideas for a Trend Micro CCO. "What will the CCO actually *be* responsible for? What will he or she do? How do you propose evaluating performance? I don't think I've even heard of this position before!"

I replied with an embarrassed chuckle and admitted that I hadn't yet worked out the details. We were indeed charting new territory. "Give me some time to work those issues through," I said.

Eva interjected with supportive words. "It sounds great! Jenny is already involved with so much relevant to corporate culture. If we're going to choose history's first chief cultural officer, I can't think of any better candidate than she."

Just like that, I transformed my withdrawal from Trend Micro into an advance into the lucrative and highly meaningful new position of our company's first chief cultural officer.

In the blink of an eye, my universe was transformed into a vast, empty canvass awaiting my brush. Although the "universe" had always been something without end, my vision and my own limitations had always somehow encouraged my confinement within familiar borders.

While Trend Micro has traveled terrain marked by beauty as well as mortal danger, it has remained singularly fixated on pursuing its entrepreneurial endeavors. While we have peered forward toward the horizon and kept a firm grip on evolving trends, we remained slaves to the electronic information streaming to us over the Internet. Certainly, we would occasionally take time to admire the blue skies above and dream of the beauty beyond our cloistered, high-tech world. But fear of falling behind, of taking our eye off "the ball," ensured that we returned sooner rather than later to our professional vigil and to the determined march forward. When the skies above us clouded over, rather than abandon the inclement weather for brighter climes, we always buckled down and looked forward to the rains that would see us through the tough times ahead.

The onerous weight of one's myriad responsibilities can only be truly appreciated when they are suddenly lifted from the shoulders. The joys of liberation are needed to bring awareness of the restricted nature of the life just abandoned. But, at least at first, I guarded carefully those sweet, new melodies so recently discovered, partly out of fear of losing myself in their beguiling charms and partly in order not to not make waves for the newly instated Eva and Connie.

Steve continued his exploration of Zen Buddhism and began practicing meditation. His high-strung, restless nature had always made Steve something of a wild stallion—unpredictable and difficult to coax away from his chosen path. Now, he was looking to find inner peace, to come to rest, and to find himself.

While I, too, had long lost my way in the deep, dark "forest" of IT, I had taken pains to remember and nourish the interests I had held dearest in youth. While my dreams of a literary career had long vanished, I still looked forward to weaving its elements into my life. Yes, while fate had blown me onto technology's "yellow-brick road," it had strewn that road with challenges and opportunities that kept alive the idea of one day returning to those relinquished interests. Setting down our daily burdens at Trend Micro, we looked up at the road ahead and found a horizon of limitless possibilities.

With little hesitation, I switched paths and dove into arts education, applying my international business management and marketing experience to the promotion of culture and art. I also tapped into personal funds I had accumulated over the years from Trend Micro dividend payments to support the expenses of two foundations: the Trend Education Foundation and the Taiwan Institute of Psychotherapy. I wanted to create a positive, mutually reinforcing loop where private-sector business resources irrigate the fertile "fields" of culture and the bountiful harvests of those fields return to inspire creativity and innovation in business. This newly emerging trend would be the stage on which I played out this new phase in my life.

For his part, Steve had truly turned his eyes from the clouds to the dust beneath his feet. To my surprise, he traveled to northern Vietnam to take part in a local reforestation project. Professing to follow water as his role model, he stayed on to foster local community businesses. In searching to find himself, Steve had stepped onto a path very different from mine.

After Trend Micro, we were a couple taking two disparate paths of self-learning and discovery. While the dreams dreamt in our shared bed shared little in common, these dreams were equally good and fulfilling.

Steve explored the realms of Buddhism and meditation, while I pursued the multifaceted interplay between the classical and modern literary arts. He planted forests; I taught people. He managed our finances; I found new ways to spend our finances. In our separate explorations, we enriched each other's perspectives and understanding. Facets of our life that continued to overlap included Trend Micro staff training, watching movies, enjoying hot spring baths, the philosophies of Confucius and Zhuangzi, and Jungian psychology.

Without planning to do so, I became the first person in the business world to wear the hat of "chief cultural officer."

Despite the impressive-sounding title, the job description for this brand-spanking new position was still quite vague and in serious need of clarification. Everyone seemed to have his or her own distinctive take on the role and responsibilities of a CCO.

Rumors flew hot and heavy at Trend Micro: "Jenny will surely continue developing and organizing interesting, team-oriented activities, right?" "If we find something in Trend Micro that doesn't quite mesh with our culture, we'll surely be able to report the problem to Jenny." "No matter what the position actually does, having a CCO gives Trend Micro the cachet culture. It sets us apart."

While everyone had an opinion, no one was sure what the CCO would be doing. After all, Trend Micro's culture was already writ large across every one of its employees. What additional value could a CCO hope to bring?

Those in the cultural world outside of Trend Micro were visibly more excited than the Trend Micro organization at the announcement of this new position. I immediately began being addressed as CCO. I received widespread encouragement peppered here and there with mirthful ribbing. My title was often used without reference to Trend Micro, which infused an extra sense of weighty importance that was certainly not deserved. It was a distraction from what I intended to achieve. An increasing number of people came to the incorrect conclusion that this title had been created to confirm my previous participation in various cultural events and to pave the way for Trend Micro to use its largess to sponsor more cultural activities.

The Unity of the "In" and the "Out"

Strictly speaking, the position of chief cultural officer should have a well-defined definition and scope ... like the narrow confines of the family well in the backyard. "Cultural arts," however, is a broad, inclusive and un-limitable concept ... analogous to a flowing river or expansive ocean. I found myself frequently asking myself whether corporate culture existed to serve corporate goals or whether it existed independently as an aspect of human culture, with the potential to further enlighten the human condition. Would it be possible, I asked, to somehow link this well in the backyard to the powerful and limitless reserves of the ocean?

This was indeed a selfish venture. I hoped to use this new title to bridge the realms of business and culture and then use this bridge to channel resources into culture and creative innovation into business.

But my decades-long experience in business had taught me that selfish motivations rarely influenced business operations. Investing corporate resources based solely on personal interests would be unfair to our shareholders—all the more so because our shareholders were spread across the globe, and my interest was to promote and revitalize traditional Chinese cultural tenets.

I thus proceeded forward with a cautious eye on propriety. I created two foundations: the Trend Education Foundation in 2000 and the Taiwan Institute of Psychotherapy in 2001. Neither drew a single dollar from Trend Micro's coffers. Rather, I encouraged our colleagues to participate in the Taiwan-based charity and culture-oriented events that these foundations organized.

In hindsight, I realize that the transformation from head of HR to head of corporate culture was an eye-opening experience that taught me to see much farther than I had ever seen before. Human society, I came to realize, had progressed through hunting and gathering and animal husbandry to intensive agriculture and industry. The overriding importance of business and commerce in our current age thus naturally made corporate-sponsored events and activities a key aspect of modern human culture. The potential scope of influence for these events and activities, if marked by honest, high-quality cultural traits, thus extends far beyond the corporation itself.

They can be engines that power society forward to a higher plane of social and cultural achievement. In this surprising revelation, concepts like *inside* and *outside*, *have* and *have not*, and *first* and *last* could each be two sides of the same coin. They were connected. Surely, finances had to be clearly accounted for. But why should the same expectation be applied to the realms of the heart and mind?

Perhaps, I thought, I would be able to use my position as CCO, Trend Micro's transnational organization, and the base already created by the two foundations to introduce Chinese humanistic cultural mores to opinion leaders around the world, ultimately introducing Eastern philosophical perspectives to a much wider audience and helping more people to see, and hopefully realize, new potentials and possibilities. At least on the world's cultural scale, we may help add a bit more weight on the "Eastern" end.

However, the key problem remained as to how to make the clear distinctions necessary to succeed with such a venture. How could an open linkage between the inside and the outside survive in a system that distinguishes clearly between the public and the private? It was like standing with one foot on two boats. A slight shift in either could send the person in the middle tumbling into the water.

I stumbled slowly forward in my efforts. Asking the opinions of my colleagues about the potential duties of a CCO elicited numerous and varied responses. Some left me dumbfounded: "A CCO shouldn't be responsible for anything … It should be a symbolic position only." Some responses were deeply touching: "Culture is for everybody. You do the groundwork and we'll join in. We'll work together as a team." Still others left me shaking my head in disagreement: "Not too much and not too little … just right, like we've been doing." If we just continued as before, what need was there of a CCO? The business world is very different from the world of government. Businesses must clearly justify every action and every position, and there is no room for patronage.

I mulled carefully over everyone's ideas and expectations. I knew that the only one that truly looked forward in anticipation to this new position was me. I remained loath to choose one side or the other, but I was cognizant of treading on thin ice and had to look out for myself.

My Duties as CCO

In the end, I elected to frame the role of Trend Micro's CCO temporarily around two principle responsibilities: increase cultural value and support social causes.

1) Increase the Value of Trend Micro's Corporate Culture through Greater/ More Effective Promotion and Education

What might the CCO do in practical terms for the company? In the language of business, he or she should add cultural value to corporation. The CCO should work to ensure a constant inward flow of creativity and innovation, foster and instill internal values that ensure these are utilized fully in business operations, and make sure current corporate culture is regularly evaluated, critiqued, and renewed.

I incorporated cultural renewal into Trend Micro's handling of V.594. Undeniably, our culture had been an indispensible part of Trend Micro's successful, team-oriented extirpation from this potentially disastrous incident. How could we ensure the continuance of this remarkable, exceptionally advantageous spirit? Also, should its inner workings be subject to some regular review and update process?

Two years after V.594, we had already launched into the realm of cloud computing and were widely recognized as the antivirus market leader in this "new frontier" for computing technology. For the CCO, then, a natural question was whether our culture could keep pace with the rapid changes inherent to the coming age of the virtual cloud.

Our earlier Paramount Culture Tour program had worked to bring all Trend Micro employees into the cultural discourse. We were now moving things up a notch. In addition to a World Coffee Break activity, we were adding new cloud-based voting and discussion programs to give everyone in the company the opportunity to participate and have their opinions heard. Looking back on these developments, the successful launch and growth of each of these could be credited largely to "creative innovation." Each had begun with a friendly, distinctly nonbureaucratic letter to everyone, inviting all to participate in a new, fun communication activity designed to let participants speak their minds. Participants joined in and discussed issues related to a theme topic. Necessary adjustments and changes were then made based on the key ideas and opinions expressed, with an announcement of each made to the employees with the understanding that their participation in the process had been both crucial and appreciated.

The Paramount Culture Tour had served its purpose but no longer fit the polished image necessary for the "age of the cloud." Therefore, we christened the new cultural program Funtastic and invited everyone to join.

On the heels of World Coffee Break discussions and a company-wide Internet vote, the 4C+T concept that had long defined Trend Micro's core values (Change, Creativity, Communication, Customer, and Trustworthiness) received an overhaul, with two key changes made. The first was the change of the word *Communication* to the more relevant term *Collaboration*. The second updated *Creativity* to *Innovation*. Through this process, it became even more apparent that employees were eager for something even more substantive and practical than mere communication. They set Trend Micro's collective sights on *collaboration*. Additionally, they refined Trend Micro's mission beyond mere creativity, giving it greater practical punch as *innovation*.

Just so, our core values had been updated from "4C+T" to "3CiT." The only apparent drawback was that the new acronym no longer fit the easy-to-remember "4 entrées + soup" meal image!

While you may at this point be thinking that I am being somewhat smug about what these cultural endeavors have accomplished, there have been colleagues who have taken me to task on the value of it all, with questions such as, "Trend Micro executives love promoting 'culture' and use big events to do it. Is it really effective? Are you considering the opinions of the recipients of your messages?"

I would smile in response. I looked forward to such reproofs. Trend Micro is a worldwide organization with more than five thousand employees. While it was no longer possible to confer personally with each, we still wanted to get everyone involved in the process. Thus, designing time- and resource-consuming activities that were both big in scale and fun for participants seemed unavoidable. It was an approach that certainly deserves more thought and improvement, but, as of now, I have yet to arrive at the "perfect" solution. In any case, Trend Micro no longer holds Funtastic programs.

The Trend Micro Learning Circle ("TLC"), a group-training program that uses a smaller-scale team format and that Steve teaches personally, has since superseded our Funtastic activities. (See chapter 16 for a more complete introduction to TLC.)

2) Invest Trend Micro Resources and Talents in Well-Targeted Social Causes

Well-established companies have an inherent social responsibility. I feel it only natural that a business meets this responsibility using the tools and resources of its particular trade and within the context of its own corporate culture. After initial consideration, I knew I wanted to use "participatory innovation" rather than a top-down approach to develop and guide our efforts in this area. Therefore, we created an Internet forum open to everyone in the company that let anyone launch a charitable activity in a few easy steps.

Trend Micro's globe-girding organization is replete with people eager to help better society. Thus, any application submitted to HR for a charitable cause that garnered the support of ten employees and a commitment of US$500 or more earned a matching donation from Trend Micro and the potential for additional funding support from the founders.

Over the years, disasters around the world have garnered the strongest funding support. Trend Micro employees have donated generously to relief efforts in the aftermath of massive flooding in the Philippines, forest fires in Italy, the Sichuan earthquake, major flooding in southern Taiwan, and tsunami devastation in Japan. Internal activism and generosity has also often been enhanced by the participation of our distributors around the world. Trend Micro's charitable works have earned a steady stream of letters thanking us for being there in time of need and for stepping up to our responsibilities as a citizen of the world. For me, it is clear that making good on a company's societal duties requires both sustained commitment and proper mechanisms.

Trend Micro's global social activism ploughed smoothly forward, carried on sails fully extended via the World Wide Web. Not that there weren't problems, mind you. Our community-development project in the

Philippines highlights some of the difficulties we have faced on the road to social responsibility.

Trend Micro partnered with local charitable organizations in the Philippines on this project. We not only sponsored project-material costs but also paid for half of our employee volunteers' travel costs and maintained volunteers on full salary during their stay in the country. We sent four teams of Trend Micro volunteers per year for project work. Team members lived with Philippine families and worked with their communities to build houses and improve the local environs. The list of those eager to volunteer was invariably long. Some employees even took their families with them to help out. But there were unavoidable, inherent risks involved, and teams had their share of injuries and illnesses. Our white-collar professionals were used to working in air-conditioned offices in front of computer screens. Manual labor was a significant, and sometimes a wholly new, challenge for our employees.

In spite of the challenges, the project was a major success for both recipients and Trend Micro participants. The completed "Trend Community" was an accomplishment in which we could all take great pride. This was a true "brick-and-mortar" accomplishment! Furthermore, our volunteers came back with a better understanding and appreciation for Philippine culture, our Philippine colleagues took even greater pride in being part of the Trend Micro team, and our international family became even more tightly knit.

Promoting online safety awareness to children is, of course, a perfect fit for Trend Micro. Our experts took pride in designing education materials and special free software. We trained our colleague volunteers to teach Internet safety and online child-protection skills at schools and other organizations. We went even further by sponsoring an annual promotional video competition that invited young people to film and share online their personal experiences about falling victim to Internet-based hazards and scams. The City of New York supported our effort by airing the winning entries in Times Square, an attention-grabbing honor that gave a further positive boost to Trend Micro's corporate image.

Corporations have a virtually endless choice of ways to contribute as citizens of their communities and of the world. However, establishing a clear set of principles and goals is essential to achieving a meaningful and lasting impact. A guiding principle required that all of our charitable initiatives tap our core competitive advantages and global organization, giving all employees a chance to contribute and participate. All initiatives were organically inspired, and none were designed to reduce Trend Micro's tax obligations or to advance our marketing and sales goals. Nothing was forced or used in self-promotion. Our program has won widespread internal recognition and support. My annual report on Trend Micro's charitable contributions for the year is invariably met with enthusiastic applause that reflects genuine organizational buy-in and consensus. It is an undeniable source of pride for this CCO!

Trend Micro's CCO has no dedicated team and must channel all cultural initiatives through the Human Resources Division. To give teeth to the firm's humanistic philosophy of management, however, this philosophy must permeate the very fiber of Trend Micro's system of rules and regulations. It was thus fortunate that my exceptional working relationship and shared goals with Connie and her team helped us avoid the normal awkwardness of the hierarchical relationship and kept us working smoothly and effectively together.

Winning Hearts and Minds

A subtler but no-less-important responsibility of the CCO is to retain talent by making the company an attractive and satisfying place to work.

Trend Micro's hiring process includes a battery of interviews and tests. However, when all is said and done, affinity and fit with our corporate culture is a necessary condition for approval. We highly value and actively recruit new employees who have a simple, honest character, are eager and ready to take on responsibility, and have both professional qualifications and a passion for learning.

Ask a Trend Micro recruiter what sort of person most likely wouldn't get the job, and you are likely to get answers like: those who create the pretense of knowing something they don't; those who are overly proud and self-centered; those who are stubborn and unwilling to consider change; and those who are unclear about their own career objectives. On the other hand, lack of experience or a spotty academic career is rarely used to reject an otherwise promising candidate. We bring in good people and give them the training and opportunity needed to shine in the professional world.

It pleases me most to see new employees blossom in their new position, gaining in confidence, learning to adapt and change, and becoming happier. It is a great comfort to think that we've done our best for all of our employees.

However, doing so has certainly not been easy.

I once read an insightful report that pointed to poor management rather than salary issues as the most important reason for employee dissatisfaction and resignation. Dissatisfaction fueled by feelings of unfair treatment by management is disconcertingly prevalent in today's white-collar companies.

A competitive salary, bonus incentives, and stock options or distributions are minimal conditions for high-tech companies to attract and retain talent. But money alone most often falls short of earning true commitment from employees. Fortunately, even in today's consumer-driven economy, there are many good people out there looking for something more than just a nice paycheck.

"Ideals" are something for which people regularly profess a willingness to strive and even sacrifice. A company able to tap into this potential reserve of energy and enthusiasm can use it to build internal consensus and strong forward momentum. Perhaps it represents an area in which a CCO should invest a significant amount of his or her time exploring and developing.

An organization without ideals has a difficult time holding on to either the minds or the hearts of its employees. It is thus Trend Micro's fondest hope to use cloud and big-data technologies in its marketing and services to foster a new global business trend underpinned by a healthy and dynamic corporate culture, social responsibility, and the spirit of "honesty, goodness, and beauty." Some people join Trend Micro out of a passion for new technology, while others are attracted by our transnational business operations. Still others join for our solid career opportunities, our opportunities for learning and advancement, and even out of strong respect for our 3CiT-nourished culture. It is thus our responsibility to include each of these disparate ideals into our organizational ideals and express each in our normal business operations.

Scaling the Heights of Management Effectiveness

Ideals are abstruse concepts that typically lose their luster if not soon realized in management practice.

Many problems in the workplace have their origins in perceived inequity and injustice. While we all have a moral compass, if a firm's systems, incentives, and rules aren't clearly stated and implemented properly, this leaves the door open for individuals to impose their own subjective ideas—a situation that is almost always contentious and divisive.

The guiding principle of Trend Micro's philosophy on human resources is that each colleague should be allowed and encouraged to realize his or her potential as part of the Trend Micro team for the greatest collective benefit.

The performance-appraisal system constructed within this philosophical construct thus looks very different from what one might expect otherwise. Rather than being announced by top management, key work goals are derived from one's personal growth plan. This plan is set and regularly adjusted so that the talents, passions, and implementation capabilities of each employee support personal objectives that align with the overall objectives of Trend Micro. Plans are reviewed regularly with supervisors and adjusted as necessary to maintain optimal alignment between employee and company goals.

The performance-evaluation process first considers the performance of the entire company in achieving stated goals. Next, the process considers the contribution of each employee to achieving these goals. This allows Trend Micro managers to maintain a holistic approach to the business. Oftentimes, a focus on details of the business or on key performance-index indicators misleads managers into "losing sight of the forest for the trees" and failing to translate personal performance into organizational performance.

When Trend Micro exceeds set targets for a certain period, everyone in the organization shares the bonus using a ratio that reflects his or her direct contribution. With regard to salary increases, Trend Micro HR takes five factors into consideration:

1) Personal performance and contribution to achieving corporate goals;
2) Level of realization of personal potential, capacity to learn and improve, etc.;

3) Possession of special/essential skills critical to continued company growth;

4) Degree of conformity with Trend Micro's vision and goals, willingness to work within the Trend Micro team, and affinity with the company's culture and values; and

5) Current availability of this individual's skills and talents in the general market.

Performance evaluations, number-crunching, and other procedures may be necessary "evils" in the business world. However, achieving the corporate vision while maintaining a fair and humanistic hand and upholding fairness and individual freedoms while inspiring innovation and creativity is something that is both a science and an art. While we constantly fiddled and adjusted in the gray area between top-down and bottom-up management styles, we never strayed from our commitment to respect and consider the individual. We always began with "the individual," with our eye on maximizing the power and potential of every Trend Micro employee.

We were acutely aware of the necessity of striking an acceptable balance between the "ideal" and the "practical." Thus, in addition to keeping a firm hand on the helm of our corporate culture and management philosophy, we developed and launched a regularly updated series of advanced training courses with topics such as "Performance Growth Planning," "360-degree Contributions to Society," "Assessing Contribution," and "Indices of Customer Satisfaction." We took an active interest in helping all employees create and realize their career plans. Moreover, we made sure to arrange opportunities for extracurricular fun and exercise.

In Taiwan, Trend Micro sponsors more than a hundred employee-run clubs and teams, including various sports, a fencing club, boxing club, flower-arranging club, yoga club, handicraft club, and a calligraphy club, among many others. Annual competitions are always highly anticipated and well-attended events. We hope to help employees strike a balance between work and home life as well as between mental and physical activities. Despite many years of efforts, I must admit that achieving this ideal is still not easy, with problems made all the more challenging because of the transnational nature of our organization. Trend Micro employees travel often, which impacts normal family life. I have firsthand experience with this problem. I can only hope that videoconferencing technologies soon reach the point where face-to-face meetings can be reduced so that travel no longer consumes a significant amount of what rightfully is family time.

Systematic and idealistic; demanding and compassionate … this is the tightrope we walk every day as we work to keep our industry's top talent.

However, if our employees simply remained cloistered within the Trend Micro organization, it would threaten stagnation and separate us from the source of our innovation and dynamism.

Staff turnover within the worldwide Trend Micro organization is roughly 12 percent each year, slightly lower than the industry average of 15 percent. I believe this is a healthy rate for the company. Too much would bring the threat of lost resources and opportunities and an organization on the decline. To little would threaten turning the Trend Micro talent pool into a "dead sea" devoid of the necessary ripples of dynamic energy and inspiration. The answer to this problem is also half art, half science. It is necessary to find just the right balance between too much and too little.

While our corporate culture is humanistic and humane, it does not blindly mollycoddle. On occasions where we did delay handling employee problems, we found that by doing so, we simply ended up hobbling our business and letting down our team players. Nevertheless, when choosing between someone with a good fit with our culture and mediocre talents and someone who fits poorly with our culture and has exceptional talents, we will normally go with the former. Skills can be trained, but character is something deeply ingrained.

Human talent is the most important asset of high-tech companies today. However, this talent cannot be meaningfully tallied on a spreadsheet. It can't even rightfully be considered something that a company "owns." Talent's intangible nature gives it exceptional value. The fact that it can come and go as it chooses raises its worth even more.

In the interest of retaining this intangible, hard-to-calculate talent, corporations often have little choice but to create an environment that delivers the freedoms, ideals, and equanimity sufficient to keep people not only in their positions but also dedicated to achieving the firm's goals and vision.

Finding My Groove, Moving Forward

After earning acceptance as Trend Micro's first CCO, I asked everyone to allow me the time necessary to find my groove. Eight years on, I feel I'm still searching for that elusive "groove."

The title and position I had created were meant as temporary placeholders. It wasn't much later that Google announced it was creating a CCO position within its organization. A book was even published in the United States entitled *Chief Culture Officer*. My once-unique position in the business world was being superseded by a growing list of companies with CCOs. I figured that the natural differences distinguishing the cultural mores of various companies would lead naturally to differences in the character and responsibilities among CCO positions. I wondered whether these new CCOs shared my tribulations about their duties. Perhaps they were plowing confidently forward? I was an inveterate worrier about the future—always consulting the opinion of others and finding it very difficult to make definitive decisions about my course of action.

I remained uncertain about how I would play out my new role. Despite its "metaphysical" nature, culture had to find practical expression in day-to-day operations. Despite its "spiritual" nature, culture could not overlook the necessity of satisfying material needs. While I was the captain of our culture, I was incessantly drawn to cultural horizons beyond our corporate confines. I found myself invariably looking for practical ways to bridge the potentials and realities of our internal culture with those of external culture.

While I exude confidence when sharing my thoughts on being a chief cultural officer, I remain torn by doubt and uncertainty inside. On paper, I have accomplished quite a bit. However, these accomplishments have necessarily relied on the assistance of others. My "full authority" has made getting results easy. I cannot thank Trend Micro's global human resources team enough for their regular and generous support. They have allowed me room to experiment, given me cover to dabble in the world of art and culture, and, most of all, upheld their mission to turn my intentions and expectations faithfully into practical action. I will always remember and remain grateful to you all.

I am Trend Micro's chief cultural officer. I feel my way forward, peer into the future, mull over philosophical and practical issues, and take three steps forward only to take one step back. My worth and accomplishments still await the test of time. The only thing I am truly qualified to state with confidence is that I have remained true to our fundamental principles. With threads made of dreams, we are weaving a cradle of brilliant, humanistic character.

CHAPTER 15

The Highest Goodness

"I'm not a caring person." Steve would often point an accusing finger at himself. His involvement in the social-enterprise field was not grounded in sympathy or caring. He didn't fight for business opportunities out of love. He didn't steer his companies with a loving hand, either. Social enterprises are carefully balanced entities, with profit on one end and the public interest on the other. Steve and Roy, two very different entrepreneurs, thus came together out of a shared vision. All that was left was to work on bringing balance to the sensitive scales of this social enterprise in order to take firm, confident steps forward to creating a sustainable ecosystem for employing the disabled.

I have always nurtured and sustained an unceasing love for business culture. After relinquishing command of Trend Micro, Steve had launched into a meandering and seemingly directionless exploration for meaning and purpose. While looking inward through meditation to find inner peace in his frequent spiritual journeys to far-flung Buddhist destinations, he also invested his passions and talent into the bourgeoning new realm of the social enterprise, hoping to use his experience to help society and do something good for his homeland, Taiwan.

He seemed to be driven forward by some unknown force. Steve continued to explore, continued to seek. He had passed "the baton" but had no intention of sitting still. Now over fifty years of age, Steve wanted to know his heaven-ordained mission. He was cognizant of his own limits and saw much ahead yet to be learned.

Steve's growing list of accomplishments that came after shedding his daily responsibilities at Trend Micro took even me by surprise. Despite his prior ignorance of the classics of Chinese literature, he now faithfully attended I-yun Hsin's weekly course on Lao-Tzu (Laozi). He even named his new company Ruo Shui, the first two words of the line from the Tao Te Ching, which mean: "Water reveals the highest goodness, benefitting all without competing." Although Steve had never been one to mix company with men of letters, he surprisingly invited author Tom Wang to join him as a Ruo Shui cofounder. They set their wives aside and set about doing business free from the interference of their "better halves" in the unfamiliar (both to themselves and to the business world) landscape of the social enterprise.

Dreams Born from Youthful Passions

In 2006, Steve's wanderings took him to Vietnam's unfamiliar interior, where he volunteered on local reforestation efforts. This is an area once devastated by the US military, which dropped chemicals that stripped the forests of leaves in hopes of depriving the Vietcong of important bases of operation. Thirty years later, those chemical-soaked soils continued to curse the area, making the once rich forestland a contaminated, barren wasteland. But new government policies were now hoping that foreign investment and land-lease agreements would help put the land on the road to recovery. Steve and his good friend Kuo-wei Wu were among the first to answer Vietnam's call for foreigners to come and help.

Where others were attracted by the land-development opportunities, Steve and Kuo-wei were enticed by the natural environment. They leased a broad swath of barren hillside and invited agriculture experts from Taiwan's National Pingtung University of Science and Technology to help remediate the damaged soils. They planted eucalyptus and acacia saplings with high hopes of seeing a healthy forest in seven or so years. This forest could be a source of material for the area's furniture industry and reduce the ongoing culling of old-growth forests. If things went as planned, Steve's plan could also help advance Vietnam's calendar for meeting Kyoto Protocol commitments and give the country valuable carbon credits that it could potentially sell to carbon-generating states.

I couldn't resist poking fun at my husband. "You are rising up the ladder of enlightenment! You've moved up from peddling virtual software to selling air!" After all, air was even less "tangible" than software.

Steve's time at the helm of Trend Micro gave him hands-on experience with every aspect of business operations. He had never, however, had the chance to work in the realm of government relations. After six years, their seedlings had grown into a healthy acacia forest. In the meantime, the Vietnamese government had had a change of heart and announced the end of its land-lease policies in order to "prevent national borderland forests from Chinese occupation." They had chosen to lump Taiwan at this time into "China" for their own policy purposes.

His acacia dreams had failed, but the forests remained. Steve consoled himself by seeing his cup as half full. It was still a good result, after all. He hadn't made any money, but Vietnam and the environment were still benefactors of his efforts. Vietnam had turned his work into an unadulterated environmental remediation project, and hundreds of thousands of trees were exhaling oxygen, doing their part to clean up the world's atmosphere.

About the same time, Ruo Shui Inc. was opening its doors for business. With Steve and renowned author Tom Wang at the helm, they were the social enterprise sector's newest addition and the spotlight of public attention.

They launched the business with an "innovative ideas" competition that attracted hundreds of entries from Taiwan and around the world. Some came from recognized NGOs, some came from social enterprise newbies, and some came from "old hands" at business innovation. The stream of interesting and innovative proposals was as impressive as it was humbling. Steve, however, quickly identified a problem. The vast majority of submissions, while offering a competitive business model, lacked a sustained value component. Thus, the proposals didn't translate into the sort of social enterprise that Steve wanted. Steve wanted to create a business that would: increase job opportunities for disadvantaged groups, be self-supporting, be a point of pride for everyone involved, and be sustainable over the long term.

Responding to its high ideals, many talented individuals with similar ideals and aspirations joined Ruo Shui, creating its strong and cohesive core. Thus, Steve's nascent venture came to be staffed by highly experienced business managers, Internet experts, and entrepreneurs.

However, his long search for the perfect path forward and continuous validation led persistently to dead ends and disappointment.

Continuing to respect our agreement to allow each other to pursue our respective paths alone, I dared not get involved in Steve's Ruo Shui venture. Nevertheless, I couldn't help but feel terribly anxious for him.

Starting any new business presents daunting challenges. This time, however, Steve's insistence on operating Ruo Shui for the benefit of society's disadvantaged, with profitability a secondary priority, while insisting that it break even in terms of earnings and expenses, made the challenges of this startup all the more difficult. A barren pond trumps the old adage of giving a person a fishing pole rather than fish. In the absence of opportunity, passing out fishing poles is frustratingly superfluous. Perhaps things had to be taken back a step further. Perhaps an entire new business sector would have to be created before thinking about fishing poles and fish markets.

The Candle of Self-Sufficiency

Steve set off at the head of his new Ruo Shui organization on a long march in search of a social enterprise "oasis in the desert." He had a voracious appetite for knowledge and eagerly attended relevant seminars and classes. International interest in the social-enterprise sector was growing. Even investment banks were starting to organize regular seminars on the subject, and cornerstone business research and media outlets such as *Harvard Business Review* and *Bloomberg Businessweek* were publishing articles and case studies on the social-enterprise phenomenon.

I remember Steve's excitement upon reading an article about a Danish entrepreneur who had created a tech-based company for of his autistic son. "I've found my model! This company has adopted the repetitive habits of autistic individuals to do software testing. Isn't this just the sort of idea I've been looking for?"

I was pleased too. "Definitely worth looking into. Something like this would let you use your Internet and software skills to help the disabled."

Although our careers had gone their separate ways, travel was a passion we continued to share. The clean and beautiful city of Copenhagen beckoned with promises of new experiences and new friends, so I joined my husband on this pilgrimage.

We arranged a meeting with the Danish company that Steve had seen featured in the *Harvard Business Review*. This social enterprise, we learned, used a business model that relied on corporate charity for much of its operating expenses. Furthermore, the firm benefitted from Danish policies that gave social enterprises priority consideration for contract work. The firm's senior executives were all highly paid financial professionals who admitted rather openly that their salaries accounted for a high percentage of their human resources expenditures. They concluded the meeting with an earnest, highly polished appeal for our financial support.

We thus left Denmark rather disappointed. This was far short of Steve's ideal and, even so, would be difficult to implement in Taiwan. Steve's hopeful sojourn overseas in search of a shortcut to his dream thus drew to an abrupt close. We came back home, and he continued groping his way slowly forward.

"Maybe it's time for me to pay Roy a visit," Steve said. He had never forgotten Roy Chang.

Victory Knocks on Ruo Shui's Door

Sitting through the stream of project-proposal presentations for Ruo Shui had been mentally exhausting on Steve and the evaluation committee. Toward the end of one particularly rough day, Steve was giving serious consideration to making his apologies and leaving early when an image cast on the projector screen caught his attention. "Hey! My father built that!" he said out loud. The presenter was polio survivor Ying-shu Chang, who said, "I'm here on behalf of Victory Home for the Disabled in Pingtung."

For Steve, long-shelved memories of childhood returned as if they were yesterday. Victory Home is a charitable Christian organization founded by donations from churches in Norway. Many Norwegian ministers and nurses have served at the home—pioneers in the fight for polio prevention and treatment.

Steve's father worked in construction and specialized in erecting churches and charity centers for foreign church organizations. While not particularly profitable, work had been steady and payment was reliable.

Victory Home was a project in which he had taken particular pride. Steve was a regular at his father's building sites and had visited with the sick children and Norwegian doctors at Victory Home. He had often recounted with pleasure the story of blue-eyed, blonde Hanna, one of the missionary doctors' children, who once introduced herself to Steve and said, "I'm a Taiwan doll!" in fluid Taiwanese tinged with a distinctive southern twang.

He hadn't thought of those carefree days for years. It was the appearance of the youthful, wheelchair-bound Roy that brought these memories back to life. Roy and Victory Home seemed an inevitable pairing. He was the founder of the Taipei-based Victory Potential Development Center for the Disabled, a nonprofit organization (NPO) with all the passion of an entrepreneurial startup company.

For more than a decade, Roy had eschewed fundraising in favor of achieving success through the application of appropriate, effective models of business management in hopes of creating sustainable work opportunities for disabled individuals. His approach dovetailed nicely with what Steve was hoping to achieve.

In the private conversations that followed, Steve proposed a cooperative endeavor that would combine Roy's management expertise with Steve's IT industry connections to create significant new software-industry job opportunities within the social-enterprise framework. After several meetings, however, it became clear both that Roy wasn't ready to leave his current enterprise and that Steve wasn't ready to compromise on his fundamental ideas for the Ruo Shi venture. The two ended their discussions with an agreement to consider rekindling the idea of cooperation once Steve had a clearer picture regarding the direction of his social enterprise and Roy had found a suitable replacement to run his NPO.

Opportunities in the Cloud

Who would have predicted that emergent cloud technologies would, in the short span of a half decade, become IT's hottest growth segment? My visionary Steve was once again leading the industry forward. He focused the Trend Micro organization on promising cloud-computing opportunities, dove headfirst into the development of open-source cloud systems, funded new cloud technology courses in universities, and launched a promising new venture with his Beijing-based friend Edward Tian that was focused on developing Cloud Valley and a big data center in Beijing. He also reached out across the Pacific to help successful Taiwanese entrepreneurs in the United States return to Taiwan to take advantage of bourgeoning opportunities "in the cloud."

On the face of it, it seemed as if Steve had stumbled back onto his familiar entrepreneurial path, exploiting his talents to develop next-generation cloud opportunities. However, his eyes never strayed from the ultimate goal of getting Ruo Shui onto the path of steady, sustained growth. The idea of creating a successful model for social enterprises that would help make disabled individuals independent, productive members of society remained his passion.

Once more, he was starting from scratch. He was looking for the threads in the cloud that could be woven into a bustling new "fish market."

The time was finally right for Roy's expertise in managing disabled employees to merge with Steve's expert grasp of the basics of the new cloud-computing sector. Their cooperative relationship was grounded in three key principles:

1) The new venture would seek out green-field cloud business opportunities and avoid competition with current business interests. Nascent cloud technologies were ripe with possibilities such as 3D scanning, 3D printing, video editing, and much more. All required a certain level of specialist training and expertise and were not necessarily tied to the office environment. This principle was common to all of Steve's cloud investments, as it offered the potential for mutual benefit while training up talent that the Trend Education Fund might employ in its online video courses. This principle brought Steve's fish market into somewhat clearer focus.

2) The new venture should offer opportunities to persons with various disabilities as well as facilitate disabled employee integration with their nondisabled peers. Roy's years of management experience had taught him that "segregation" of the workforce was something to be studiously avoided. In Taiwan, the disabled are still often shunted into stereotyped careers such as masseurs (the blind)

and lottery ticket sellers (the lame). A mixed labor force not only offers opportunities to overcome individual shortcomings but also encourages close cooperation to ensure that everyone's skills are put to full and productive use.

3) While some or all of an individual's work may be done from the home, it is important to establish an appropriate, disabled-friendly office that employees can call "home." This office will be where staff members work, meet, network, and foster team spirit and focus.

"I'm not a caring person." Steve would often point an accusing finger at himself. His involvement in the social enterprise field was not grounded in sympathy or caring. He didn't fight for business opportunities out of love. He didn't steer his companies with a loving hand either.

Social enterprises are carefully balanced entities, with profit on one end and the public interest on the other. Maintaining this balance is exceptionally tricky. Steve and Roy brought their own unique talents, with the former having the business vision and business management insights of Trend Micro's founder and CEO and the latter having in-depth knowledge of the structural issues involved in successfully employing disabled staff as well as experience leveraging NPO and government resources. Together, they were committed to creating a model to train the disabled for business success.

Two very different entrepreneurs thus came together out of a shared vision. All that was left was to work on bringing balance to the sensitive scales of this social enterprise in order to take firm, confident steps forward to creating a sustainable ecosystem for employing the disabled.

The path Steve was building would be long and slow. My cultural ambitions, while more interesting, seemed rather selfish and easily achieved by comparison. I admired Steve for once again taking the road less traveled … for doing something wholly different from everyone else. But what made me happiest was that Steve had finally found his way "home" and was involved in something intimately tied to his childhood experience and roots. His new endeavors created new, positive ties to his parents and to his childhood community. This was something precious and rare in the fast-paced, migratory lives of most people today.

CHAPTER 16

Awakening

Steve and I shared the conviction that the best environment, even in the workplace, was free of limiting interference. We eschewed supervision and control mechanisms and avoided pragmatism in favor of helping employees find their individual passions and strengths so that they could successfully, and happily, realize their true potential. Furthermore, by putting all of these intelligent, motivated people together, there was no telling what the true extent of their collective potential was! Alternatively, over-saddling our people with goals and objectives would naturally impose limitations that could end up stymieing growth and interfering with creativity and innovation.

It was the autumn of 2013—Trend Micro's silver anniversary and eight years since Steve passed the baton to Eva. Eva had continued to grow steadily in both confidence and stature. There was little question that she had risen to become one of the most influential women in global IT. Wherever Internet security was discussed, especially in the realm of cloud security, Trend Micro was almost always part of the conversation. We had been a global team just shy of three thousand when Steve stepped down. Now, Trend Micro was an organization of five thousand.

With twenty-five years in the game, Trend Micro was now an established and trusted brand. No longer an upstart, adventure-seeking startup, we had become a stable, reliable place to build a career. Data exchange was moving bodily onto new platforms such as tablet PCs and smartphones. The chronic global shortage of experienced engineers and tech-savvy professionals able to not only keep up with but also lead these changes made Trend Micro's well-trained tech managers and engineers in Taiwan, Silicon Valley, Tokyo, Nanking, Manila, and elsewhere hot commodities.

The headhunting threat from across the Taiwan Strait was particularly pronounced, with quite a few senior managers leaving Trend Micro for lucrative offers in China. They invariably wrote heartfelt letters of farewell to their Trend Micro colleagues before departure. The messages I received typically read something like this: "I bought my house and car and raised a family during my more than ten years with Trend Micro. While it is painful for me to leave the warm, accommodating embrace of the Trend Micro family, the time seems right for change. I look forward to new challenges. I will never forget all that I have learned here." How could I argue against a decision couched in the desire for "change"? I also understood the almost irresistible lure of a twofold increase in salary and the need for additional security for our employees moving into their forties. Launching a bidding war to keep our people in place was considered by our human resources team.

However, doing so would destabilize our existing salary and compensation system and potentially end up causing more harm than good. While we encouraged our staff to stay, we wouldn't compromise our underlying business principles.

"Work to be a dynamic influence for good at your new company," I encouraged those who chose to accept an outside offer. "Help take good corporate cultural values to others."

Eva remarked resignedly that, "We must get used to the new reality. Trend Micro has become a training ground for IT talent. Our turnover rate is much higher than it's ever been."

Like Steve had once said, "No one at any level of the company should ever be irreplaceable." The wisdom in those words had held true across the years. After all, the company had continued to grow and prosper even after the replacement of its founder and first president.

I still couldn't help but take the departure of so many good colleagues lightly. "What's the value of culture," I couldn't help blurting out at a get-together with old colleagues, "if it collapses at the first whiff of a better salary? Maybe we should just stop trying so hard!"

Raofu Liu, a longtime colleague who had left Trend Micro to start a management-consulting firm, replied after a moment of thoughtful consideration. "Without its good culture, Trend Micro would probably be losing a lot more colleagues than it is. Also, the decision to leave Trend Micro wouldn't be so heart-rending. At least those who leave know they are losing something special when they move to another company. If we didn't place such a high value on Trend Micro's culture, we wouldn't always be coming back for get-togethers like this."

Charlie Lee, a comrade from Trend Micro's earliest days, chimed in: "Do you really think we haven't been tempted? Why do you think we chose to stay?" He looked at me seriously and, in a voice tinged with rebuke, said, "It's been Trend Micro's culture that's kept us here! Why are you so quick to write it all off?"

The discussion set my mind a bit more at ease. As I thought back over the years, I realized that those who had left Trend Micro had done so amicably. None had walked off with proprietary information or publicly attacked our shareholders. Indeed, quite a few had returned to Trend Micro after gaining experience at other companies. Perhaps I should not be so hard on myself. As Trend Micro's well-trained people rose to take key positions elsewhere, they were surely having a positive, long-term impact on the IT competitiveness of Taiwan and Asia, right? At least it gave me food for thought and consoled me for the moment.

Strategy: Culture in the Driver's Seat

If it weren't for Steve's steady and firm support, Trend Micro's cultural foundations would have long since stagnated and buckled under the weight of immediate business needs. Without Steve, culture would also have never achieved its current prominence in management decision-making.

When I began to doubt the vale of corporate culture, Steve came predictably to its defense. "Corporate culture," he reminded me, "is the key to strategy. You may not be able to see it, but you know it's there. It is *very* important."

Steve had a refined knack for talking about how to develop a good strategy. Many both inside and outside of Trend Micro had taken his course on strategy development. It was one of his most highly rated courses. But his syllabus included little on the connection between strategy and culture.

"Really?" I snapped back. "Explain what you mean, Steve." I needed him to show me that there was substance to what he was saying and that he wasn't just trying to make me feel better or to get me to drop it and get back to work. I needed to know.

"The way I see it," he said, "strategic decision-making requires three things. Firstly, a shared vision; secondly, consensus on who is the competition and where you are competing; and thirdly, how you plan to define *victory*." He always gets more serious when discussing theories of strategy, and when he saw my stale expression, he chuckled and altered course. "Remember that story I told you? Three workers are at a construction site hammering nails. The first says, 'I always make sure my nails hold things in place.' The second says, 'When I put in a foundation, I make sure it's stable to support the structure above.' The third says, 'I'm building a temple and will make it a fine place of worship.'"

"You've told me stories like that before," I said. "You're saying that people need a vision ... need to have some expectation for the future."

He continued. "Can a vision be viable if only the head of the company knows about it? Those three workers are doing the same job, but the approach and mindset of each are totally different, right? Vision is something that has to be visible and clear to everyone in the company. What's more, in order to realize a vision, it must be perceived by everyone as a 'common cause.'"

"True," I replied. "The ideal is that everyone understands what he or she is fighting for."

"Exactly! And how are you going to achieve that ideal without promoting culture,

without constant communication and without regularly reinforcing this shared vision?" Steve was making his point. "You can't just sit back and wait for everyone to figure it out on his or her own! That third worker didn't have any unique wisdom. He was simply inspired," he finished.

I smiled and said, "Okay, okay ... you've made your first point. I'll accept that culture is relevant to achieving shared vision. What about number two—who you are competing with and where you're competing? This is not culture, but rather an issue of position!"

Steve was ready. "It's not that simple. You're talking about 'position' like it's a point on a map indicating your direction and where you plan to do battle. The problem is that you have to prepare well in advance of those kinds of decisions." Steve certainly was one to look before leaping. "You've been in marketing long enough to know the overriding importance of first understanding the root nature of your customers' problems before attempting to figure out their true needs."

"Yes." I cut Steve off. "That is the way to create solutions that are of real value to your target customers."

He continued on the same train of thought. "While developing a blue-ocean market with no apparent competition may be considered the highest accomplishment, it may be also that you find yourself picking fights with another ocean. Southwest Airlines is a prime example. In creating an entirely new market niche with their focus on short-distance flights, they extirpated themselves from direct competition with other airlines only to start competing with other transportation services like Amtrak and Greyhound that operate according to entirely different sets of pricing and service strategies."

Steve had used this example many times in his classes, and the story was familiar to everyone at Trend Micro. "Sure. The strategy is clear, but where's the connection to culture?" I asked.

"You have to have the foresight to see the full range of disparate possibilities. Inspired thinking is not a substitute for careful planning. Leaders have to keep an even keel, avoid becoming trapped in immediate issues, seriously consider their customers' needs, and create appropriate new solutions." He looked intently at me. "This approach to thinking comes only after much experience and training. In other words, it is the vision instilled through corporate culture. It guides employees' decision-making and keeps them from choosing the wrong battles and squandering their firm's limited resources."

"Are you saying that corporate culture holds the potential to shape the fundamentals of how a business operates?" I pondered the issue a bit more and continued, "I appreciate how it can influence personal character. I hadn't considered how it might influence strategy-making."

"Creating an open, autonomous environment and a clear vision is critical to encouraging everyone involved to think broadly while staying firmly rooted to your predetermined guiding principles. It's an approach that opens potential for innovation across the full spectrum of technologies, products, strategies, business models, and executive functions.

Finished with number two, he moved on to his third point. "Now, 'defining victory' is an executive function. It is easy to see how that connects into business culture, right?" Steve was like a teacher challenging one of his students.

I didn't want to play dumb for fear of damaging my CCO credentials. "Yes, comprehensive implementation requires a full understanding of a firm's core competitiveness, organizational strengths, and various latent human and integrative team impact factors." My appreciation for the executive side of the business was particularly sharp.

"But," Steve said, again demonstrating his sharper insight on the subject, "culture wields its influence at a level that is difficult to perceive. Everyone has a chance to make decisions. When no one is looking over their shoulder, will people be able to make the necessary tough decisions? Will they be able to conserve resources? Can they take a sufficiently macro perspective and set personal considerations aside? These issues all harken back to the long-term development and nurturing of corporate culture."

He pressed his concerns further and said, "Strategy isn't about doing things better but about doing different things. Making choices is a fundamental part of strategizing. Once decisions have been made, you need to constantly work on reinforcing and enhancing your core competitiveness in order to create unique value for customers. See? Culture underpins every step of the process ... from initial discussions of vision through to the setting and implementation of strategy!"

"All right." I caved. "You've convinced me." Nevertheless, I couldn't help but add, "But isn't it still nearly impossible to evaluate the effectiveness of our cultural efforts?"

"You can only evaluate what can be perceived. How can you truly capture the imperceptible?" He smugly added, "The spirit of the Valley dies not. It is called the 'mysterious female.'"[8]

---

[8] From Chapter 6 of the *Tao Te Ching* by Chinese philosopher Laozi (Lao-Tzu). Here, the spirit of the Valley refers to the intangibility of "nothingness"—a quality essential to accepting and creating everything.

How things had changed! My husband was using a quote from Laozi's classic work, the *Tao Te Ching*, to teach me a lesson!

Assignment: Discover Your True Self

Without self-awareness of one's life path and goals, one is fated to remain trapped in a circle chasing after riches and fame, never having the opportunity to look inward.

Since stepping down as Trend Micro president, Steve had withdrawn from the competitive world of business and embarked upon a journey of inward-looking self-discovery. In addition to his careful readings of Laozi's *Tao Te Ching*, he took to frequent meditation. He had spent time at temples across Taiwan, at Zen Buddhist retreats in the United States, and at *Vipassanas* in India. His passion for this new inward journey was equal to that when he first launched his career as an entrepreneur.

I accompanied him on several of his meditation quests. The last was in Sri Lanka. It was memorable for the sore knees and muscles I got from the long hours of meditative sitting and for the incessant onslaught of mosquitos and leeches, which kept me totally off my game.

I finally confessed to Steve. "This is not my road. I had best return to my own path of literature, history, and philosophy." After all, when sequestered together in silent meditation, we couldn't talk. We weren't even supposed to look at one another. Accepting my request, he no longer invited me on his meditative journeys.

Steve's increasing focus inward clashed with Eva's increasingly urgent requests that Steve find the time to organize and lead new courses for Trend Micro's senior managers—especially in the critical arena of strategy. Steve fended off these requests long enough that Eva finally asked Connie, head of Trend Micro's global human resources organization, to reassign Steve's older sister Julie from her position in the US human resources office to head up the company's training curriculum. Steve was doomed to eventually cave in to his sister's soft-spoken urgings. They thus began working together on a comprehensive new training curriculum for Trend Micro that they christened "The Trend Micro Learning Circle," or "TLC."

He approached his latest mission from an entirely new perspective. Gone were his former long-winded pronouncements on strategy, management, and the global Trend Micro organization.

"What I really want is to transform Trend Micro into a learning-oriented organization," he shared with me. "During your Paramount Culture Tours, you shared Peter Senge's thoughts on the 'fifth discipline', right? How effective was that?"

During my brief time as an editor and translator at Commonwealth Publishing, I came into contact with many books on business management. After entering business myself, I continued reading books by many of the business world's leading lights. Of all of those I had read, *The Fifth Discipline* by Peter Senge impacted me most deeply.

"I shared that in our reading group. We discussed the five perspectives of personal mastery, shared vision, systematic thinking, mental model, and group learning. We actually didn't delve into the topic to any great depth." I reflected on the experience and added, "But everyone liked the concept of a learning-oriented organization."

Steve chimed in. "But afterward, when we invited Peter to speak at our senior manager's meeting, why did his approach to the subject differ so diametrically?"

I laughed. It was true. When I had invited Dr. Senge to speak on his learning-organization ideas to a gathering of more than a hundred Trend Micro senior managers from around the world, he pulled me aside and confided, "I've been studying Eastern philosophy with Nam Huai-jin and have a wholly new perspective on that issue. I really don't want to revisit that twenty-year-old theory." So, Peter formatted his presentation as a question-and-answer session and gave his audience the opportunity to participate and address hot-button issues. He ended up avoiding discussions of theory, with the exception of his "U" theory developed in his later book *Presence*. Thus, half of the audience left feeling warm and touched by Peter's unexpectedly personal approach, while the other half left feeling disappointed and confused.

"Perhaps there are still those in the world of business who still tow a tight theoretical line. Everything fits into a predefined box with little room for discussions of quixotic subtleties." That was my take on the issue.

"Then, in teaching lessons that involve less tangible emotional or introspective topics, it is still important to incorporate elements of rationalism and theory. Is that right?" he asked himself.

"I think so," I replied. "After all, most people like most to learn from practical, real-world cases." I was thinking about Harvard's case-study courses. Weren't they widely recognized as the most efficient model for business study?

Julie, responsible for Trend Micro's training programs, spoke up with a practical suggestion. "Peter Senge runs an academic program dedicated to teaching about the learning-oriented organization. They hold a convention every year to train their own educators on how to help organizations continuously learn and improve. Why don't we join in on the next one?" It was the perfect suggestion at just the right time.

Arrangements were made for Steve, Julie, Connie, and I to travel to Seattle for Peter's annual trainers' convention. I loved travel, and with my oldest son working for Microsoft at their headquarters not far from the convention venue, I looked forward to the prospect of spending some extracurricular time with him.

What most impressed me at the convention was the success they made of breaking out the more than one thousand attendees into small discussion groups. The groups, made up of not more than eight people each, changed tables three times during what he dubbed his "World Café." It proved effective at bringing this otherwise unwieldy convention to quick consensus on the core elements of the day's topic: environmental protection. All had a chance to see their voice and opinions not only heard but also to impact results.

"This discussion format is *perfect* for helping get Trend Micro toward its goal of participatory innovation." I was over the moon at having learned this new approach to communication. From then on, a "World Café" featured prominently in Trend Micro's internal communications. We now had a tool of communication that not only helped us quickly converge on consensus but also broadened employees' circles of communication and interaction. Our internal World Café discussions were invariably lively, and time frequently ran out before everyone's grievances had been heard.

The Trend Micro Learning Circle

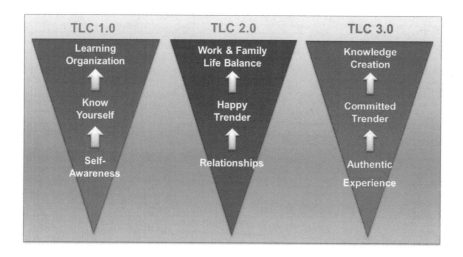

I remain indebted to Charles Kao for introducing Peter Senge to us and for opening the door to all that we have since learned from him. Steve paid a visit to Peter one snowy evening at his house in a suburb of Boston. Peter had just recently published *Presence: An Exploration of Profound Change in People, Organizations, and Society* and I had written the preface for the Chinese edition, entitled "The Sixth Discipline: Embracing the 'U' from Head to Heart." While reading his latest effort, I realized that this electrical engineer academician had fundamentally transformed his perspective on life.

Late into that wintry night, he and Steve's discussion wandered from business management to organizational management and then to aesthetic contemplations of Zen Buddhist philosophy. They clicked from the start, and afterward, when Peter visited Taiwan, he frequently stayed with us at our home. He abhorred staying in hotels with their windowless rooms, he said.

Steve worked closely with Peter's consultative group to tailor an appropriate curriculum for the Trend Micro Learning Circle. It was built on the theoretical foundations of Peter's *Fifth Discipline* and supplemented with many practical activities designed to achieve experiential learning. Steve adjusted his teaching techniques to the curriculum and added many new case examples from Trend Micro and his own experience. His material settled out naturally into a three-stage curriculum. He named them "Self-Awareness," "Interpersonal Relationships," and "Group Learning," respectively.

The next step was for Steve to identify and personally invite those Trend Micro colleagues he felt were best fit to teach the new courses. They all withdrew to a secluded, scenic venue far from the din of the office, where they discussed, shared ideas, and plumbed the deeper intent of the new Learning Circle curriculum. These "seed teachers" started off teaching small-group classes in order to "train the trainers." Trend Micro would spread the key messages embodied in the Learning Circle outward from the core to the outermost periphery.

Steve announced, "I'm no longer interested in discussing theory. I hope to help everyone achieve self-awareness." His own "enlightenment" had taught him that, in the absence of self-awareness, all knowledge is an exercise in superficiality. "A method that sparks inspiration and awareness is key to achieving true personal transformation. It should be something that everyone can take part in."

On several occasions, he asked everyone to rise early with him to meditate. Of course, some were too groggy to get much out of the experience, while others drifted back off to sleep. But some came out a bit better because of the experience. It reflected the truth of the old adage: the master may lead the student to the gate, but only the student can walk through. Julie, Steve's sister, summed it up in practical terms. "The ultimate objective of this curriculum," she said, "is to provide a common learning experience and a shared vocabulary to everyone at Trend Micro in order to enhance each employee's understanding and strengthen internal cohesion and teamwork."

They developed the Learning Circle with this in mind, creating myriad opportunities for students to interact and learn from the experience. Each course began with a group "check in" session that, rather than talking shop, asked students questions like, "Talk about something that's made you happy recently;" "Share your most touching moment;" and "Share something that is troubling you now." Sometimes, there would be one-on-one sessions, called "walk and talk," when students were asked to take a walk together outdoors and share thoughts on some topic. Other times, we would have students break out into groups of threes to practice the art of effective listening. Still other times, we would ask teams to break out based on sibling order in order to understand the different perspectives held by eldest, second, third, and only children.

I discovered that most people enjoy sharing their inner selves. This, after all, is the engine driving the success of Facebook and other social-networking sites. Our courses were always greatly anticipated and always lively, even when participants were unfamiliar with one another. It may just be that the need to communicate is part of our hard-wiring, part of our very nature, and that it is society that has made communication seem awkward and unnatural by imposing countless rules, conventions, and taboos. After all, opening up a discussion with employees about the management hierarchy or promotion policies is almost fated to end in either awkward silence or, at most, guarded opinions. However, once hierarchical levels are removed and all are free to communicate as equals, the floodgates to unfettered, honest communication swing open!

Of course, the natural tendency to guard one's opinions, to speak only after hearing others' opinions, or even to parrot the perceived dogma remains a stubborn obstacle to honest and open communication in group settings.

This is why the "left-hand column" was such an epiphany to so many people. This activity separated everyone out into groups of twos, one of whom was asked to talk about a discussion experience while the other listened carefully and then tried to analyze what was said and assess the speaker's real motivations. Sometimes the motivation was discomfited apology; sometimes it was redirected anger; other times it was a desire for harmony; and at still other times, it was the subconscious expression of an innate bias. Whatever the reason, it caused the speaker to present her or himself insincerely. The intent hidden behind our words is what is known as the "left-hand column." Better understanding your own or others' left-hand columns is a positive move forward toward becoming more empathetic and understanding and, perhaps, expressing your true thoughts and intentions. The activity is an excellent tool for improving communication skills.

Many Learning Circle students also began applying what they learned at home, to exceptional result. This side effect of the courses was an unexpected bonus and a great source of encouragement to us. It is only natural that communication skills in the home and the workplace be on an equal footing. As no one should pretend they are someone else at work, no one should leave work to face a silent, noncommunicative household.

Steve, adept at applying basic psychology theory into practice, used the Johari window diagram to present an engaging description of the four "quadrants" of everyone's inner self. These include the "known to me, known to others" quadrant (e.g., one's name, academic history, title); the "known to me, not known to others" quadrant (e.g., a secret love); the "not known to me, known to others" quadrant (e.g., a piece of food on one's chin, bad breath); and the "known only to the heavens" or "subconscious" quadrant (e.g., a psychological complex one has yet to discover).

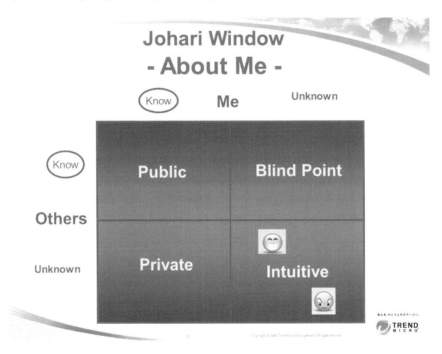

"I'm constantly encouraging you all to be yourself," Steve announced to his attentive class. "But if you don't know yourself, how can you ever truly *be* yourself?" He continued with emotive earnestness, "Try to understand yourself. Listen to the feedback from others to get a better handle on aspects of yourself that you may still be unaware of. Self-reflect and turn your subconscious realm into a conscious, observable aspect of your existence. The less you conceal, the more open and self-assured you will become. Expanding the realm within you that is conscious and understood will make it all the more easy for others to understand and appreciate you." This was one of the deep revelations Steve came upon through his meditations, readings, and coursework. His position as living testimony to this principle he was now teaching simply made the lesson all the more profound.

The process of self-awakening, with its emphasis on life goals and deep-set desires, is a very subjective process, and thus traditionally *not* seen as a realm particularly suited to exploration in the business setting. However, although the narrow goals of business give short shrift to the personal problems of individual employees, there is an obvious paradox: it is *precisely* these problems that keep employees from achieving their potential and, ultimately, limit overall business performance.

The Trend Micro Learning Circle thus looked to provide a starting point. Like the shepherd boy pointing to the sanctuary of a village during a rainstorm in the poem "Qingming" by Du Mu, we could only point the way and offer suggestions. Would students follow our advice? Would they find self-awakening on the other side? It all depended on the personal initiative of the individual and the vagaries of fortune.

The Management Philosophy of P=p-i

"Why do you spend so much time in your organization teaching on self-awakening?" a US-based business journalist once challenged us in an interview. "Aren't you taking a risk that, once self-aware, your employees will want more than you are able to offer?"

This problem did indeed come up. The former head of the Trend Education Foundation had discovered that her true calling was as a yoga instructor. She finally got up the courage to launch her own business. We all went and took her classes and encouraged her, and we continue to keep in touch. It has been a learning and growing experience for her as well as for us.

One of our customer service engineers from Norway enjoyed his volunteer work in the Philippines so much that he decided to stay on as a long-term volunteer. Human Resources panicked. "He is our most experienced CS engineer! The customers love him. What should we do?" I answered, "Help him launch successfully onto his chosen path. Let him try and experience for himself. He may be back." I was actually very happy for him. Perhaps, I thought, he had found his path to self-awareness.

With self-awareness comes the potential for major shifts in life trajectory. Efforts to keep someone against his or her will are ultimately fruitless. Why not then give your open and sincere blessing? Although the loss will certainly cause disruptions and inconvenience for a time, isn't that preferable to crushing the dreams of a valued employee?

Steve took to explaining our management philosophy using the formula P=p-i. Neither of us is now sure whether he had adopted it from something he had read or whether it had come to Steve in an inspired moment.

The uppercase *P* stands for *performance*; in other words, how effectively an organization performs overall. The lowercase *p* stands for *potential*, or the collective potential of that organization's constituent members. Finally, the lowercase *i* stands for *interference*, or the amount of unnecessary interference.

Mind capital is the most important asset held by firms in so-called "smart industries." As Steve often said, "When our people leave for home at the end of the workday, the value of our assets drops to zero."

Everyone, regardless of intellect, has limitless potential. Giving employees an open, supportive environment geared to turn that potential into forward momentum toward our collective goals thus seemed the natural path forward to maximizing Trend Micro's collective potential.

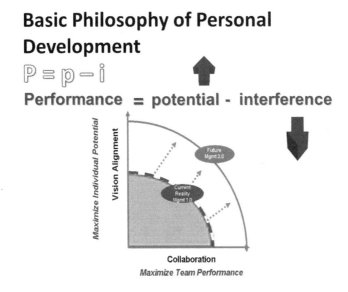

Basic Philosophy of Personal Development

$$P = p - i$$

Performance = potential - interference

Steve and I shared the conviction that the best environment was free of limiting interference. Perhaps this conviction was born out of Steve's lifelong hostility toward "playing by the rules" and my youthful desire to escape a prim and proper upbringing. We thus both allowed our children a wide berth to experiment, experience, and find their own ways in life. We gave them myriad opportunities while growing up in hopes that it would better prepare them to make their own choices. Beyond our hope that they would be healthy, happy, and have a good moral grounding, we did little to steer their courses down life's path.

We worked hard to apply these ideals to Trend Micro as well. We eschewed supervision and control mechanisms and avoided pragmatism in favor of helping employees find their individual passions and strengths so that they could successfully, and happily, realize their true potential. Furthermore, by putting all of these intelligent, motivated people together, there was no telling what the true extent of their collective potential was! Alternatively, over-saddling our people with goals and objectives would naturally impose limitations that could end up stymieing growth and interfering with creativity and innovation.

Admittedly, this approach to management philosophy is idealistic and carries a certain measure of risk. Trust in your employees is essential, as is a willingness to embrace chaos, accept situations that don't necessarily make sense, and face up to the stream of frequent troubles erupting within the organization.

However, it often takes only self-awareness, self-acceptance, and the embracing of fate to realize one's full potential. Freed from the fetters of practical concerns over immediate gains and losses, one may embark on an unabashed course of giving. It is only natural that this course will ultimately release far more latent energy and talent than a course set by preordained objectives and priorities.

These are ideas that have underpinned Trend Micro's management philosophy since the very beginning. Perhaps we have been overly idealistic. Full and honest implementation of this philosophy is fraught with difficulties, and assessing results is practically impossible. Moreover, even now, there remain voices within Trend Micro that advocate for a different, more conventional management approach.

While the road forward has been all but smooth, we have managed to continue Trend Micro's steady growth in the highly competitive world of the Internet. Continuous innovation, a tight-knit global organization, and universally high rates of customer satisfaction are all essential factors in seeing us through to our twenty-sixth year in business.

Live Your Destiny

Apple Inc. co-founder Steve Jobs passed away in 2011 at the relatively young age of fifty-six. His death elicited worldwide expressions of regret and commiseration from across the social spectrum. On hearing the news, my Steve remarked dolefully, half out of self-congratulation and half out of self-reflection, "I've now lived a year more than he did."

For my part, I had no qualms about using Steve Job's widely publicized passing for more base purposes. "See," I quipped in my public-speaking engagements, "the United States has one by one lost its superstars. Johnny Cash, Bob Hope, and Steve Jobs have all passed on. It's true. The US has no Cash, has lost Hope, and doesn't have any more Jobs." Once the chuckles died down, I used the joke to springboard into a discussion of corporate responsibility.

"These may be the three basic things a company has to provide to its employees: a job, a salary, and a reason for hope. But I'm always thinking ... can't we do even better? Wouldn't it be better if companies provided professional careers rather than just jobs? Provided financial security rather than just a salary? Offered an attainable dream rather than just hope?"

I've never been comfortable with public speaking, and I invariably spend hours with Steve preparing my presentations and slides. However, the groundswell of interest in corporate culture in recent years has led to a steady stream of invitations for me to speak on my experience and perspectives as a chief cultural officer (CCO). Only when I am unable to politely decline do I accept, with a due sense of reluctance. Each speaking engagement presents a nerve-racking new challenge. I can only do my best to speak on corporate culture within the limited context of Trend Micro's experience. As I look back through the years, it is clear how both Steve and I have sought consistently to shed fixed formalities in the pursuit of a more personally satisfying and flexible lifestyle. We naturally also both sought to imbue our Trend Micro venture with an open and accommodating work environment suited to helping everyone realize his or her full potential.

Psychologist Abraham Maslow's Hierarchy of Needs puts physiological needs at the base of a human-needs "pyramid." Atop this follows, in turn: safety, love and belonging, and esteem, with self-actualization occupying the highest layer. Later in life, Dr. Maslow revised his pyramid to add yet another layer over self-actualization. This new layer, which he called over-actualization, may be properly interpreted as the human need to contribute back to society. This pyramid was an impressive, pioneering attempt to conduct an analytical dissection of human need. It framed my thoughts on business management, and I referenced it frequently in discussions of corporate culture. It spurred me to think how much more preferable it would be if we could somehow satisfy the entirety of the needs pyramid simultaneously rather than working up step by step. After all, doesn't that better reflect how we live and function in the real world? There is nothing that requires you to make your fortune before doing charitable work, right?

It was always our hope that our company might strike an optimal balance between all of the hierarchical needs. Most important is the provision of "meaning." This includes infusing purpose and meaning into work, team cooperation, wealth creation, and life. Why should I choose to work for this company? Will it help me fulfill *my* objectives and ideals? Do I enjoy teamwork with these people? I'm contributing to company growth and profitability, so is my company making sufficient contributions back to society? What is the significance of my life and work here?

In providing a positive, encouraging environment and confirming our employees' professional passions and talents, helping them develop their potential, encouraging the pursuit of knowledge and self-discovery, and fostering positive energies, we may indeed be on the right track to creating the sustainable "learning organization" envisioned by Peter Senge. Moreover, shouldn't it be possible for the individual to exceed organizational strictures and learn without limit or end?

But this brings up the question: What, precisely, do we mean by "learning"?

Learning vs. Awareness

I held strong hopes for picking up and continuing my literary studies once Eva was firmly at the helm of Trend Micro. As a student, I had been most drawn to the Taoist philosophies of Laozi and Zhuangzi, although my readings were mostly the genre's better-known works and my appreciation was largely superficial.

My participation in the stage production of the Peony Pavilion introduced me to Hsin Yi-yuen, one of the play's scriptwriters. "You're looking to take a class in Chinese philosophy? Professor Hsin is one of the best," Ken Pai once told me.

I began listening in earnest to his regular radio programs on the Confucian *Analects* and the philosophy of Zhuangzi. Later, I attended his course at the National Taipei University of Education entitled "The Seven Books Everyone Needs to Read," which focused on the *Analects*, *Mencius*, *Zhuangzi*, Laozi's *Tao Te Ching*, the *Platform Sutra*, *Records for Reflection* (*Jinsilu*), and *Records for Teaching & Practicing* (*Chuanxilu*), as well as his course on Mencius at the Taipei Lecture Hall. Inspired by my enthusiasm, Steve also joined me in my studies and courses.

My undergraduate studies of Zhuangzi and Laozi had focused on appreciating the aesthetical aspects of the literature that underpins their philosophies. We barely touched their philosophical ideas. Studying under Professor Hsin was thus an eye-opening new experience. He analyzed each word in each brilliantly constructed line of text to elucidate its meaning and importance first in the context of contemporary social ethics and then in terms of modern society. Every element was enveloped in philosophical import, and every class inspired continued discussions between us. Steve and I shared our thoughts and impressions. We were fully immersed in the joys of learning.

Years before, we had studied the philosophy of Carl Jung and explored the meaning of dreams and the subconscious. Professor Hsin encouraged us to once again ponder the meaning and value of life. This renewed journey was particularly eye-opening for Steve, who was for the first time seeing deep, purposeful truths and practical wisdom in those philosophical classics he had once dismissed as pedantic. The "learning circle" curriculum he was developing was increasingly flavored with traditional Chinese philosophy.

Professor Hsin succinctly explained the concept of "learning" by quoting from the first chapter of the Confucian *Analects*.

> *Isn't it a pleasure to study and practice what you have learned? Isn't it also great when friends visit from distant places? If one remains not annoyed when he is not understood by those around him, isn't this man a sage?*

It seems to convey easily understood, sensible messages: practice what you learn, and enjoy the fruits of doing so. Your friends are happy when you are happy. A wise man will keep his cool when others don't understand what he is trying to explain. This was my long-held superficial explanation of the venerable opening lines of the *Analects*. I had never once considered why its author had put these words at the front of this compilation of wisdom or what its deeper meaning might be.

That is why listening to Professor Hsin's radio show on the *Analects* was such a revelation for me. These three seemingly unrelated sentences actually fit tightly together and encapsulated the wisdom that is the fertile soil nourishing all learning. Each expresses a distinct stage of both learning and life.

Thus, I hope in the following to convey my small new insight into learning.

Learning may be considered synonymous with *awareness*. You may also think of learning as the positive action that flows from becoming aware. Comprehension of life and of your own existence is awareness. Awareness of oneself and of existence opens the door to self-exploration, learning, and the pursuit of life's ultimate meaning.

Practice evokes the image of chicks trying out their new wings for the first time and then practicing, repeatedly, for the day they will finally take to the skies and move forward up the ladder of life. The knowledge that emerges from such awareness gradually elicits understanding of and appreciation for the essence of life. Is this not, then, a true cause for joy?

Therefore, "practicing what you have learned" is an activity born from awareness and the first stage in the pursuit of learning. It is fundamental to self-consciousness and brings true inner happiness.

The second stage of learning necessitates interaction with others. "Friends from distant places" thus refers to those friends also in the process of learning to spread their wings. In fact, the first character *peng* of the Chinese word for friend (*pengyou*) traces its origin to an ancient word for "spreading wings." Those who appreciate their new awareness can seek out those on a similar path and work to refine each other's perspectives as a way to both continue learning and improving and earn approval and validation. Isn't this the epitome of happiness? Bolstered by external confirmation, this happiness satisfies one's internal as well as external self and lies along a plane quite distinct from the first stage of internal happiness elicited by the act of "learning."

The third stage returns yet again to the inner self—to an even deeper level. While learning confirmed and appreciated by others delivers happiness on two levels, life can truly only be an indelibly introspective experience. Each of us is responsible for our own learning and deliberations along life's pathway. Personal values and perspectives that fall out of sync with those around you should never be a cause of self-doubt or concern. They reflect your own personal life choices and, as such, deserve to remain unaffected by externally imposed definitions of success, accomplishment, wealth, and fame.

Such an internal endeavor, independent of outside interference, may, I believe, epitomize the self-aware sage.

Confucius, the model of patient, sage advice, sought concurrence by asking pointed questions such as, "Is this not happiness? Is it not something truly joyous? Isn't this a sage?" He avoided the pitfall of definitive statements, perhaps out of his desire to make his students think and experience for themselves. Professor Hsin follows the same tenets.

We who had only recently extirpated ourselves from the "ego"-centric world of business were busy at work catching up with this new take on "learning."

Fate Unavoidable vs. Fate of One's Own Choosing

Although the Internet's buoyant, youthful dynamism had propelled us forward along life's pathway, we both remained beholden to fate's uncompromising rules.

While even now, I am unsure regarding the true meaning of fate, I nevertheless have an abiding awareness of some degree of predestination at work. Feeling our way forward in life has gradually engendered a cautious respect for the power of fate. While "she" leaves ample room for human will and creativity, the general flow of the affairs of life remains beyond our ken and our ability to wield any formative influence.

Narrowing our focus to a discussion of entrepreneurism, we would have a hard time arguing that the Internet is the creation of a small number of individuals. Rather, those involved in its creation and expansion may well number in the hundreds of millions, as every user around the world has been and continues to affect the face of the globe's new digital nervous system. Trends have thus long migrated beyond anyone's control. It was within this unstoppable current that Trend Micro flourished and grew. Holding tight to our singularly unique values through multiple storms, we were seemingly forging our own destiny … seemingly in control of our very fate.

Narrowing our focus further still to the individual—to Steve, Eva, and myself, although we share a close, synergistic relationship, we are each very different in terms of both personality and talents. So much is already hardwired into our DNA from birth. Much of our personality and talents are resistant to change, even with the investment of time and dedicated effort. Otherwise, what other excuse do I have for still being such a high-tech "outsider" despite more than two decades in the business? Why, after so many years, have I again returned to my youthful predilections for the humanities? Why also, after so many years in the global technology sector, have I returned to the relatively more narrow confines of Chinese culture? Aren't these examples of personal choice? If I presume as an explanation the intervention of fate, I would still have to explain all the hard work put into my decisions. However, if I claim the credit, how then do I explain all those fingerprints of serendipity clearly visible throughout my life?

At the crossroads of heaven and man, there are implacable rules as well as ample room to write one's own future. This is truly a remarkable road that we are on!

The three of us created Trend Micro together within the confines permitted by fate. We also each invested our individual strengths and talents to forge our own distinct path through life.

I've recently had a recurring dream in which I approach a dense forest shaded by giant trees with branches that reach down to the ground from the heavens. I push back on the branches and wander inward to find the air dense with the aroma of forest greenery and the understory still and silent. Sometimes I see a flock of beautiful birds arrayed on one of the branches; sometimes I encounter a phoenix preening its wings; sometimes I see a golden monkey coquettishly brushing its eyelashes. Still other times, I am completely alone.

I wake up content and peaceful, wishing I could shut my eyes once again and go back.

It is no longer like my dreams before … when my dreams had me disoriented, lost and alone in Italy, on stage in a ballet, in some unfamiliar place, or in my family home. Back then, when I woke up, the fears of my imagined experience would linger, sometimes for hours afterward.

Steve's dreams had changed too. A swirling, dark vortex threatening to suck him deep down into its gaping maw was a recurring element in his dreams as a child. He confided after the Trend Micro succession, "I haven't had that nightmare in a long time. I now dream more about fish, shrimp, crabs … about animals that live in the water."

In response to my question about her dreams, Eva answered, "I've no idea! I forget it all when I wake up." With full sails forward at the helm of Trend Micro, she likely has little time or inclination to commune with her dreams. Nevertheless, Eva's creative paintings have become brighter and more colorful. My sister the ballerina has more energy and vibrancy than ever before.

She has opened a space all her own, while I have found my way back "home" to explore my inner being. For his part, Steve continues tinkering with dreams of new horizons, new markets, and new opportunities.

"At 15, I honed my mind for learning; at 30, I held firm to my beliefs; at 40, I had no doubts; at 50, I knew the will of heaven; at 60, my ears knew to listen; and at 70, I could follow my heart's desire while remaining upright and blameless."

In reflecting on this well-memorized passage of the *Analects,* if I interpret "learning" to be Professor Hsin's "awareness," I fear my path to enlightened wisdom began rather late in the game. My path to awareness didn't begin until I was well into my twenties. My life afterward, however, truly seems to have mirrored Confucius's description. I grew in confidence and gradually shed my doubts. Only now was I learning, albeit slowly, to perceive the will of heaven.

On my road ahead, I look forward to becoming one who knows how to listen and, ultimately, to following my heart's desires into a beautiful sunset.

As for Trend Micro, our entrepreneurial offspring has only just moved into its "firm-belief thirties." It still has quite a ways to go, with every stage offering up new challenges and new fruit ready for harvest. I have every confidence that our core values and human-centric approach to business will see Trend Micro, like its entrepreneurial founders, further along the path of continuous learning and improvement.

I would like to express my deep gratitude to those ahead of me on the path of life. Thank you for your trailblazing efforts in finding a path forward for humanity and in giving us so many role models worthy of emulation.

I would also like to extend a hand of invitation to those of you sharing the road with me. Let us proceed forward together, pry away the boulders blocking our path, discover our shared dreams and ideals, and make this road a bit easier for those still on their way.

Additionally, I would like to encourage those who will be coming after us to continue pushing forward. The road ahead crosses a landscape of exceptional beauty and is carpeted in succulent, satisfying fruit. Open your eyes and ears ... savor every flavor. With each purposeful step, make sure to reach out and assume new challenges. Be sure also to stop and smell the roses! Find yourself while you live your destiny. Try never to rush through things or risk missing the beauty that lines your pathway.

The path is the purpose, and a firm, stable footing is key to continuing the journey for a lifetime. Where does your path end, you ask? Listen to the heavens, follow in the footsteps of those before you, follow the current, and launch onto a new path all your own! While sometimes your chosen path may turn onto a dead end, always remember that heaven's boulevard is immeasurably broad and forgiving!

In closing, I would like to share with my readers a poem that has much meaning to me, written by the Irish poet William Butler Yeats.

The Coming of Wisdom with Time
Though leaves are many, the root is one;
Through all the lying days of my youth
I swayed my leaves and flowers in the sun;
Now I may wither into the truth.

ABOUT THE AUTHOR

Jenny Chang co-founded Trend Micro, where she promotes and maintains its core values and open-minded, transnational culture. She formerly worked with Hewlett-Packard Taiwan, was chief editor of Common Wealth Publishing, and was the marketing director of AsiaTek Computer. She graduated from National Taiwan University and Lehigh University.